THE WILEY BICENTENNIAL–KNOWLEDGE FOR GENERATIONS

Each generation has its unique needs and aspirations. When Charles Wiley first opened his small printing shop in lower Manhattan in 1807, it was a generation of boundless potential searching for an identity. And we were there, helping to define a new American literary tradition. Over half a century later, in the midst of the Second Industrial Revolution, it was a generation focused on building the future. Once again, we were there, supplying the critical scientific, technical, and engineering knowledge that helped frame the world. Throughout the 20th Century, and into the new millennium, nations began to reach out beyond their own borders and a new international community was born. Wiley was there, expanding its operations around the world to enable a global exchange of ideas, opinions, and know-how.

For 200 years, Wiley has been an integral part of each generation's journey, enabling the flow of information and understanding necessary to meet their needs and fulfill their aspirations. Today, bold new technologies are changing the way we live and learn. Wiley will be there, providing you the must-have knowledge you need to imagine new worlds, new possibilities, and new opportunities.

Generations come and go, but you can always count on Wiley to provide you the knowledge you need, when and where you need it!

WILLIAM J. PESCE PRESIDENT AND CHIEF EXECUTIVE OFFICER	PETER BOOTH WILEY CHAIRMAN OF THE BOARD

WORKING PAPERS
Volume I / Chapters 1-12
to accompany

ACCOUNTING PRINCIPLES

8TH Edition

Jerry J. Weygandt, Ph.D., C.P.A.
Arthur Andersen Alumni Professor of Accounting
University of Wisconsin - Madison
Madison, Wisconsin

Donald E. Kieso, Ph.D., C.P.A.
KPMG Peat Marwick Emeritus Professor of Accountancy
Northern Illinois University
DeKalb, Illinois

Paul D. Kimmel, Ph.D., C.P.A.
Associate Professor of Accounting
University of Wisconsin - Milwaukee
Milwaukee, Wisconsin

Prepared By
Dick D. Wasson, M.B.A., C.P.A.
Southwestern College
San Diego State University
University of Phoenix

John Wiley & Sons, Inc.

Cover photo credit: Peter Turner / The Image Bank / Getty Images

To order books or for customer service call 1-800-CALL-WILEY (225-5945).

ISBN 978-0-470-07406-0

Printed in the United States of America

10 9 8 7 6 5 4 3 2

Printed and bound by Courier Kendallville, Inc.

CONTENTS

Working Paper templates are provided for end-of-chapter brief exercises, exercises, problems, and broadening your perspective problems. Working Paper templates are not provided for solutions that are textual in nature.

Name

Section

Date

BE1-1	Assets	Liabilities	Owner's Equity	
(a)	$ 90000	$ 50000		
(b)		40000	70000	
(c)	94000		60000	

BE1-2

(a)

(b)

(c)

BE1-3

(a)

(b)

(c)

BE1-4

(a)	(d)
(b)	(e)
(c)	(f)

BE1-5	Assets	Liabilities	Owner's Equity	
(a)				
(b)				
(c)				

BE1-6	Assets	Liabilities	Owner's Equity	
(a)				
(b)				
(c)				

BE1-7

(a)	(e)
(b)	(f)
(c)	(g)
(d)	

Name

Section

Date

BE1-8

(a)

(b)

(c)

BE1-9

Lopez Company

Balance Sheet

December 31, 2008

Assets

Liabilities and Owner's Equity

BE1-10

(a)

(b)

(c)

(d)

(e)

Name Exercise 1-8

Section

Date S. Moses & Co.

(a)

1.

2.

3.

4.

5.

6.

7.

8.

9.

10.

(b)

(c)

Name

Section

Date

Exercise 1-9

S. Moses & Co.

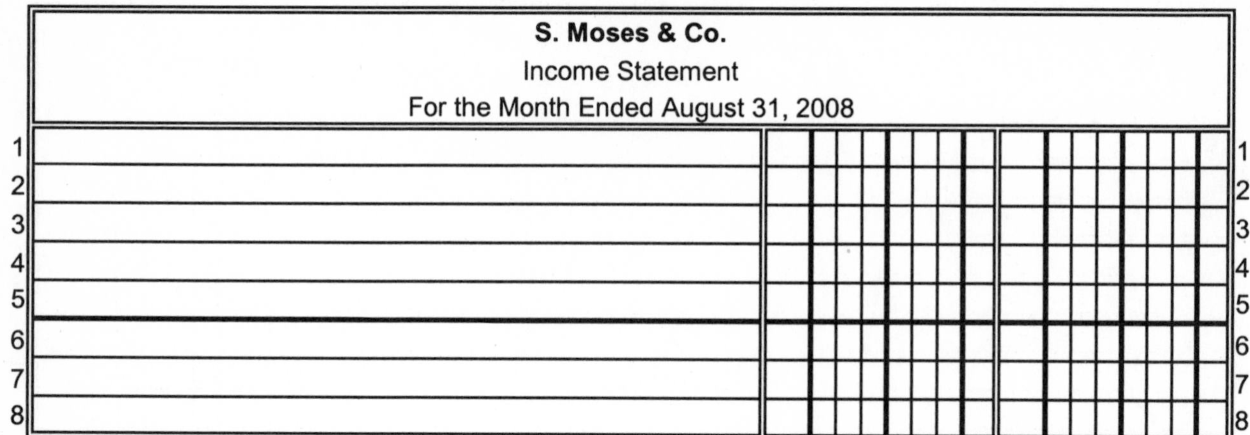

S. Moses & Co.

Income Statement

For the Month Ended August 31, 2008

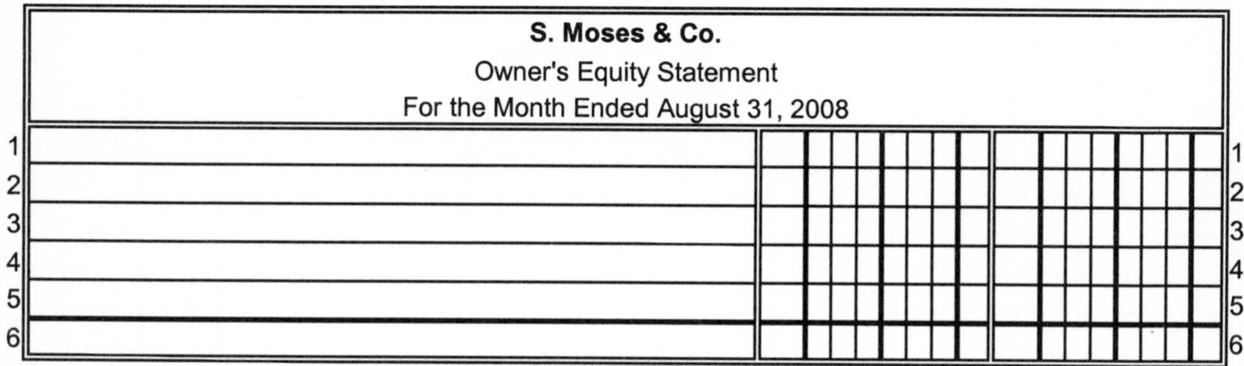

S. Moses & Co.

Owner's Equity Statement

For the Month Ended August 31, 2008

S. Moses & Co.

Balance Sheet

August 31, 2008

Assets

Liabilities and Owner's Equity

Name

Section

Date

Exercise 1-10

Lily Company

(a)

(b)

(c)

Name

Section

Date

Exercise 1-11

Craig Cantrel & Mills Enterprises

(a)

(b)

(c)

(d)

Name | Exercise 1-12
Section
Date | Linda Stanley Co.

Linda Stanley Co.
Income Statement
For the Year Ended December 31, 2008

Linda Stanley Co.
Owner's Equity Statement
For the Year Ended December 31, 2008

Name

Section

Date

E1-13

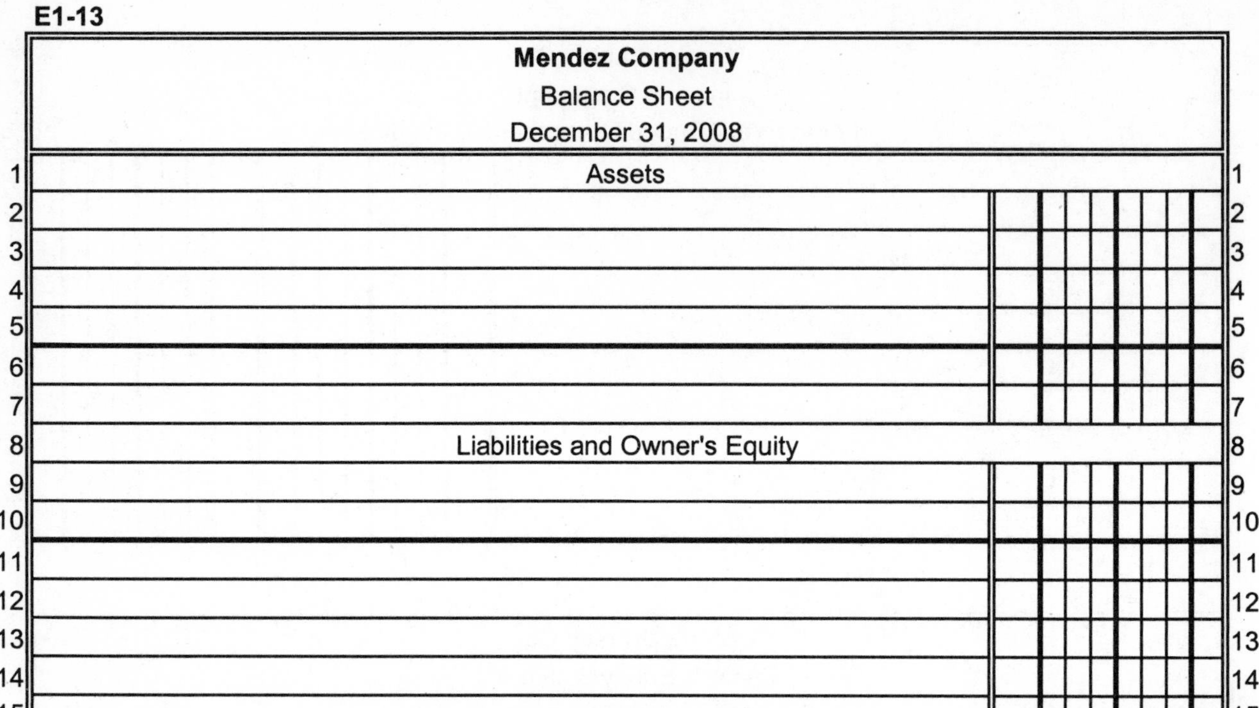

Mendez Company

Balance Sheet

December 31, 2008

Assets

Liabilities and Owner's Equity

E1-15

Summers Cruise Company

Income Statement

For the Year Ended December 31, 2008

Name | Exercise 1-14
Section
Date | Deer Park

(a)

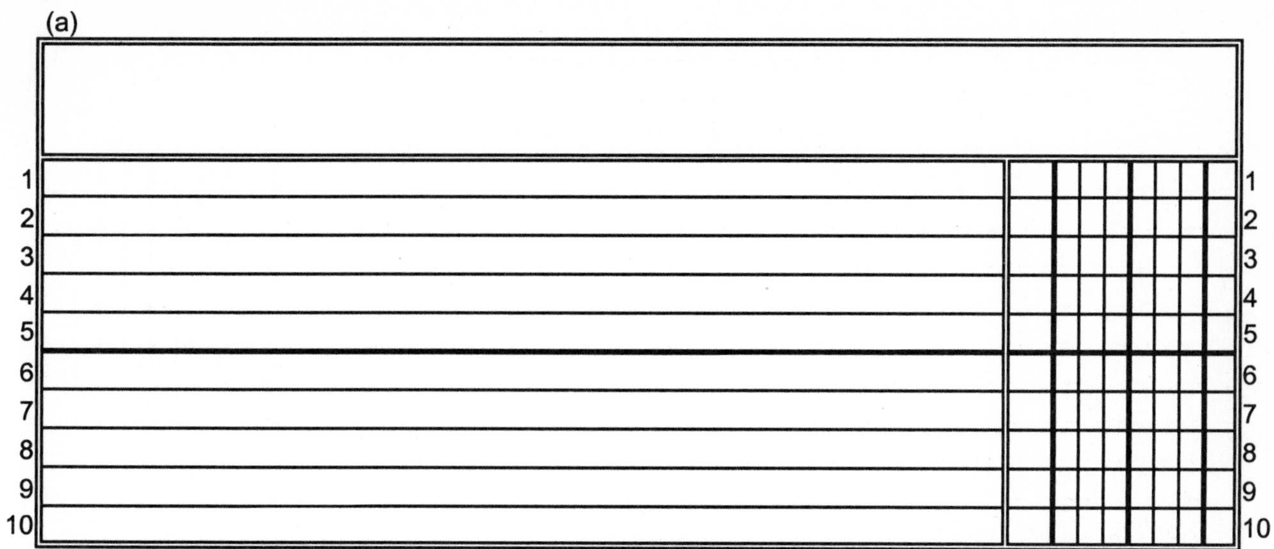

(b)

Deer Park
Balance Sheet
December 31, 2008

Assets

Liabilities and Owner's Equity

Name

Exercise 1-16

Section

Date

Kevin Johnson, Attorney

Kevin Johnson, Attorney

Owner's Equity Statement

For the Year Ended December 31, 2008

Supporting Computations

Problem 1-1A

Barone's Repair Shop

See Appendix

Name

Section

Date

Problem 1-1A

Barone's Repair Shop

(b)

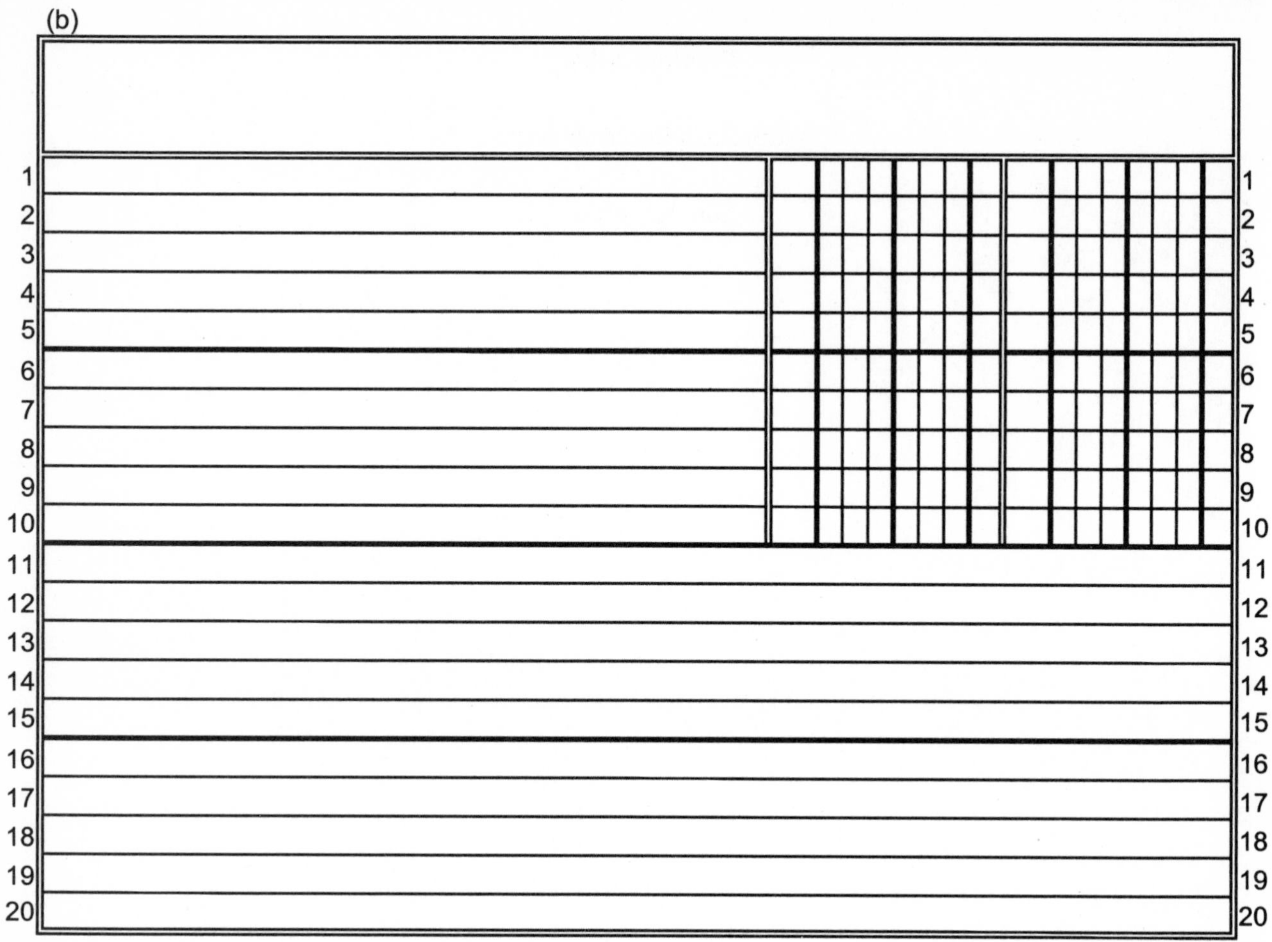

Problem 1-2A

Maria Gonzalez, Veterinarian

See Appendix

Name
Section
Date

Problem 1-2A Continued

Maria Gonzalez, Veterinarian

(b)

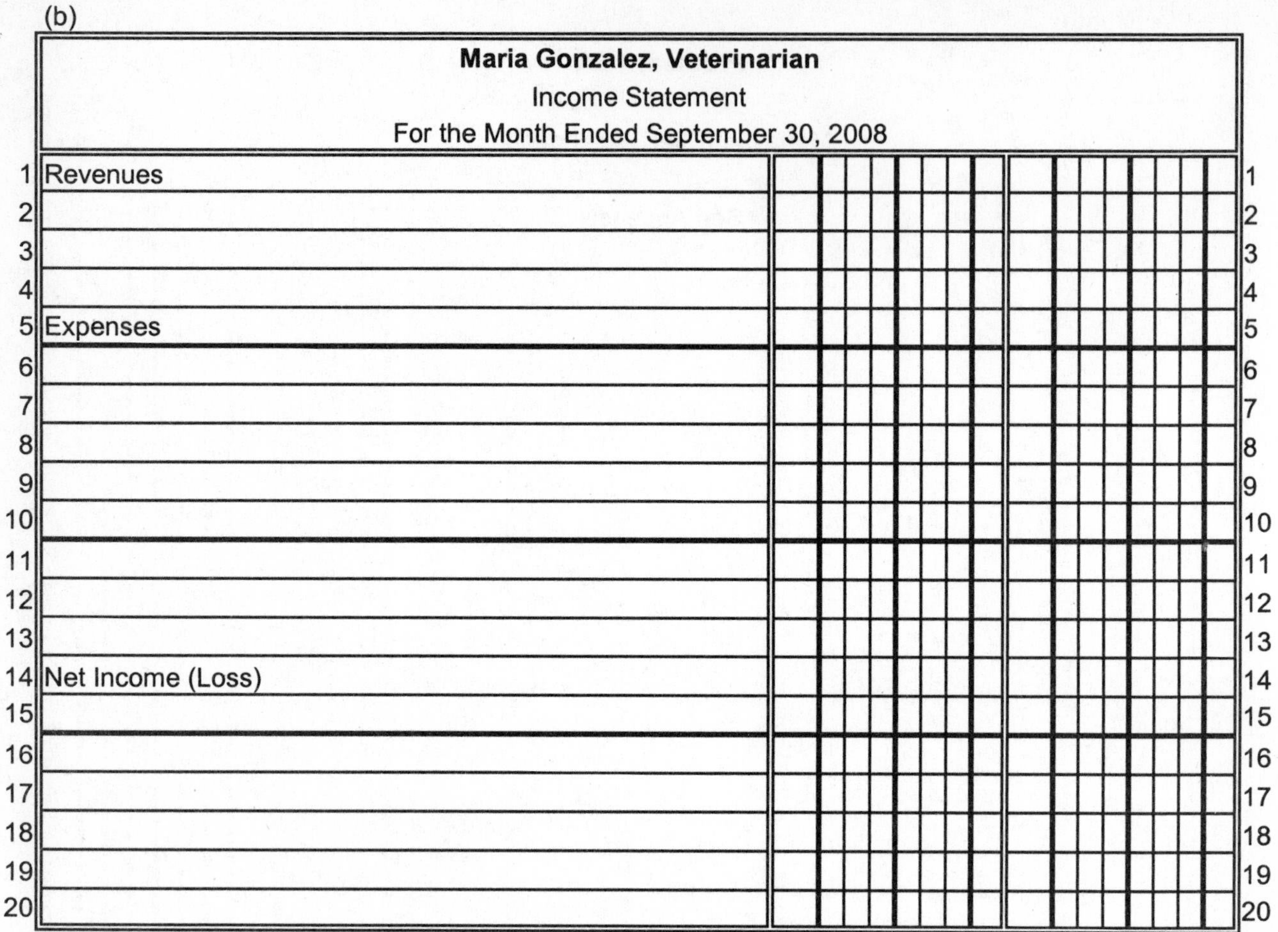

Maria Gonzalez, Veterinarian
Income Statement
For the Month Ended September 30, 2008

Revenues

Expenses

Net Income (Loss)

Maria Gonzalez, Veterinarian
Owner's Equity Statement
For the Month Ended September 30, 2008

(b) (Continued)

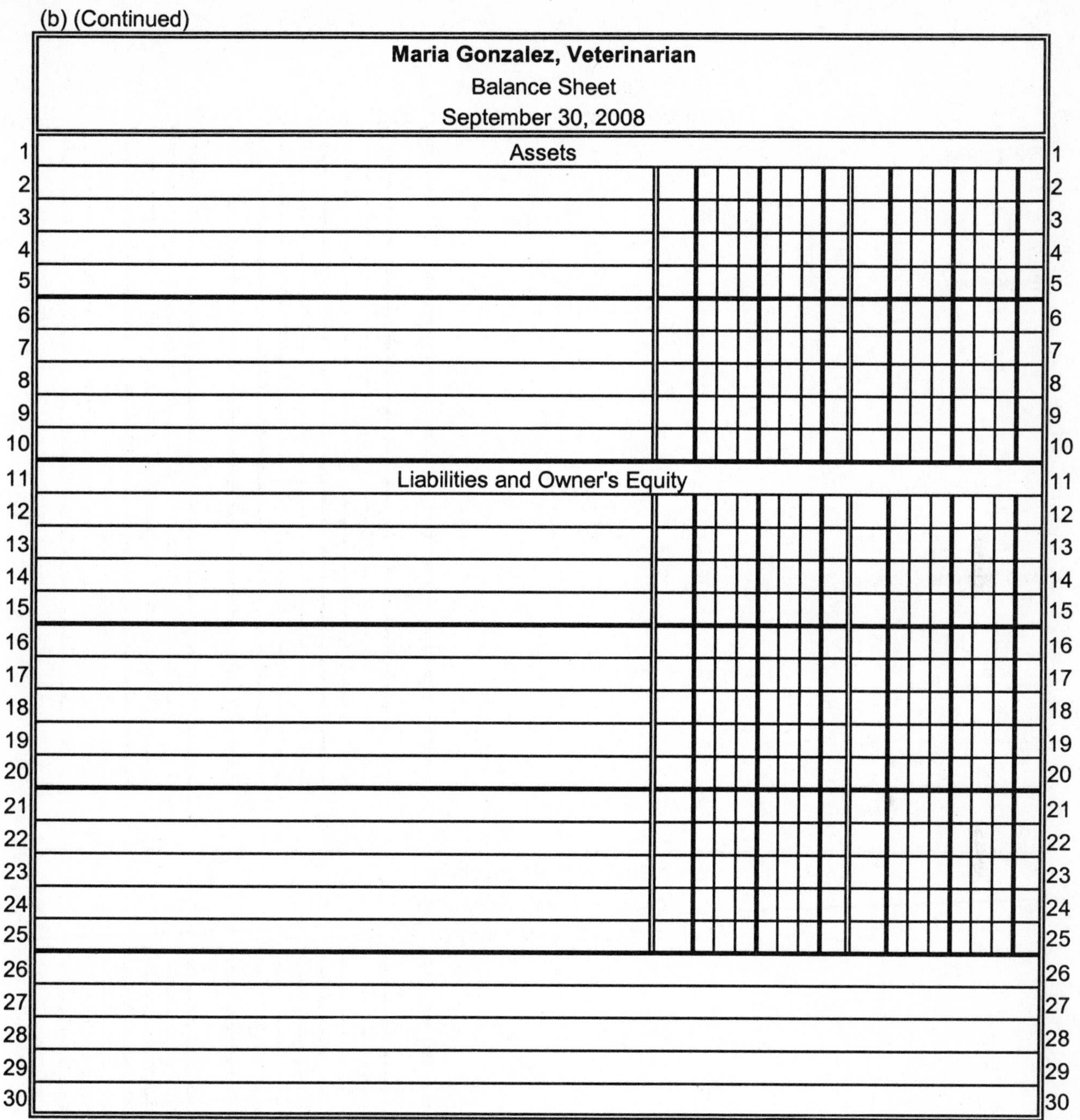

Maria Gonzalez, Veterinarian
Balance Sheet
September 30, 2008

Assets

Liabilities and Owner's Equity

Name

Section

Date

Problem 1-3A

Skyline Flying School

(a)

Skyline Flying School

Income Statement

For the Month Ended May 31, 2008

Revenues

Expenses

Net Income (Loss)

Skyline Flying School

Owner's Equity Statement

For the Month Ended May 31, 2008

(a) Continued

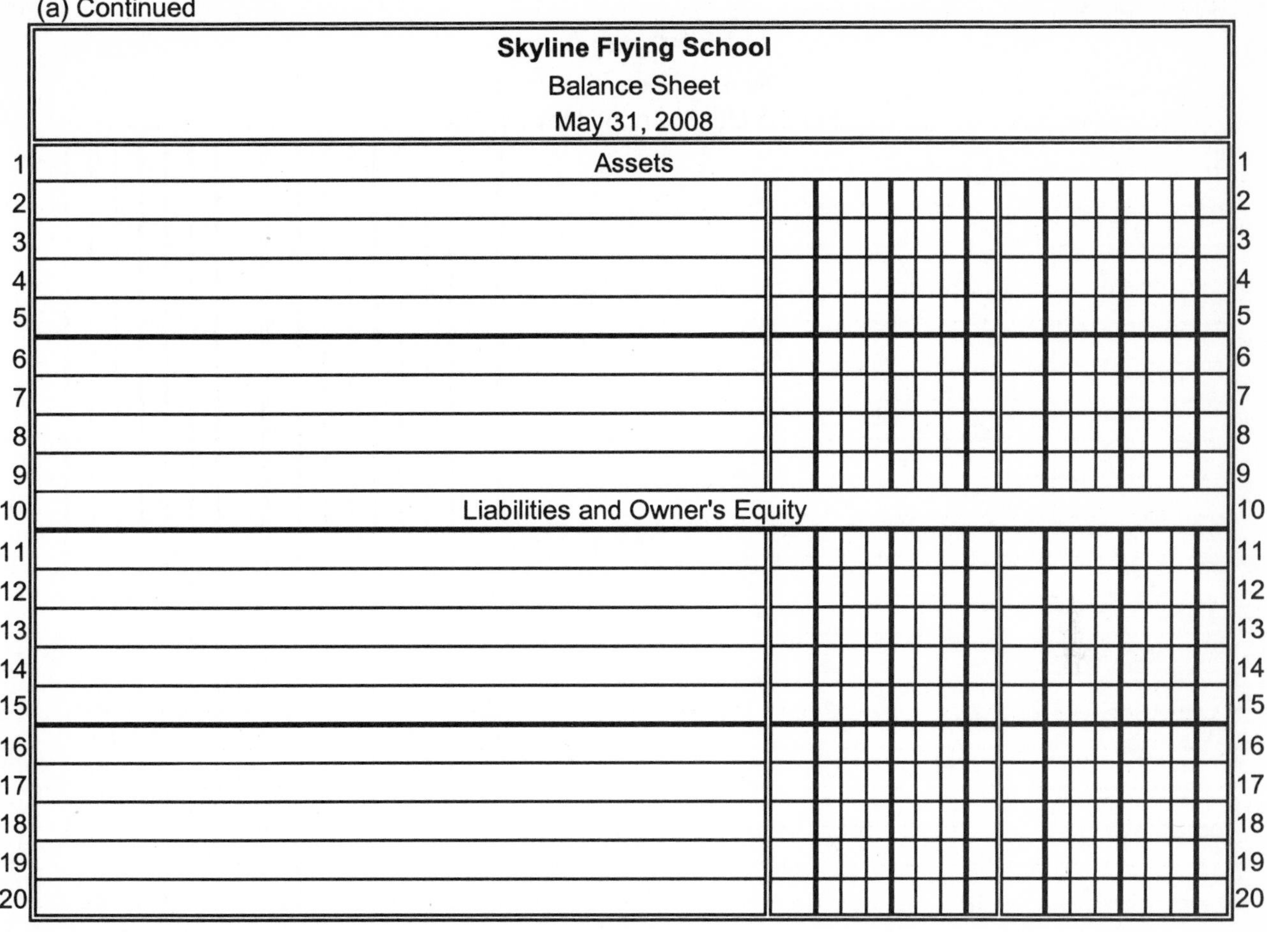

Skyline Flying School

Balance Sheet

May 31, 2008

Assets

Liabilities and Owner's Equity

(b)

Skyline Flying School

Income Statement

For the Month Ended May 31, 2008

Revenues

Expenses

Net Income (Loss)

(b) Concluded

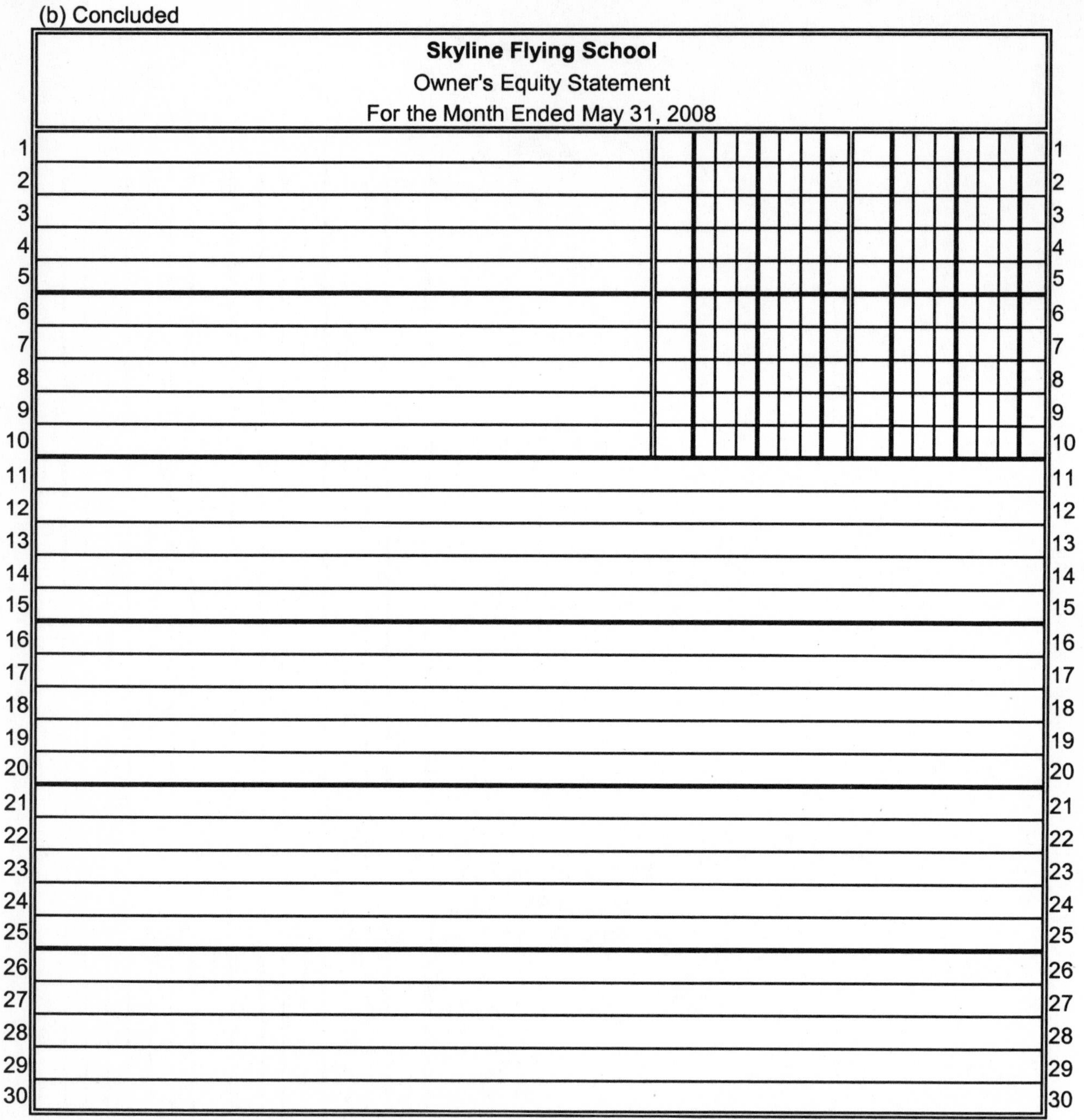

Skyline Flying School

Owner's Equity Statement

For the Month Ended May 31, 2008

Problem 1-4A

Miller Deliveries

See Appendix

Name | Problem 1-5A

Section

Date | Yates Company

(a)

	Karma Company	Yates Company	McCain Company	Dench Company
January 1, 2008				
Assets	$ 95000	$ 110000		$ 170000
Liabilities	50000		75000	
Owner's Equity		60000	40000	90000
December 31, 2008				
Assets		137000	200000	
Liabilities	55000	75000		80000
Owner's Equity	60000		130000	170000
Owner's equity changes in year				
Add'l investment		15000	10000	15000
Drawings	25000		14000	20000
Total revenues	350000	420000		520000
Total expenses	320000	385000	342000	

(b)

Yates Company

Owner's Equity Statement

For the Year Ended December 31, 2008

(c)

Problem 1-1B

Matrix Travel Agency

See Appendix

(b)

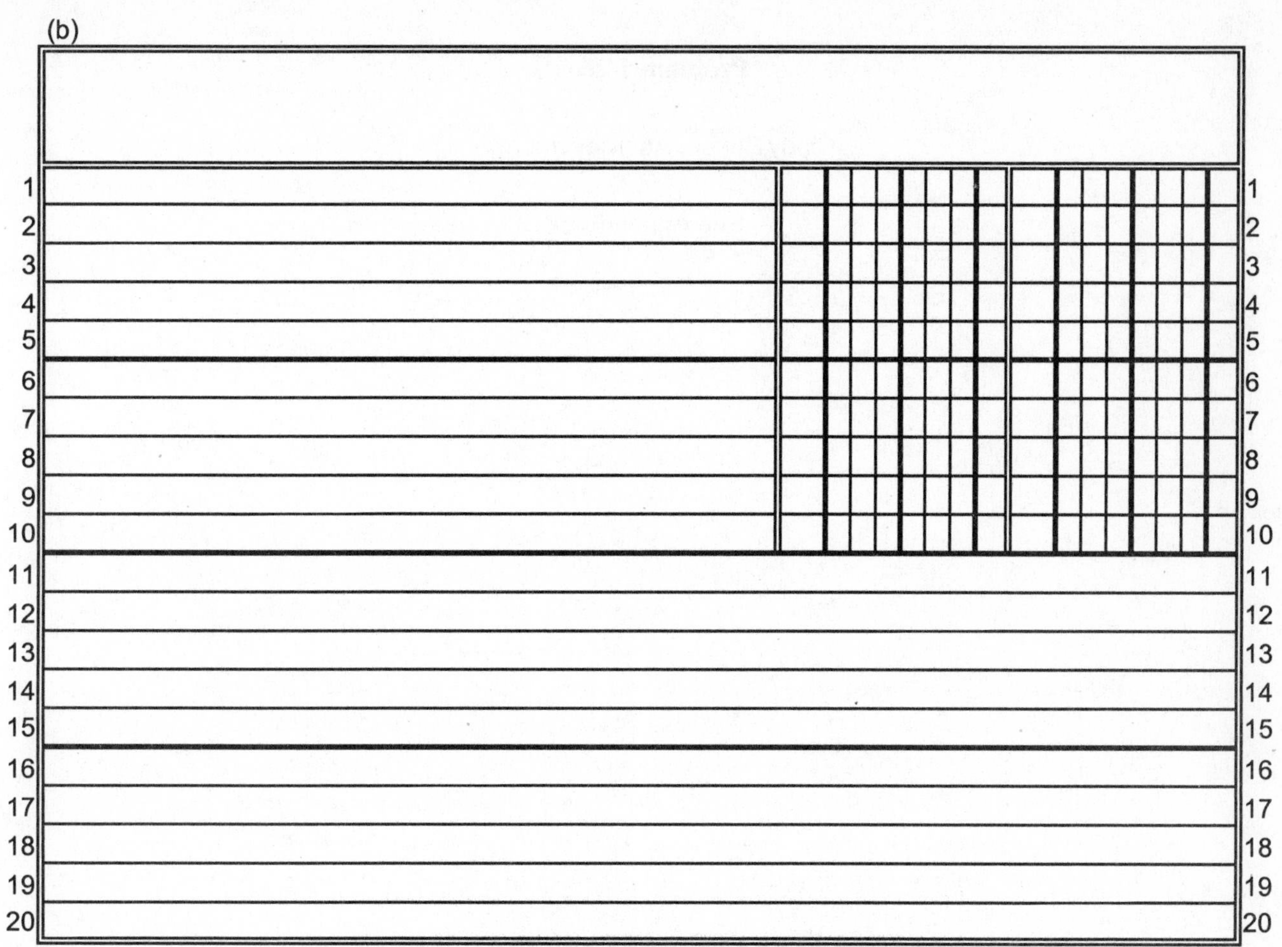

Problem 1-2B

Cindy Belton, Attorney at Law

See Appendix

(b)

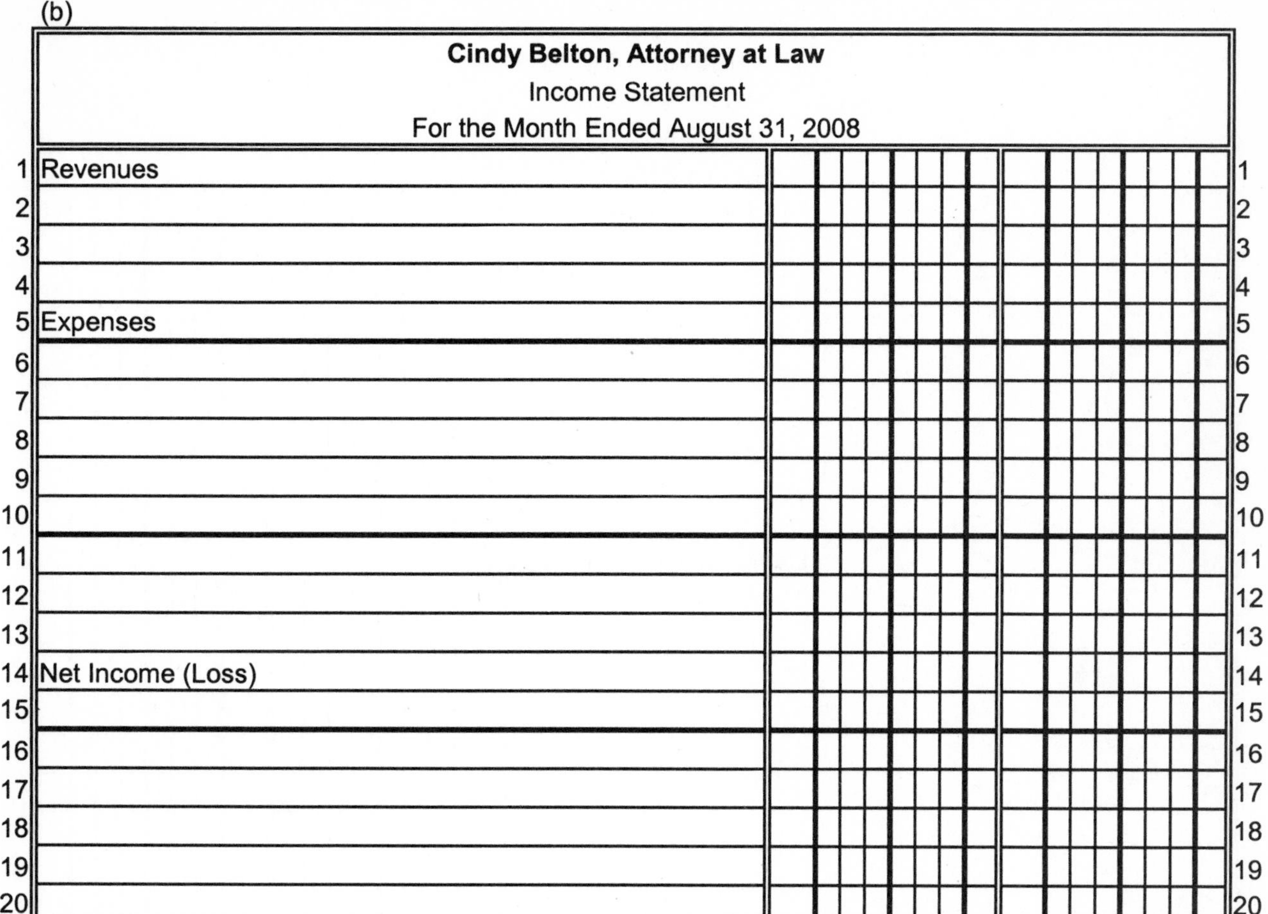

Cindy Belton, Attorney at Law
Income Statement
For the Month Ended August 31, 2008

Revenues		
Expenses		
Net Income (Loss)		

Cindy Belton, Attorney at Law
Owner's Equity Statement
For the Month Ended August 31, 2008

(b) (Continued)

Cindy Belton, Attorney at Law

Balance Sheet

August 31, 2008

Assets

Liabilities and Owner's Equity

Name Problem 1-3B

Section

Date Divine Cosmetics Co.

(a)

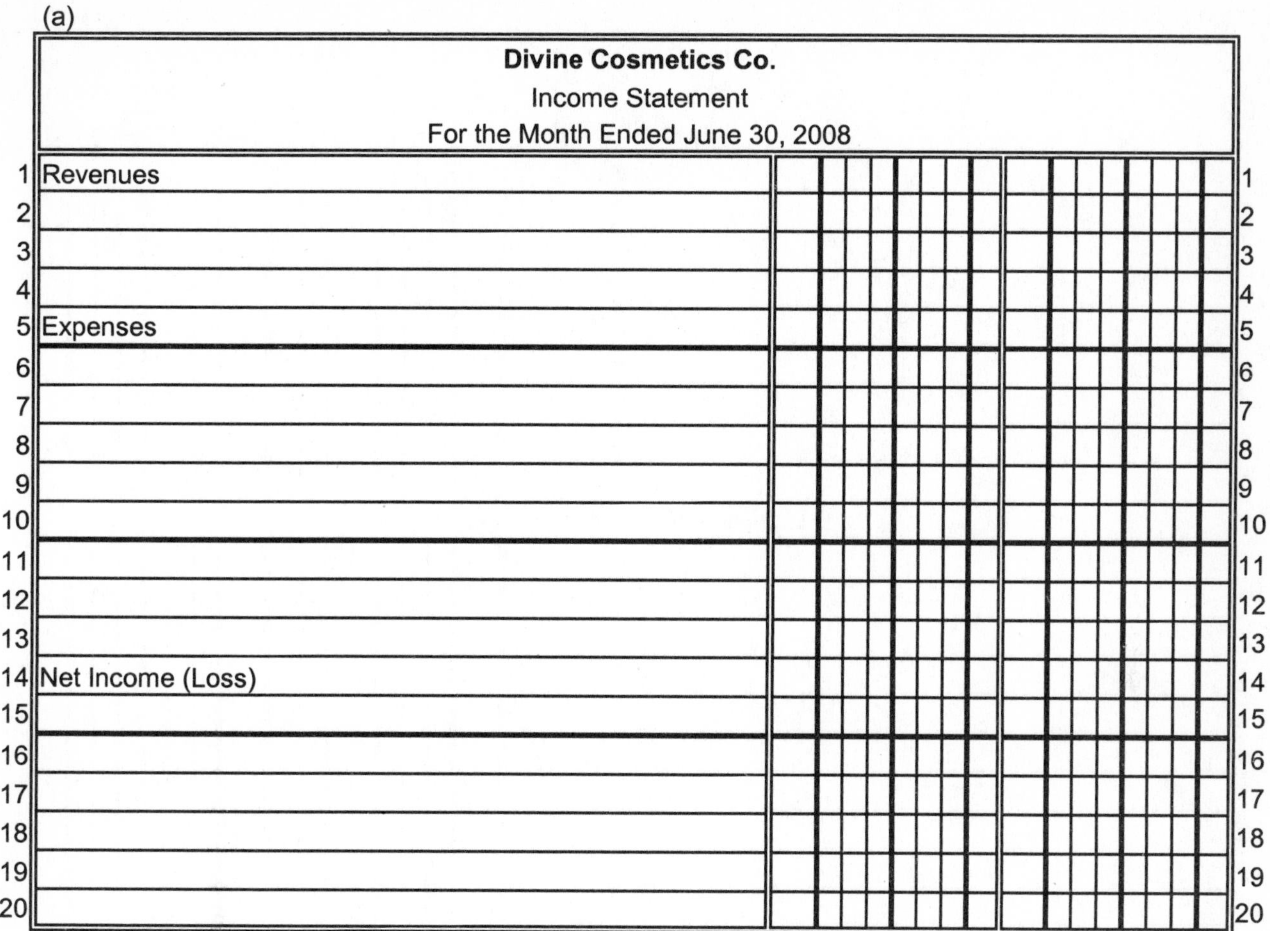

Divine Cosmetics Co.

Income Statement

For the Month Ended June 30, 2008

Revenues		
Expenses		
Net Income (Loss)		

Divine Cosmetics Co.

Owner's Equity Statement

For the Month Ended June 30, 2008

Name | Problem 1-3B Continued

Section

Date | Divine Cosmetics Co.

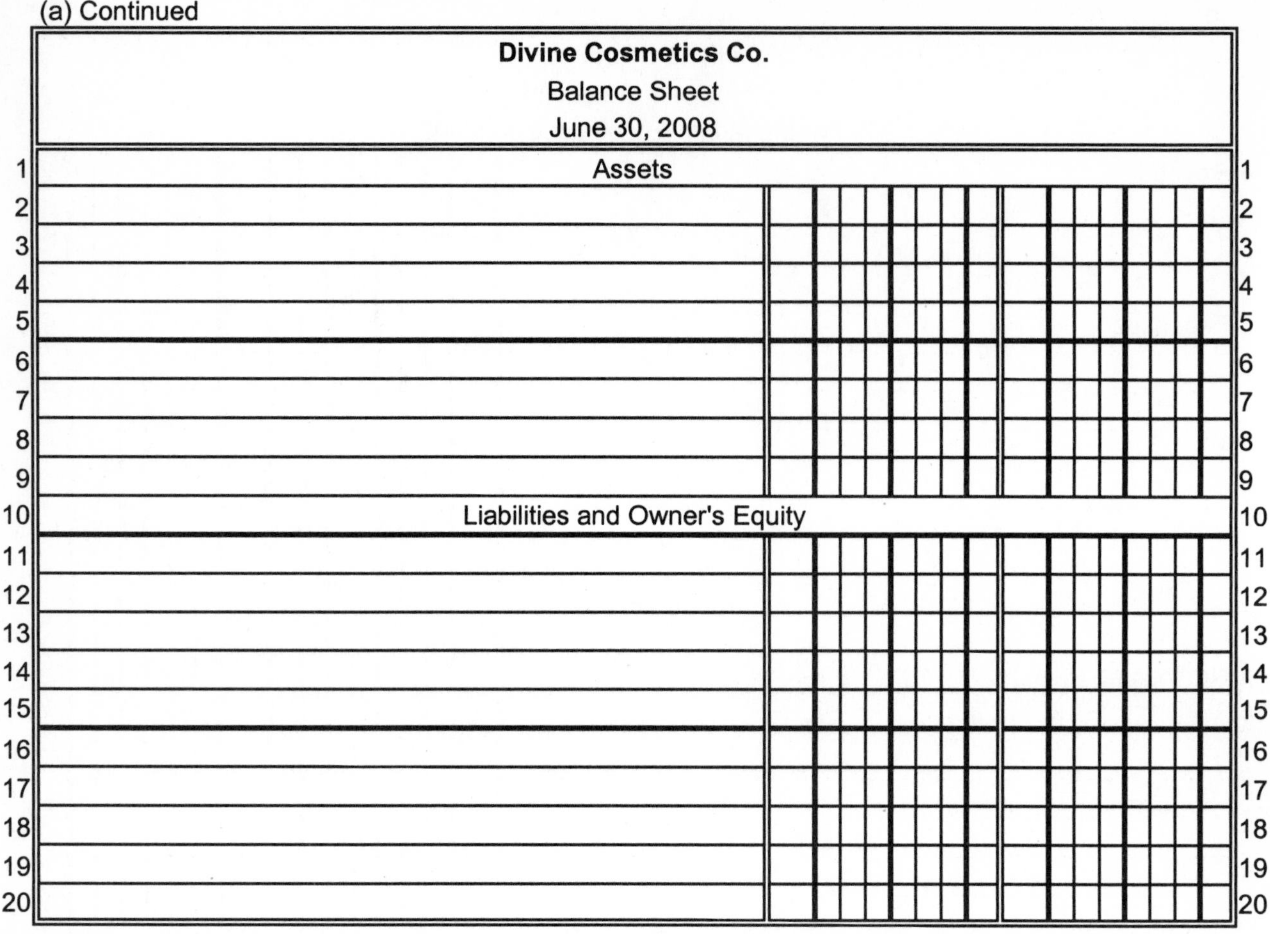

(a) Continued

Divine Cosmetics Co.
Balance Sheet
June 30, 2008

Assets

Liabilities and Owner's Equity

(b)

Divine Cosmetics Co.
Income Statement
For the Month Ended June 30, 2008

Revenues

Expenses

Net Income (Loss)

Name Problem 1-3B Concluded

Section

Date Divine Cosmetics Co.

(b) Concluded

Divine Cosmetics Co.

Owner's Equity Statement

For the Month Ended June 30, 2008

Problem 1-4B

Geller Consulting

See Appendix

(b)

Geller Consulting
Income Statement
For the Month Ended May 31, 2008

1	Revenues		
2			
3			
4	Expenses		
5			
6			
7			
8			
9			
10			
11			
12	Net income		
13			
14			

(c)

Geller Consulting
Balance Sheet
May 31, 2008

1	Assets		
2			
3			
4			
5			
6			
7			
8	Liabilities and Owner's Equity		
9			
10			
11			
12			
13			
14			
15			
16			
17			
18			

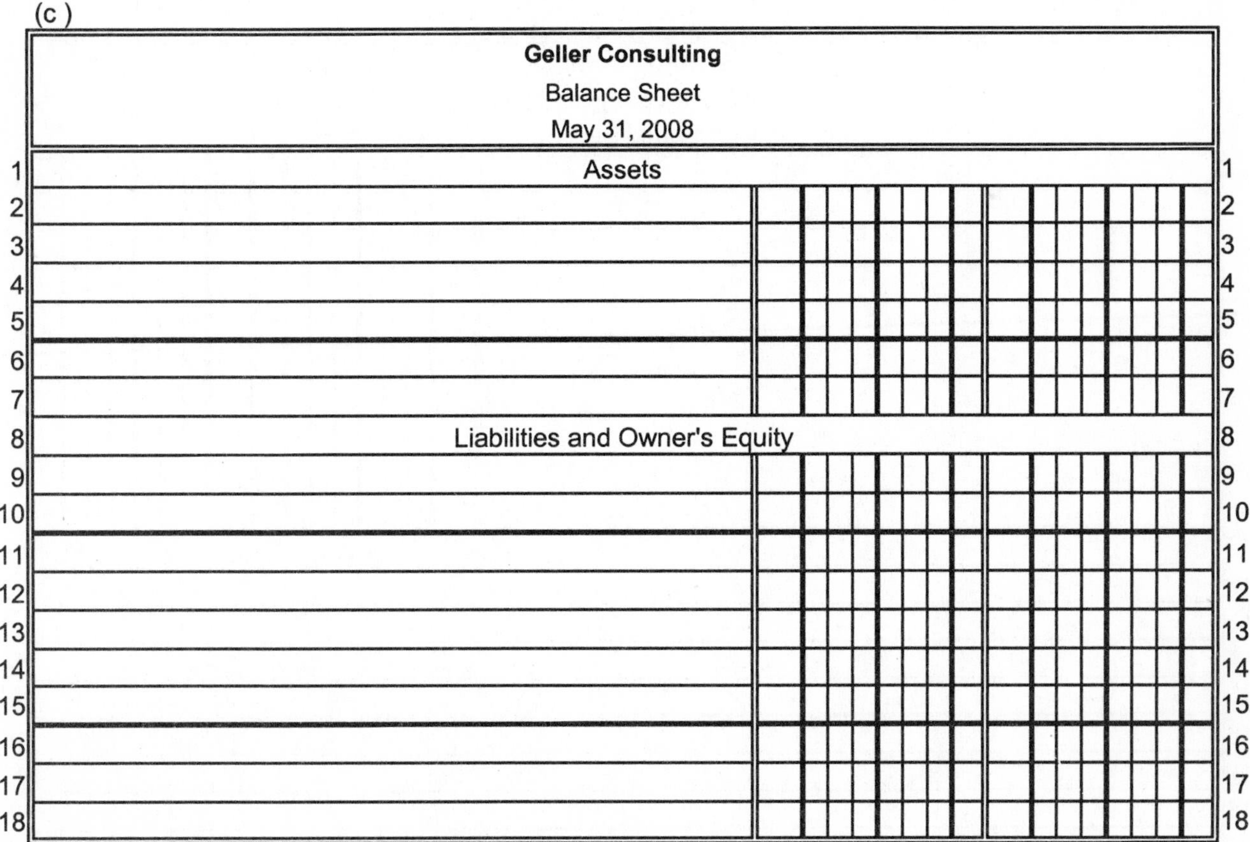

Name	Problem 1-5B
Section	
Date	McKane Company

(a)

	McKane Company	Selara Company	Gordon Company	Hindi Company
January 1, 2008				
Assets	$ 80000	$ 90000		$ 150000
Liabilities	50000		75000	
Owner's Equity		50000	49000	100000
December 31, 2008				
Assets		117000	180000	
Liabilities	55000	72000		80000
Owner's Equity	40000		100000	145000
Owner's equity changes in year				
Add'l investment		8000	10000	15000
Drawings	10000		12000	10000
Total revenues	350000	400000		500000
Total expenses	335000	385000	360000	

(b)

McKane Company

Owner's Equity Statement

For the Year Ended December 31, 2008

(c)

Name

Section

Date

(a)

(b)

(c)

(d) Net sales - 2003:

2004:

2005:

(e)

Name
Section
Date

Chapter 1 Comparative Analysis Problem

PepsiCo, Inc. versus Coca-Cola Company

	PepsiCo	Coca-Cola
(a) (in millions)		
1. Total assets		
2. Accounts receivable(net)		
3. Net sales		
4. Net income		

(b)

(a)

(b)

Chip-Shot Driving Range
Balance Sheet
March 31, 2008

Assets

Liabilities and Owner's Equity

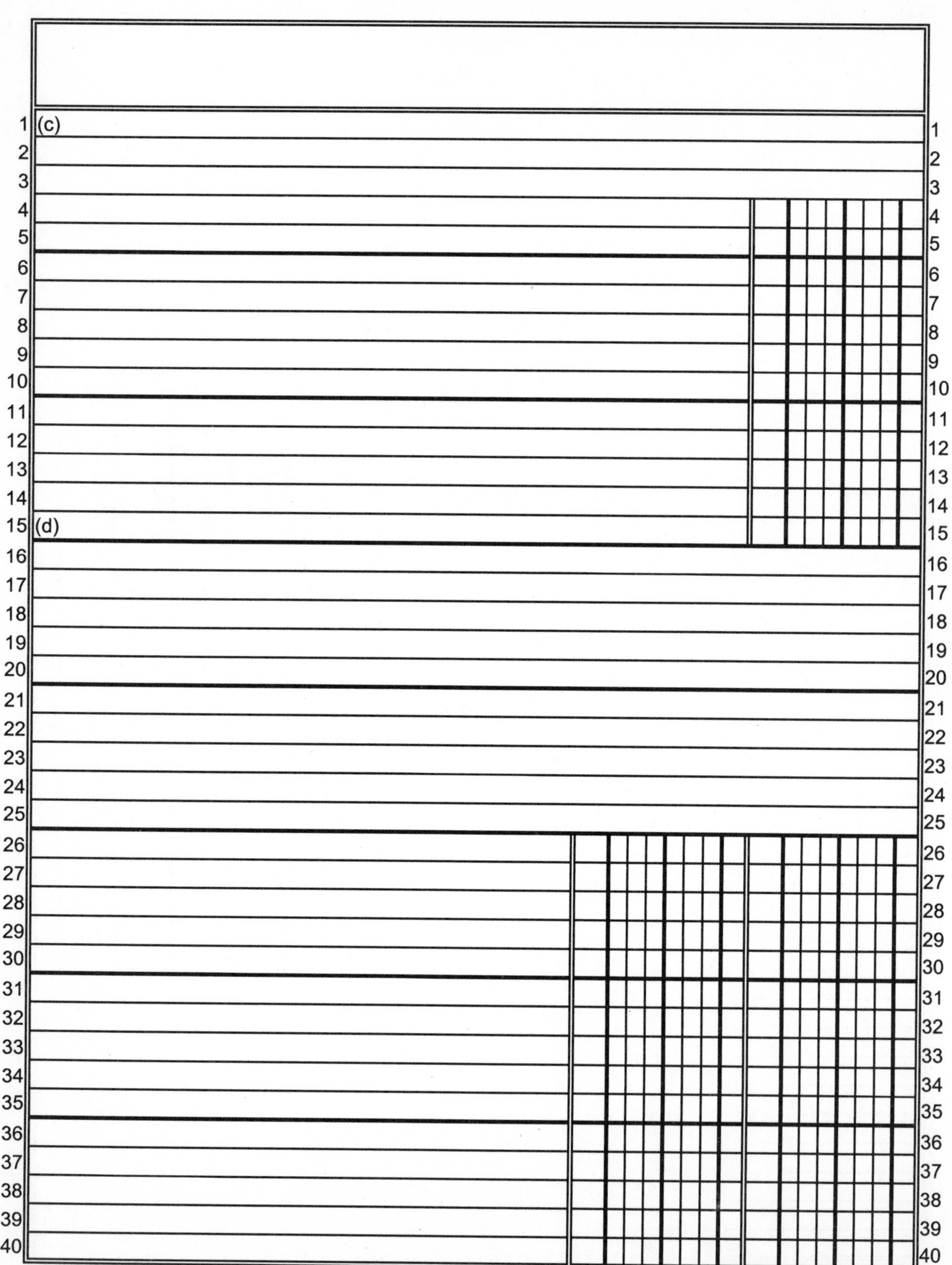

(c)

(d)

Name | Chapter 1 Communication Activity

Section

Date | New York Company

New York Company
Balance Sheet
December 31, 2008

Assets

Liabilities and Owner's Equity

Name

Section

Date

BE2-1	(a) Debit Effect	(b) Credit Effect	(c) Normal Balance
1. Accounts Payable			
2. Advertising Expense			
3. Service Revenue			
4. Accounts Receivable			
5. A.J. Ritter, Capital			
6. A.J. Ritter, Drawing			

BE2-2	Accounted Debited	Account Credited
June 1		
2		
3		
12		

BE2-3

Date	Account Titles	Debit	Credit
June 1			
2			
3			
12			

BE2-4

Name

Section

Date

BE2-5

Date	(a) Effect on Accounting Equation	(b) Debit - Credit Analysis
Aug. 1		
4		
16		
27		

BE2-6

Date	Account Titles	Debit	Credit
Aug. 1			
4			
16			
27			

Name
Section
Date

BE2-7

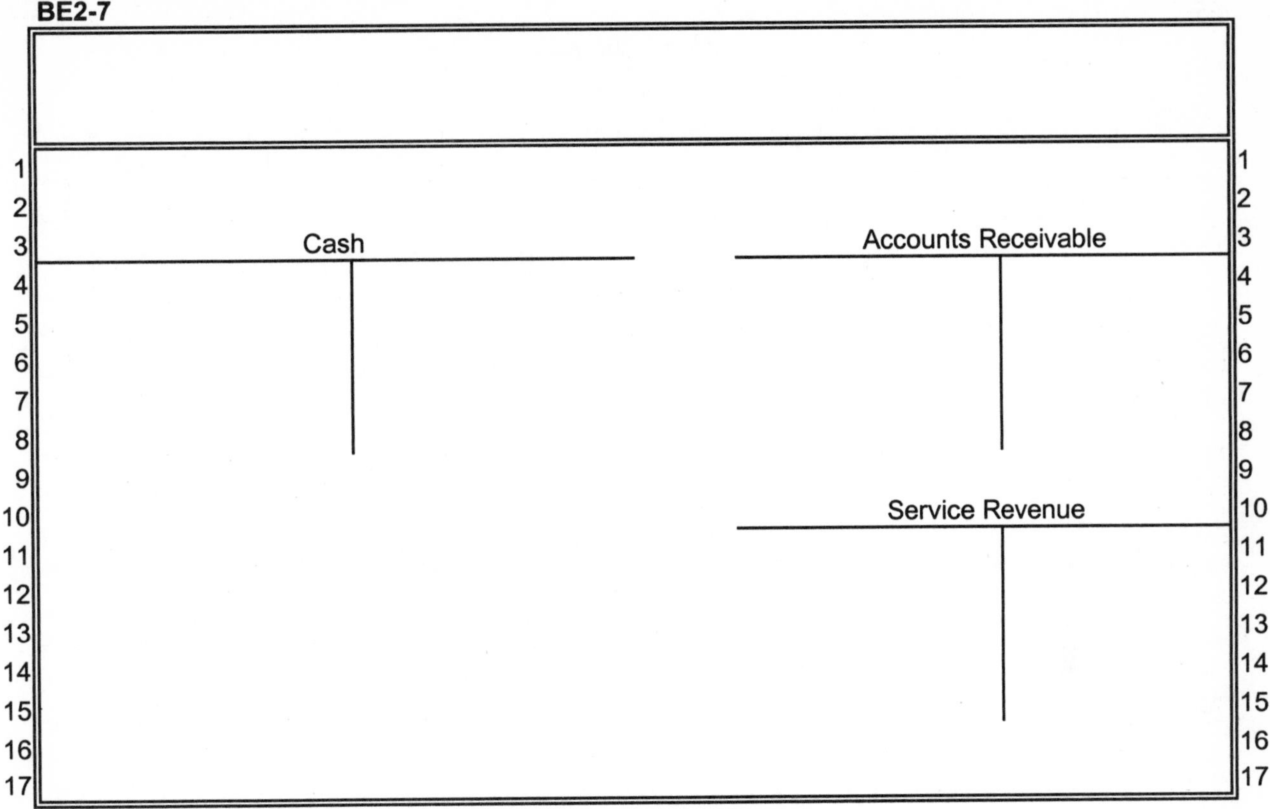

BE2-8

Cash

Date	Explanation	Ref	Debit	Credit	Balance

Accounts Receivable

Date	Explanation	Ref	Debit	Credit	Balance

Service Revenue

Date	Explanation	Ref	Debit	Credit	Balance

Name

Section

Date

BE2-9

Cleland Company
Trial Balance
June 30, 2008

	Debit	Credit

BE2-10

Kwun Company
Trial Balance
December 31, 2008

	Debit	Credit

Name

Section

Date

E2-1

1.	
2.	
3.	
4.	
5.	

E2-3 General Journal J1

Date	Account Titles	Ref.	Debit	Credit
Jan. 2				
3				
9				
11				
16				
20				
23				
28				

Name | Exercise 2-2
Section
Date | D. Reyes

Trans-action No.	Account Debited				Account Credited			
	(a) Basic Type	(b) Specific Account	(c) Effect	(d) Normal Balance	(a) Basic Type	(b) Specific Account	(c) Effect	(d) Normal Balance
Jan. 2	Asset	Cash	Increase	Debit	Owner's	D. Reyes,	Increase	Credit
					Equity	Capital		
3								
9								
11								
16								
20								
23								
28								

Name

Section

Date

Exercises 2-4 and 2-5

E2-4

Date	
Oct. 1	
2	
3	
6	
27	
30	

E2-5

Date	Account Titles	Ref.	Debit	Credit
Oct. 1				
2				
3				
6				
27				
30				

Name
Section
Date

E2-6

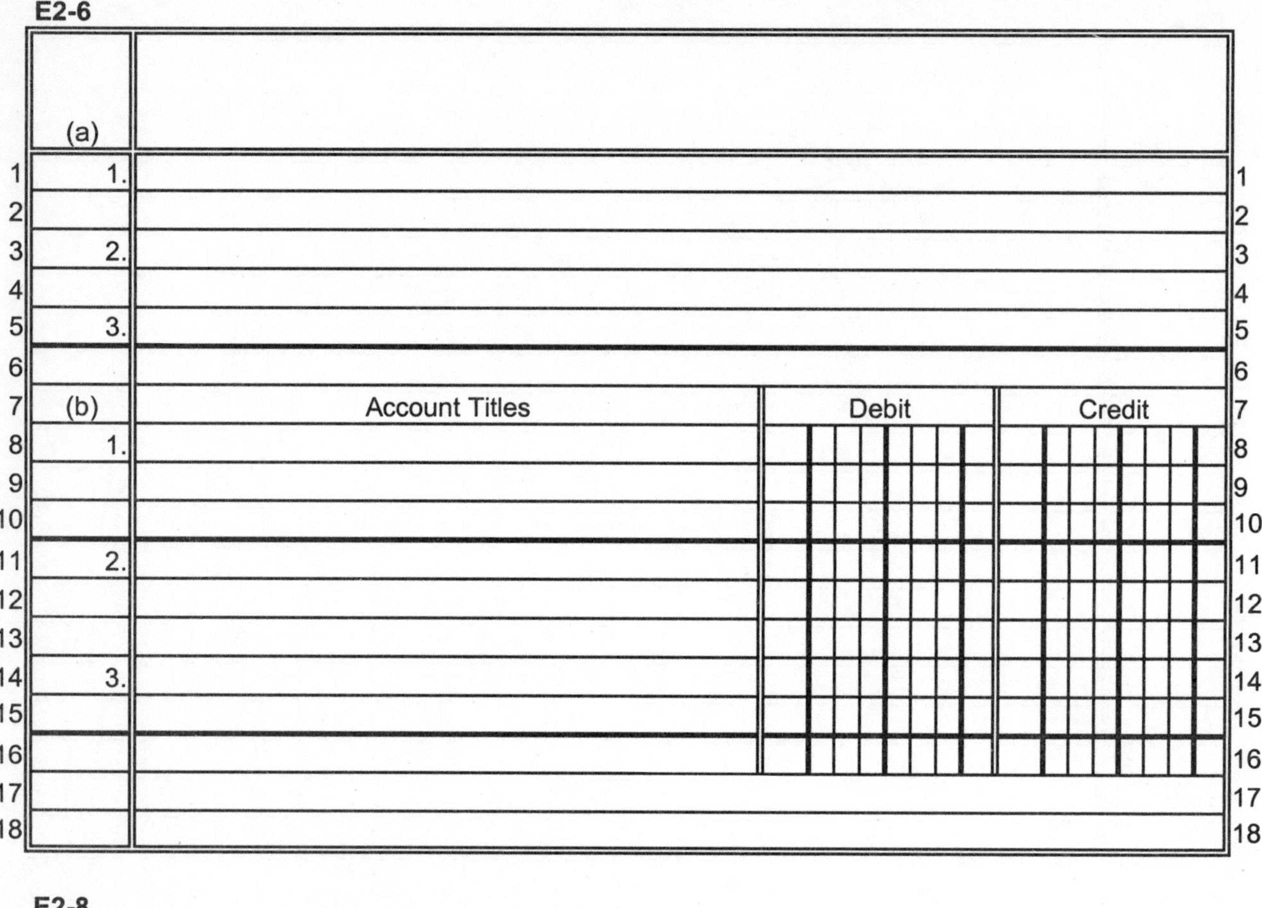

(a)

1.

2.

3.

(b)	Account Titles	Debit	Credit
1.			
2.			
3.			

E2-8

1.

2.

3.

4.

5.

Name | Exercise 2-7

Section

Date | Rowand Enterprises

(a)		Assets =	Liabilities +	Owners' Equity
1.				
2.				
3.				
4.				

(b)	Account Titles	Debit	Credit
1.			
2.			
3.			
4.			

Name

Section

Date

Exercise 2-9

Teresa Gonzalez, Investment Broker

(a)

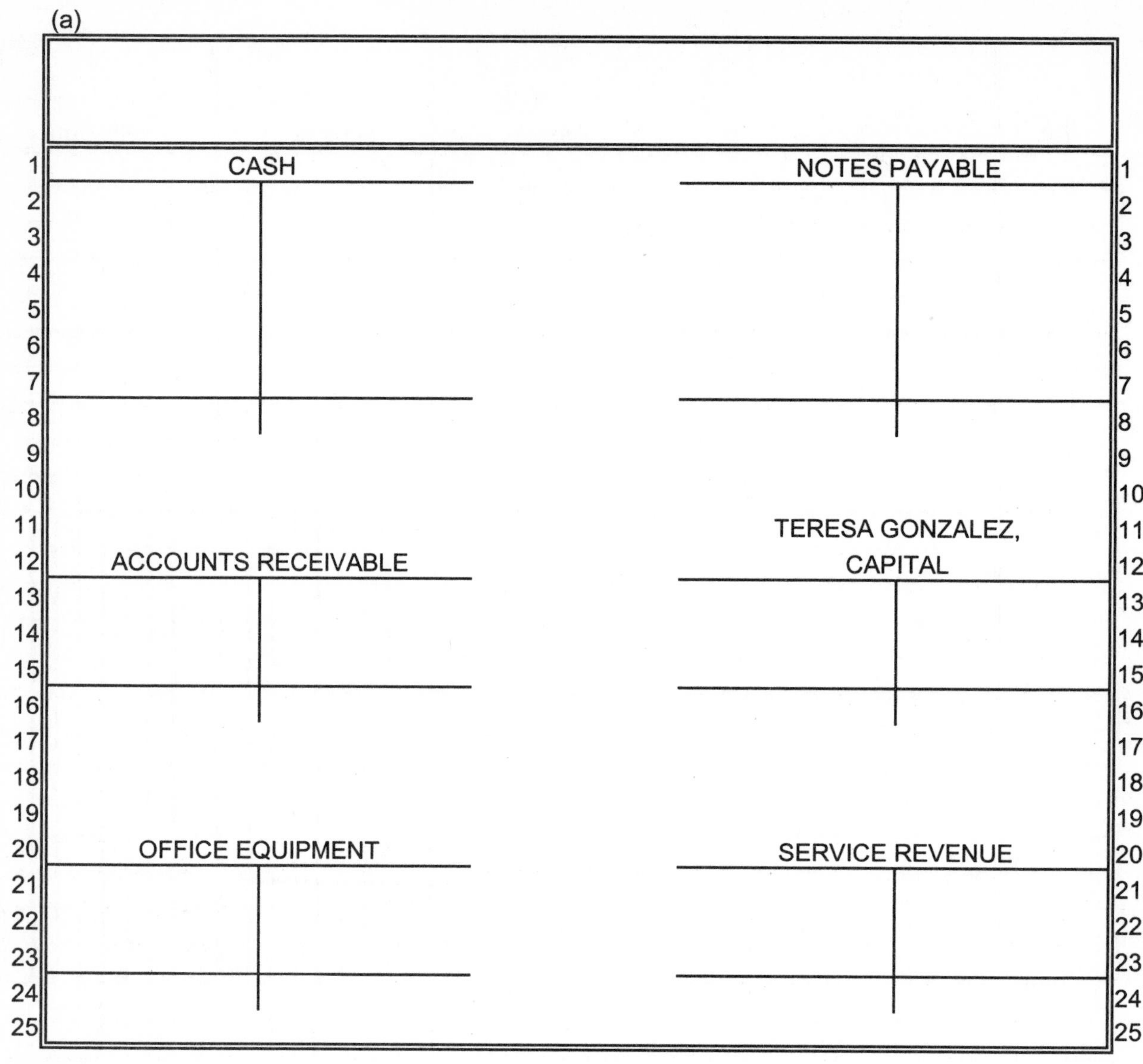

(b)

Teresa Gonzalez, Investment Broker

Trial Balance

August 31, 2008

	Debit	Credit

Name Exercise 2-10

Section

Date Simon Landscaping Company

(a)

General Journal

Date	Account Titles	Ref.	Debit	Credit
Apr. 1				
12				
15				
25				
29				
30				

(b)

Simon Landscaping Company

Trial Balance

April 30, 2008

	Debit	Credit

Name	Exercise 2-11
Section	
Date	Heerey Co.

(a)

General Journal

Date	Account Titles	Ref.	Debit	Credit
Oct. 1				
10				
10				
20				
20				

(b)

Heerey Co.
Trial Balance
October 31, 2008

	Debit	Credit

Name
Section
Date

Exercise 2-12

Tina Cordero Company

(a) General Journal J1

Date	Account Titles	Ref.	Debit	Credit
Sept. 1				
5				
25				
30				

(b)

Cash No. 101

Date	Explanation	Ref.	Debit	Credit	Balance

Equipment No. 157

Date	Explanation	Ref.	Debit	Credit	Balance

Accounts Payable No. 201

Date	Explanation	Ref.	Debit	Credit	Balance

Tina Cordero, Capital No. 301

Date	Explanation	Ref.	Debit	Credit	Balance

Tina Cordero, Drawing No. 306

Date	Explanation	Ref.	Debit	Credit	Balance

Name

Section

Date

E2-13

Error	(a) In Balance	(b) Difference	(c) Larger Column
1. A credit posting of $400 to Accounts Receivable was omitted.	No	$400	Debit
2. A debit posting of $750 for Prepaid Insurance was debited to Insurance Expense.			
3. A collection from a customer of $100 in payment of its account owed was journalized and posted as a debit to Cash for $100 and a credit to Service Revenue $100.			
4. A credit posting of $300 to Property Taxes Payable was made twice			
5. A cash purchase of supplies for $250 was journalized and posted as a debit to Supplies $25 and a credit to Cash $25.			
6. A debit of $475 to Advertising Expense was posted as $457.			

E2-14

Sanford Delivery Service

Trial Balance

July 31, 2008

	Debit	Credit

Name

Section

Date

Problem 2-1A

Frontier Park

General Journal J1

Date	Account Titles	Ref.	Debit	Credit
Apr. 1				
4				
8				
11				
12				
13				
17				
20				
25				
30				
30				

Name | Problem 2-2A
Section
Date | Jane Kent, CPA

(a) General Journal J1

Date	Account Titles	Ref.	Debit	Credit
May 1				
2				
3				
7				
11				
12				
17				
31				
31				

(b)

Cash No. 101

Date	Explanation	Ref.	Debit	Credit	Balance

Accounts Receivable No. 112

Date	Explanation	Ref.	Debit	Credit	Balance

Supplies No. 126

Date	Explanation	Ref.	Debit	Credit	Balance

Accounts Payable No. 201

Date	Explanation	Ref.	Debit	Credit	Balance

Unearned Revenue No. 205

Date	Explanation	Ref.	Debit	Credit	Balance

Jane Kent, Capital No. 301

Date	Explanation	Ref.	Debit	Credit	Balance

(b) (Continued)

Service Revenue No. 400

Date	Explanation	Ref.	Debit	Credit	Balance

Salaries Expense No. 726

Date	Explanation	Ref.	Debit	Credit	Balance

Rent Expense No. 729

Date	Explanation	Ref.	Debit	Credit	Balance

(c)

Jane Kent, CPA
Trial Balance
May 31, 2008

		Debit	Credit	
1	Cash			1
2	Accounts Receivable			2
3	Supplies			3
4	Accounts Payable			4
5	Unearned Revenue			5
6	Jane Kent, Capital			6
7	Service Revenue			7
8	Salaries Expense			8
9	Rent Expense			9
10				10
11				11

Name Problem 2-3A

Section

Date Byte Repair Service

(a) & (c)

Cash

Debit	Credit
Bal. 8,000	

Accounts Receivable

Debit	Credit
Bal. 15,000	

Parts Inventory

Debit	Credit
Bal. 13,000	

Prepaid Rent

Debit	Credit
Bal. 3,000	

Shop Equipment

Debit	Credit
Bal. 21,000	

Accounts Payable

Debit	Credit
	Bal. 19,000

Jack Shellenkamp, Capital

Debit	Credit
	Bal. 41,000

Jack Shellenkamp, Drawings

Repair Services Revenue

Advertising Expense

Miscellaneous Expense

Repair Parts Expense

Wage Expense

Name Problem 2-3A Continued

Section

Date Byte Repair Service

(b) General Journal J1

Date	Account Titles and Explanation	Ref.	Debit	Credit
1.				
2.				
3.				
4.				
5.				
6.				
7.				
8.				
9.				

Name Problem 2-3A Concluded

Section

Date Byte Repair Service

(d)

Byte Repair Service

Trial Balance

January 31, 2008

	Debit	Credit
Cash		
Accounts Receivable		
Parts Inventory		
Prepaid Rent		
Shop Equipment		
Accounts Payable		
Jack Shellenkamp, Capital		
Jack Shellenkamp, Drawings		
Repair Services Revenue		
Advertising Expense		
Miscellaneous Expense		
Repair Parts Expense		
Wage Expense		
Totals		

Name Problem 2-4A

Section

Date Sterling Company

Sterling Company

Trial Balance

May 31, 2008

	Debit	Credit

Journal Entry Aids:

Name	Problem 2-5A
Section	
Date	Lake Theater

(a) and (c)

Cash — No. 101

Date	Explanation	Ref.	Debit	Credit	Balance
Apr. 1	Balance	√			6000

Accounts Receivable — No. 112

Date	Explanation	Ref.	Debit	Credit	Balance

Prepaid Rentals — No. 136

Date	Explanation	Ref.	Debit	Credit	Balance

Land — No. 140

Date	Explanation	Ref.	Debit	Credit	Balance
Apr. 1	Balance	√			10000

Buildings — No. 145

Date	Explanation	Ref.	Debit	Credit	Balance
Apr. 1	Balance	√			8000

Equipment — No. 157

Date	Explanation	Ref.	Debit	Credit	Balance
Apr. 1	Balance	√			6000

Accounts Payable — No. 201

Date	Explanation	Ref.	Debit	Credit	Balance
Apr. 1	Balance	√			2000

(a) and (c) (Continued)

Mortgage Payable — No. 275

Date	Explanation	Ref.	Debit	Credit	Balance
Apr. 1	Balance	√			8000

Tony Carpino, Capital — No. 301

Date	Explanation	Ref.	Debit	Credit	Balance
Apr. 1	Balance	√			20000

Admission Revenue — No. 405

Date	Explanation	Ref.	Debit	Credit	Balance

Concession Revenue — No. 406

Date	Explanation	Ref.	Debit	Credit	Balance

Advertising Expense — No. 610

Date	Explanation	Ref.	Debit	Credit	Balance

Film Rental Expense — No. 632

Date	Explanation	Ref.	Debit	Credit	Balance

Salaries Expense — No. 726

Date	Explanation	Ref.	Debit	Credit	Balance

Name	Problem 2-5A Continued
Section	
Date	Lake Theater

(b) General Journal J1

Date	Account Titles	Ref.	Debit	Credit
Apr. 2				
3				
9				
10				
11				
12				
20				
25				
29				
30				
30				

(d)

Lake Theater
Trial Balance
April 30, 2008

	Debit	Credit
Cash		
Accounts Receivable		
Prepaid Rentals		
Land		
Buildings		
Equipment		
Accounts Payable		
Mortgage Payable		
Tony Carpino, Capital		
Admission Revenue		
Concession Revenue		
Advertising Expense		
Film Rental Expense		
Salaries Expense		

Name Problem 2-1B

Section

Date Surepar Miniature Golf and Driving Range

General Journal J1

Date	Account Titles	Ref.	Debit	Credit
Mar. 1				
3				
5				
6				
10				
18				
19				
25				
30				

Name

Section

Date

Problem 2-1B Concluded

Surepar Miniature Golf and Driving Range

General Journal

J1

Date	Account Titles	Ref.	Debit	Credit
Mar. 30				
31				

Name

Section

Date

Problem 2-2B

Rosa Perez, Architect

(a)

General Journal

J1

Date	Account Titles	Ref.	Debit	Credit
Apr. 1				
1				
2				
3				
10				
11				
20				
30				
30				

(b)

Cash No. 101

Date	Explanation	Ref.	Debit	Credit	Balance

Accounts Receivable No. 112

Date	Explanation	Ref.	Debit	Credit	Balance

Supplies No. 126

Date	Explanation	Ref.	Debit	Credit	Balance

Accounts Payable No. 201

Date	Explanation	Ref.	Debit	Credit	Balance

Unearned Revenue No. 205

Date	Explanation	Ref.	Debit	Credit	Balance

Rosa Perez, Capital No. 301

Date	Explanation	Ref.	Debit	Credit	Balance

(b) (Continued)

Service Revenue No. 400

Date	Explanation	Ref.	Debit	Credit	Balance

Salaries Expense No. 726

Date	Explanation	Ref.	Debit	Credit	Balance

Rent Expense No. 729

Date	Explanation	Ref.	Debit	Credit	Balance

(c)

Rosa Perez, Architect
Trial Balance
April 30, 2008

		Debit	Credit	
1	Cash			1
2	Accounts Receivable			2
3	Supplies			3
4	Accounts Payable			4
5	Unearned Revenue			5
6	Rosa Perez, Capital			6
7	Service Revenue			7
8	Salaries Expense			8
9	Rent Expense			9
10				10
11				11

Name

Section

Date

Problem 2-3B

Slocombe Services

(a) General Journal

Trans.	Account Titles	Ref.	Debit	Credit
1.				
2.				
3.				
4.				
5.				
6.				
7.				
8.				
9.				
10.				
11.				
12.				

(b)

Cash

Accounts Receivable

Office Supplies

Prepaid Insurance

Prepaid Rent

Furniture & Equipment

Accounts Payable

Ronald Slocombe, Capital

Service Revenue

Salaries Expense

Utility Expense

(c)

Slocombe Services
Trial Balance
May 31, 2008

	Debit	Credit
Cash		
Accounts Receivable		
Office Supplies		
Prepaid Insurance		
Prepaid Rent		
Furniture and Equipment		
Accounts Payable		
Ronald Slocombe, Capital		
Service Revenue		
Salaries Expense		
Utility Expense		

Name | Problem 2-4B

Section

Date | Don Kelso Co.

Don Kelso Co.
Trial Balance
June 30, 2008

	Debit	Credit

Journal Entry Aids:

Name

Section

Date

Problem 2-5B

Quinn Theater

(a) and (c)

Cash — No. 101

Date	Explanation	Ref.	Debit	Credit	Balance
Mar. 1	Balance	√			16000

Accounts Receivable — No. 112

Date	Explanation	Ref.	Debit	Credit	Balance

Land — No. 140

Date	Explanation	Ref.	Debit	Credit	Balance
Mar. 1	Balance	√			42000

Buildings — No. 145

Date	Explanation	Ref.	Debit	Credit	Balance
Mar. 1	Balance	√			18000

Equipment — No. 157

Date	Explanation	Ref.	Debit	Credit	Balance
Mar. 1	Balance	√			16000

Accounts Payable — No. 201

Date	Explanation	Ref.	Debit	Credit	Balance
Mar. 1	Balance	√			12000

M. Quinn, Capital — No. 301

Date	Explanation	Ref.	Debit	Credit	Balance
Mar. 1	Balance	√			80000

(a) and (c) (Continued)

Admission Revenue No. 405

Date	Explanation	Ref.	Debit	Credit	Balance

Concession Revenue No. 406

Date	Explanation	Ref.	Debit	Credit	Balance

Advertising Expense No. 610

Date	Explanation	Ref.	Debit	Credit	Balance

Film Rental Expense No. 632

Date	Explanation	Ref.	Debit	Credit	Balance

Salaries Expense No. 726

Date	Explanation	Ref.	Debit	Credit	Balance

Name

Section

Date

Problem 2-5B Continued

Quinn Theater

(b) General Journal J1

Date	Account Titles	Ref.	Debit	Credit
Mar. 2				
3				
9				
10				
11				
12				
20				
20				
31				

(b) (Cor

General Journal

J1

Date	Account Titles	Ref.	Debit	Credit
Mar. 31				
31				

(d)

Quinn Theater
Trial Balance
March 31, 2008

	Debit	Credit
Cash		
Accounts Receivable		
Land		
Buildings		
Equipment		
Accounts Payable		
M. Quinn, Capital		
Admission Revenue		
Concession Revenue		
Advertising Expense		
Film Rental Expense		
Salaries Expense		

(a)

Date	Account Titles	Debit	Credit
May 1			
5			
7			
14			
15			
20			
30			
31			

(b)

(c)

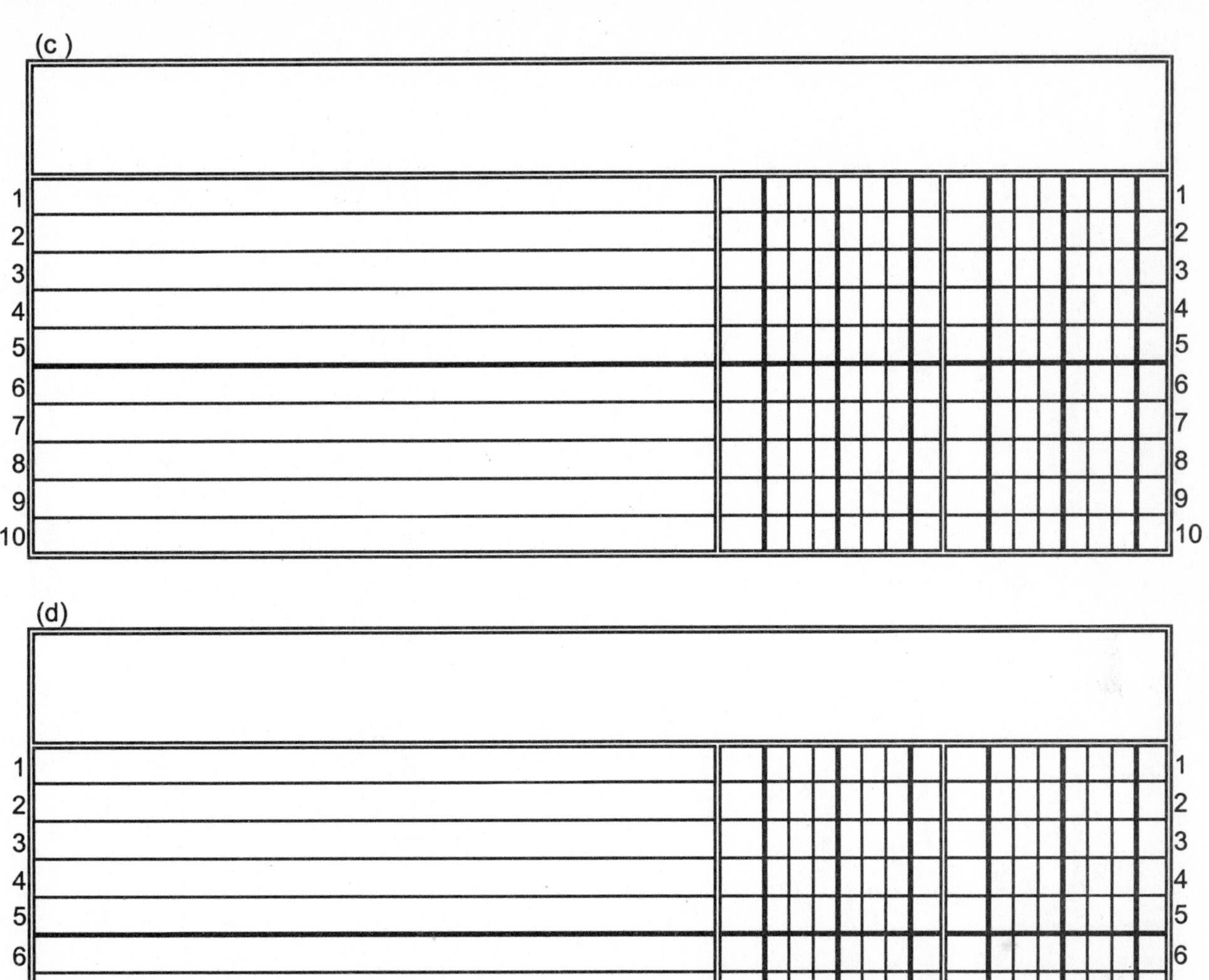

(d)

Name

Section

Date

BE3-3

Date	Account Titles	Debit	Credit
Dec. 31			

Advertising Supplies

Advertising Supplies Expense

BE3-4

Date	Account Titles	Debit	Credit
Dec. 31			

Depr. Expense - Equipment

Accum. Depreciation - Equipment

Balance Sheet:

BE3-5

Date	Account Titles	Debit	Credit
July 1			
Dec. 31			

Prepaid Insurance

Insurance Expense

Name

Section

Date

BE3-6

Date	Account Titles	Debit	Credit
July 1			
Dec. 31			

Unearned Insurance Revenue		Insurance Revenue	

BE3-7

Date	Account Titles	Debit	Credit
Dec. 31			
31			
31			

BE3-8

Account	(a) Type of Adjustment	(b) Related Account
Accounts Receivable		
Prepaid Insurance		
Accum. Depr. - Equipment		
Interest Payable		
Unearned Service Revenue		

Name

Section

Date

BE3-9

Harmony Company
Income Statement
For the Year Ended December 31, 2008

BE3-10

Harmony Company
Owner's Equity Statement
For the Year Ended December 31, 2008

***BE3-11**

Date	Account Titles	Debit	Credit
(a)			
Apr. 30			
(b)			
Apr. 30			

Name

Section

Date

E3-1

1.

2.

3.

4.

5.

6.

E3-3

(a)

(b)

Name Exercises 3-4 and 3-5

Section

Date

E3-4

Item	Type of Adjustment
1.	
2.	
3.	
4.	
5.	
6.	
7.	
8.	
9.	
10.	
11.	

E3-5

Item	Account Titles	Debit	Credit
1.			
2.			
3.			
4.			
5.			
6.			
7.			

Name
Section
Date

E3-6

Item	(a) Type of Adjustment	(b) Accounts before Adjustment
1.		
2.		
3.		
4.		
5.		
6.		

E3-7

Date	Account Titles	Debit	Credit
Mar. 31			
31			
31			
31			
31			

Name

Section

Date

E3-8

Date	Account Titles	Debit	Credit
Jan. 31			
31			
31			
31			
31			
31			

E3-9

Date	Account Titles	Debit	Credit
Oct. 31			
31			
31			
31			
31			
31			
31			

Name

Section

Date

E3-10

Benning Co.
Income Statement
For the Month Ended July 31, 2008

Revenues:		
Expenses:		

E3-11

Answer	Computation	
(a)		
(b)		
(c)		
(d)		

Name Exercise 3-12

Section

Date Tabor Company

Date	Account Titles	Debit	Credit
(a)			
July 10			
14			
15			
20			
(b)			
July 31			
31			
31			
31			

Name

Section

Date

E3-13

Date	Account Titles	Debit	Credit
Aug. 31			
31			
31			
31			
31			
31			

E3-14

Garcia Company Income Statement For the Year Ended August 31, 2008		
Revenues:		
Expenses:		

Name

Section

Date

Exercise 3-14 Concluded

Garcia Company

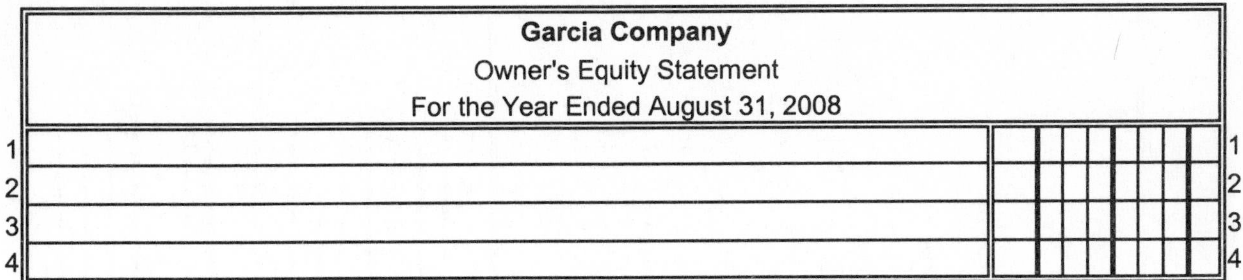

Garcia Company

Owner's Equity Statement

For the Year Ended August 31, 2008

Garcia Company

Balance Sheet

August 31, 2008

Assets

Liabilities and Owner's Equity

Name

Section

Date

	Account Titles	Debit	Credit
(a)			
1.			
2.			
3. (a)			
(b)			
4.			
5.			

(b)

***E3-16**

	Account Titles	Debit	Credit
1.			
2.			
3.			

Name *Exercise 3-17

Section

Date Natasha Company

(a)

Date	Account Titles	Debit	Credit
Jan. 2			
10			
15			

(b)

Date	Account Titles	Debit	Credit
Jan. 31			
31			
31			

CASH

PREPAID INSURANCE

INSURANCE EXPENSE

SUPPLIES

SUPPLIES EXPENSE

UNEARNED REVENUE

SERVICE REVENUE

Name

Section

Date

*Exercise 3-17 Concluded

Natasha Company

(c)

Insurance Expense	
Supplies Expense	
Service Revenue	
Prepaid Insurance	
Supplies	
Unearned Revenue	

Name Problem 3-1A

Section

Date Masasi Company

(a) General Journal J3

Date	Account Titles	Ref.	Debit	Credit
2008				
June 30				
30				
30				
30				
30				
30				
30				

(b)

Cash — No. 100

Date	Explanation	Ref.	Debit	Credit	Balance
2008					
June 30	Balance	√			7150

Accounts Receivable — No. 110

Date	Explanation	Ref.	Debit	Credit	Balance
2008					
June 30	Balance	√			6000

Prepaid Insurance — No. 120

Date	Explanation	Ref.	Debit	Credit	Balance
2008					
June 30	Balance	√			3000

Supplies — No. 130

Date	Explanation	Ref.	Debit	Credit	Balance
2008					
June 30	Balance	√			2000

Office Equipment — No. 135

Date	Explanation	Ref.	Debit	Credit	Balance
2008					
June 30	Balance	√			15000

Accumulated Depreciation - Office Furniture — No, 136

Date	Explanation	Ref.	Debit	Credit	Balance

Accounts Payable — No. 200

Date	Explanation	Ref.	Debit	Credit	Balance
2008					
June 30	Balance	√			4500

(b) (Continued)

Utilities Payable No. 210

Date	Explanation	Ref.	Debit	Credit	Balance

Salaries Payable No. 220

Date	Explanation	Ref.	Debit	Credit	Balance

Unearned Service Revenue No. 230

Date	Explanation	Ref.	Debit	Credit	Balance
2008					
June 30	Balance	√			4000

T. Masasi, Capital No. 300

Date	Explanation	Ref.	Debit	Credit	Balance
2008					
June 30	Balance	√			21750

Service Revenue No. 400

Date	Explanation	Ref.	Debit	Credit	Balance
2008					
June 30	Balance	√			7900

Salaries Expense No. 510

Date	Explanation	Ref.	Debit	Credit	Balance
2008					
June 30	Balance	√			4000

Rent Expense No. 520

Date	Explanation	Ref.	Debit	Credit	Balance
2008					
June 30	Balance	√			1000

Name

Section

Date

Problem 3-1A Continued

Masasi Company

(b) (Continued)

Depreciation Expense

No. 530

Date	Explanation	Ref.	Debit	Credit	Balance

Insurance Expense

No. 540

Date	Explanation	Ref.	Debit	Credit	Balance

Utilities Expense

No. 550

Date	Explanation	Ref.	Debit	Credit	Balance

Supplies Expense

No. 560

Date	Explanation	Ref.	Debit	Credit	Balance

(c)

Masasi Company
Adjusted Trial Balance
June 30, 2008

	Debit	Credit
Cash		
Accounts Receivable		
Prepaid Insurance		
Supplies		
Office Equipment		
Accumulated Depreciation - Office Equipment		
Accounts Payable		
Utilities Payable		
Salaries Payable		
Unearned Service Revenue		
T. Masasi, Capital		
Service Revenue		
Salaries Expense		
Rent Expense		
Depreciation Expense		
Insurance Expense		
Utilities Expense		
Supplies Expense		
Totals		

Name

Section

Date

Problem 3-2A

Neosho River Resort

(a)

General Journal

J1

Date	Account Titles	Ref.	Debit	Credit
Aug. 31				
31				
31				
31				
31				
31				
31				
31				

(b)

Cash

No. 101

Date	Explanation	Ref.	Debit	Credit	Balance
Aug. 31	Balance	√			19600

Accounts Receivable

No. 112

Date	Explanation	Ref.	Debit	Credit	Balance

(b) (Continued)

Supplies — No. 126

Date	Explanation	Ref.	Debit	Credit	Balance
Aug. 31	Balance	√			3300

Prepaid Insurance — No. 130

Date	Explanation	Ref.	Debit	Credit	Balance
Aug.31	Balance	√			6000

Land — No. 140

Date	Explanation	Ref.	Debit	Credit	Balance
Aug.31	Balance	√			25000

Cottages — No. 143

Date	Explanation	Ref.	Debit	Credit	Balance
Aug. 31	Balance	√			125000

Accumulated Depreciation - Cottages — No. 144

Date	Explanation	Ref.	Debit	Credit	Balance

Furniture — No. 149

Date	Explanation	Ref.	Debit	Credit	Balance
Aug. 31	Balance	√			26000

Accumulated Depreciation - Furniture — No. 150

Date	Explanation	Ref.	Debit	Credit	Balance

Accounts Payable — No. 201

Date	Explanation	Ref.	Debit	Credit	Balance
Aug. 31	Balance	√			6500

Unearned Rent — No. 208

Date	Explanation	Ref.	Debit	Credit	Balance
Aug. 31	Balance	√			7400

Salaries Payable — No. 212

Date	Explanation	Ref.	Debit	Credit	Balance

(b) (Continued)

Interest Payable — No. 230

Date	Explanation	Ref.	Debit	Credit	Balance

Mortgage Payable — No. 275

Date	Explanation	Ref.	Debit	Credit	Balance
Aug. 31	Balance	√			80000

P. Harder, Capital — No. 301

Date	Explanation	Ref.	Debit	Credit	Balance
Aug. 31	Balance	√			100000

P. Harder, Drawing — No. 306

Date	Explanation	Ref.	Debit	Credit	Balance
Aug. 31	Balance	√			5000

Rent Revenue — No. 429

Date	Explanation	Ref.	Debit	Credit	Balance
Aug. 31	Balance	√			80000

Depreciation Expense - Cottages — No. 620

Date	Explanation	Ref.	Debit	Credit	Balance

Depreciation Expense - Furniture — No. 621

Date	Explanation	Ref.	Debit	Credit	Balance

Repair Expense — No. 622

Date	Explanation	Ref.	Debit	Credit	Balance
Aug. 31	Balance	√			3600

Supplies Expense — No. 631

Date	Explanation	Ref.	Debit	Credit	Balance

Interest Expense — No. 718

Date	Explanation	Ref.	Debit	Credit	Balance

(b) (Continued)

Insurance Expense No. 722

Date	Explanation	Ref.	Debit	Credit	Balance

Salaries Expense No. 726

Date	Explanation	Ref.	Debit	Credit	Balance
Aug. 31	Balance	√			51000

Utilities Expense No. 732

Date	Explanation	Ref.	Debit	Credit	Balance
Aug. 31	Balance	√			9400

(c)

Neosho River Resort
Adjusted Trial Balance
August 31, 2008

		Debit	Credit	
1	Cash			1
2	Accounts Receivable			2
3	Supplies			3
4	Prepaid Insurance			4
5	Land			5
6	Cottages			6
7	Accumulated Depreciation - Cottages			7
8	Furniture			8
9	Accumulated Depreciation - Furniture			9
10	Accounts Payable			10
11	Unearned Rent			11
12	Salaries Payable			12
13	Interest Payable			13
14	Mortgage Payable			14
15	P. Harder, Capital			15
16	P. Harder, Drawing			16
17	Rent Revenue			17
18	Depreciation Expense - Cottages			18
19	Depreciation Expense - Furniture			19
20	Repair Expense			20
21	Supplies Expense			21
22	Interest Expense			22
23	Insurance Expense			23
24	Salaries Expense			24
25	Utilities Expense			25
26	Totals			26

Name
Section
Date

Problem 3-2A Continued

Neosho River Resort

(d)

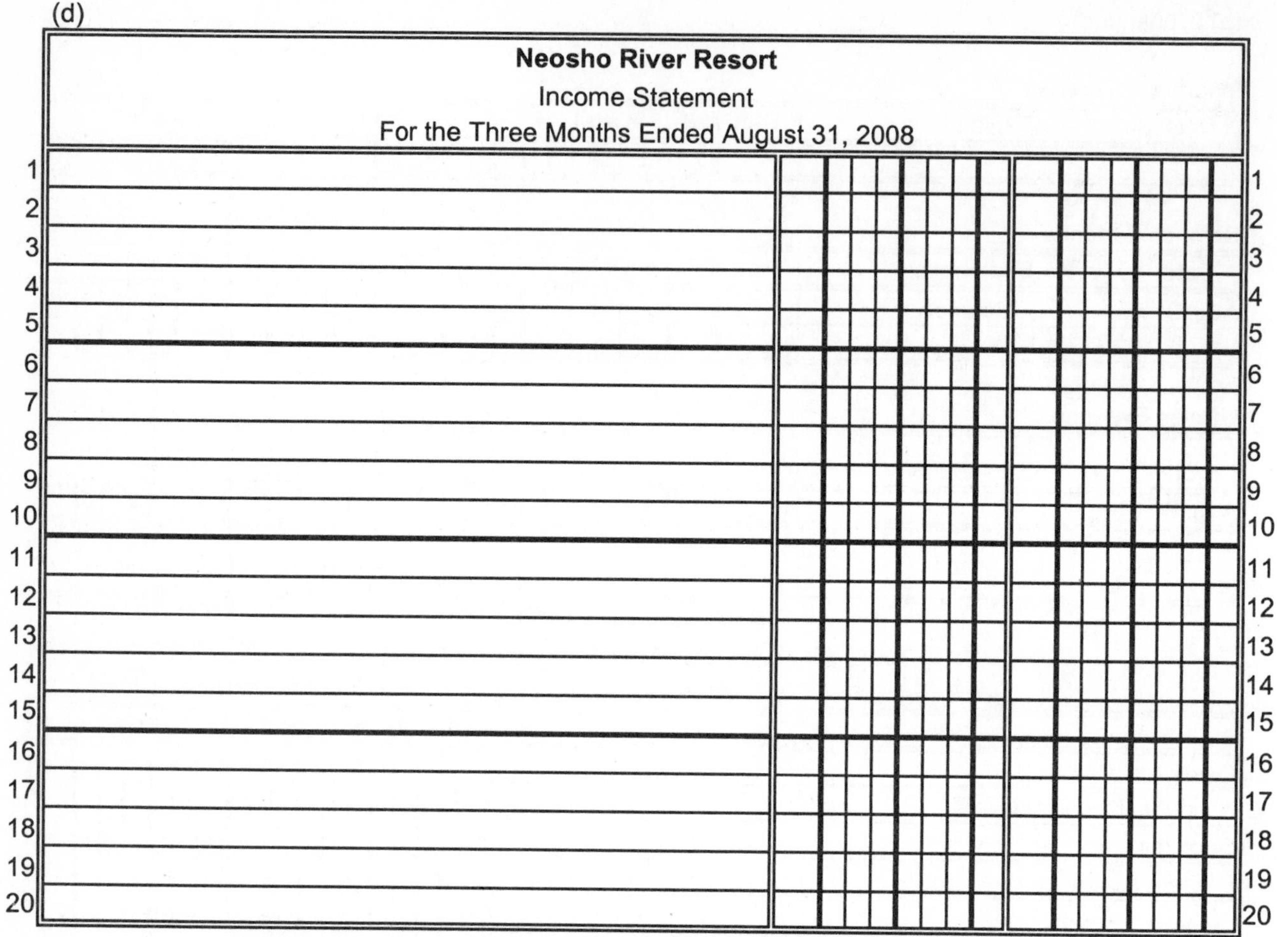

Neosho River Resort
Income Statement
For the Three Months Ended August 31, 2008

Neosho River Resort
Owner's Equity Statement
For the Three Months Ended August 31, 2008

(d) (Continued)

Neosho River Resort
Balance Sheet
August 31, 2008

Assets

Liabilities and Owner's Equity

Name

Section

Date

Problem 3-3A

Fernetti Advertising Agency

(a)

Date	Accounts Titles	Debit	Credit
Dec. 31			
31			
31			
31			
31			
31			
31			

(b)

Fernetti Advertising Agency

Income Statement

For the Year Ended December 31, 2008

(b) (Continued)

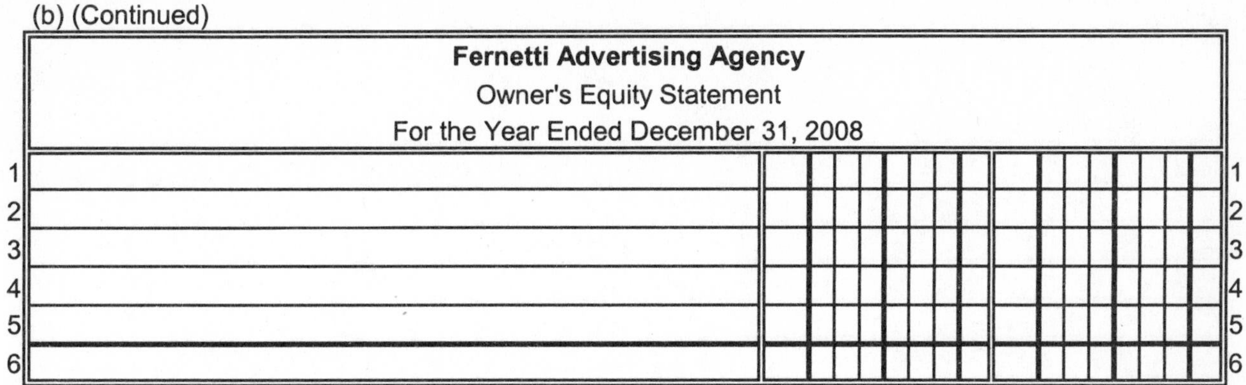

Fernetti Advertising Agency
Owner's Equity Statement
For the Year Ended December 31, 2008

Fernetti Advertising Agency
Balance Sheet
December 31, 2008

Assets

Liabilities and Owner's Equity

(c)

Name | Problem 3-4A

Section

Date | Remington Company

General Journal

Date	Accounts Titles	Debit	Credit
1.			
Dec. 31			
2.			
Dec. 31			
3.			
Dec. 31			
4.			
Dec. 31			

Name Problem 3-5A

Section

Date Rand Equipment Repair

(a), (c) and (e)

Cash No. 101

Date	Explanation	Ref.	Debit	Credit	Balance
Sept. 1	Balance	√			4880

Accounts Receivable No. 112

Date	Explanation	Ref.	Debit	Credit	Balance
Sept. 1	Balance	√			3520

Supplies No. 126

Date	Explanation	Ref.	Debit	Credit	Balance
Sept. 1	Balance	√			2000

Store Equipment No. 153

Date	Explanation	Ref.	Debit	Credit	Balance
Sept. 1	Balance	√			15000

Accumulated Depreciation - Equipment No. 154

Date	Explanation	Ref.	Debit	Credit	Balance
Sept. 1	Balance	√			1500

Accounts Payable No. 201

Date	Explanation	Ref.	Debit	Credit	Balance
Sept. 1	Balance	√			3400

(a), (c) and (e) (Continued)

Unearned Service Revenue No. 209

Date	Explanation	Ref.	Debit	Credit	Balance
Sept. 1	Balance	√			1400

Salaries Payable No. 212

Date	Explanation	Ref.	Debit	Credit	Balance
Sept. 1	Balance	√			500

J. Rand, Capital No. 301

Date	Explanation	Ref.	Debit	Credit	Balance
Sept. 1	Balance	√			18600

Service Revenue No. 407

Date	Explanation	Ref.	Debit	Credit	Balance

Depreciation Expense No. 615

Date	Explanation	Ref.	Debit	Credit	Balance

Supplies Expense No. 631

Date	Explanation	Ref.	Debit	Credit	Balance

Salaries Expense No. 726

Date	Explanation	Ref.	Debit	Credit	Balance

Rent Expense No. 729

Date	Explanation	Ref.	Debit	Credit	Balance

Name

Section

Date

Problem 3-5A Continued

Rand Equipment Repair

(b) General Journal J1

Date	Account Titles	Ref.	Debit	Credit
Sept. 8				
10				
12				
15				
17				
20				
22				
25				
27				
29				

Name

Section

Date

Problem 3-5A Continued

Rand Equipment Repair

(d) & (f)

Rand Equipment Repair

Trial Balances

September 30, 2008

	Before Adjustment		After Adjustment	
	Dr.	Cr.	Dr.	Cr.
Cash				
Accounts Receivable				
Supplies				
Store Equipment				
Accumulated Depreciation				
Accounts Payable				
Unearned Service Revenue				
Salaries Payable				
J. Rand, Capital				
Service Revenue				
Depreciation Expense				
Supplies Expense				
Salaries Expense				
Rent Expense				
Totals				

(e) General Journal J1

Date	Account Titles	Ref	Debit	Credit
1.				
Sept. 30				
2.				
Sept. 30				
3.				
Sept. 30				
4.				
Sept. 30				

(g)

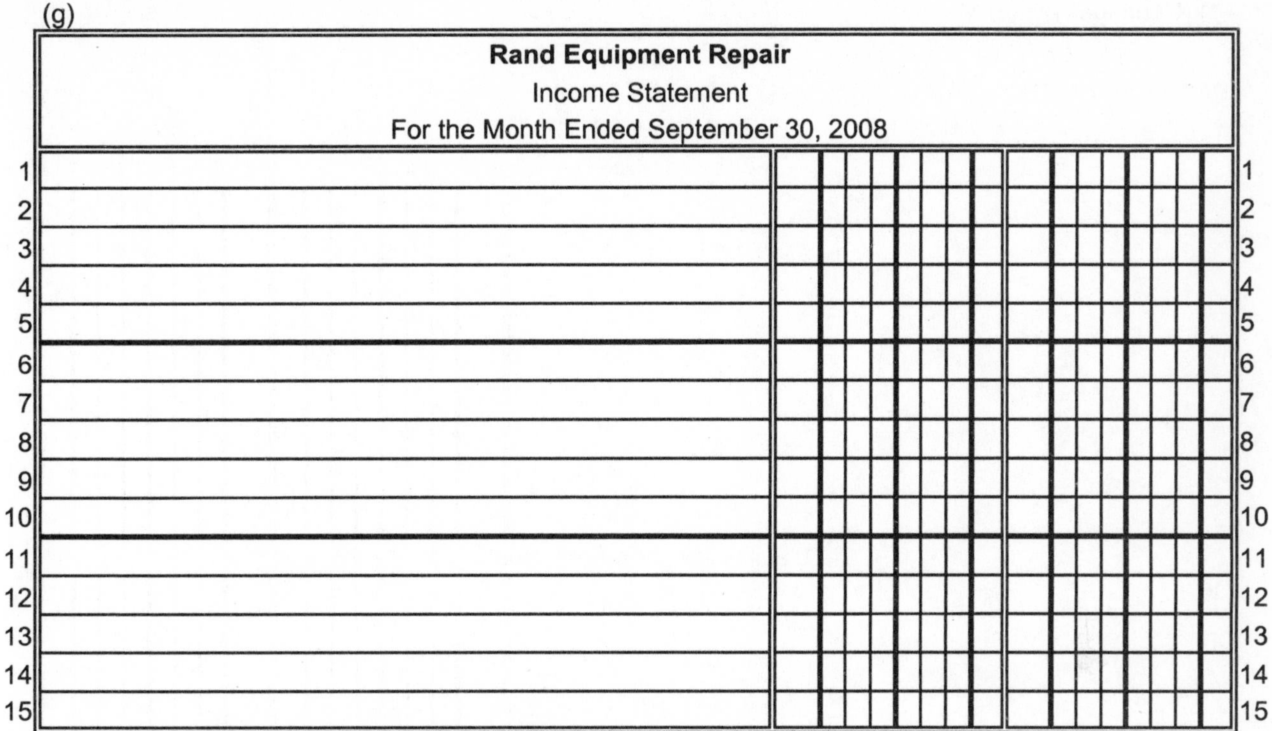

Rand Equipment Repair

Owner's Equity Statement

For the Month Ended September 30, 2008

(g) (Continued)

Rand Equipment Repair
Balance Sheet
September 30, 2008

Assets

Liabilities and Owner's Equity

Name *Problem 3-6A

Section

Date Givens Graphics Company

(a)

Date	Account Titles	Debit	Credit
1.			
June 30			
2.			
June 30			
3.			
June 30			
4.			
June 30			
5.			
June 30			
6.			
June 30			

(b)

Givens Graphics Company
Adjusted Trial Balance
June 30, 2008

	Debit	Credit

(c)

Givens Graphics Company

Income Statement

For the Six Months Ended June 30, 2008

Givens Graphics Company

Owner's Equity Statement

For the Six Months Ended June 30, 2008

(c) (Continued)

Givens Graphics Company
Balance Sheet
June 30, 2008

Assets

Liabilities and Owner's Equity

Name Problem 3-1B

Section

Date Modine Consulting

(a) General Journal J4

Date	Account Titles	Ref.	Debit	Credit
2008				
May 31				
31				
31				
31				
31				
31				
31				

Name | Problem 3-1B Continued
Section
Date | Modine Consulting

(b)

Cash | No. 101

Date	Explanation	Ref.	Debit	Credit	Balance
2008					
May 31	Balance	√			7700

Accounts Receivable | No. 110

Date	Explanation	Ref.	Debit	Credit	Balance
2008					
May 31	Balance	√			4000

Prepaid Insurance | No. 120

Date	Explanation	Ref.	Debit	Credit	Balance
2008					
May 31	Balance	√			4800

Supplies | No. 130

Date	Explanation	Ref.	Debit	Credit	Balance
2008					
May 31	Balance	√			1500

Office Furniture | No. 135

Date	Explanation	Ref.	Debit	Credit	Balance
2008					
May 31	Balance	√			9600

Accumulated Depreciation - Office Furniture | No, 136

Date	Explanation	Ref.	Debit	Credit	Balance

Accounts Payable | No. 200

Date	Explanation	Ref.	Debit	Credit	Balance
2008					
May 31	Balance	√			3500

(b) (Continued)

Travel Payable No. 210

Date	Explanation	Ref.	Debit	Credit	Balance

Salaries Payable No. 220

Date	Explanation	Ref.	Debit	Credit	Balance

Unearned Service Revenue No. 230

Date	Explanation	Ref.	Debit	Credit	Balance
2008					
May 31	Balance	√			3000

L. Ace, Capital No. 300

Date	Explanation	Ref.	Debit	Credit	Balance
2008					
May 31	Balance	√			19100

Service Revenue No. 400

Date	Explanation	Ref.	Debit	Credit	Balance
2008					
May 31	Balance	√			6000

Salaries Expense No. 510

Date	Explanation	Ref.	Debit	Credit	Balance
2008					
May 31	Balance	√			3000

Rent Expense No. 520

Date	Explanation	Ref.	Debit	Credit	Balance
2008					
May 31	Balance	√			1000

(b) (Continued)

Depreciation Expense No. 530

Date	Explanation	Ref.	Debit	Credit	Balance

Insurance Expense No. 540

Date	Explanation	Ref.	Debit	Credit	Balance

Travel Expense No. 550

Date	Explanation	Ref.	Debit	Credit	Balance

Supplies Expense No. 560

Date	Explanation	Ref.	Debit	Credit	Balance

(c)

Modine Consulting
Adjusted Trial Balance
May 31, 2008

	Debit	Credit
Cash		
Accounts Rdeceivable		
Prepaid Insurance		
Supplies		
Office Furniture		
Accumulated Depreciation - Office Furniture		
Accounts Payable		
Travel Payable		
Salaries Payable		
Unearned Service Revenue		
L. Ace, Capital		
Service Revenue		
Salaries Expense		
Rent Expense		
Depreciation Expense		
Insurance Expense		
Travel Expense		
Supplies Expense		
Totals		

Name Problem 3-2B

Section

Date Elston Motel

(a)

General Journal J1

Date	Account Titles	Ref.	Debit	Credit
May 31				
31				
31				
31				
31				
31				
31				

(b)

Cash No. 101

Date	Explanation	Ref.	Debit	Credit	Balance
May 31	Balance	√			2500

Supplies No. 126

Date	Explanation	Ref.	Debit	Credit	Balance
May 31	Balance	√			1900

(b)

Prepaid Insurance — No. 130

Date	Explanation	Ref.	Debit	Credit	Balance
May 31	Balance	√			2400

Land — No. 140

Date	Explanation	Ref.	Debit	Credit	Balance
May 31	Balance	√			15000

Lodge — No. 141

Date	Explanation	Ref.	Debit	Credit	Balance
May 31	Balance	√			70000

Accumulated Depreciation - Lodge — No. 142

Date	Explanation	Ref.	Debit	Credit	Balance

Furniture — No. 149

Date	Explanation	Ref.	Debit	Credit	Balance
May 31	Balance	√			16800

Accumulated Depreciation - Furniture — No. 150

Date	Explanation	Ref.	Debit	Credit	Balance

Accounts Payable — No. 201

Date	Explanation	Ref.	Debit	Credit	Balance
May 31	Balance	√			5300

Unearned Rent — No. 208

Date	Explanation	Ref.	Debit	Credit	Balance
May 31	Balance	√			3600

Salaries Payable — No. 212

Date	Explanation	Ref.	Debit	Credit	Balance

Interest Payable — No. 230

Date	Explanation	Ref.	Debit	Credit	Balance

Name

Section

Date

(b) (Continued)

Mortgage Payable No. 275

Date	Explanation	Ref.	Debit	Credit	Balance
May 31	Balance	√			40000

Mary Lerner, Capital No. 301

Date	Explanation	Ref.	Debit	Credit	Balance
May 31	Balance	√			55000

Rent Revenue No. 429

Date	Explanation	Ref.	Debit	Credit	Balance
May 31	Balance	√			9200

Advertising Expense No. 610

Date	Explanation	Ref.	Debit	Credit	Balance
May 31	Balance	√			500

Depreciation Expense - Lodge No. 619

Date	Explanation	Ref.	Debit	Credit	Balance

Depreciation Expense - Furniture No. 621

Date	Explanation	Ref.	Debit	Credit	Balance

Supplies Expense No. 631

Date	Explanation	Ref.	Debit	Credit	Balance

Interest Expense No. 718

Date	Explanation	Ref.	Debit	Credit	Balance

Insurance Expense No. 722

Date	Explanation	Ref.	Debit	Credit	Balance

Salaries Expense No. 726

Date	Explanation	Ref.	Debit	Credit	Balance
May 31	Balance	√			3000

(b) (Continued)

Utilities Expense | No. 732

Date	Explanation	Ref.	Debit	Credit	Balance
May 31	Balance	√			1000

(c)

Elston Motel
Adjusted Trial Balance
May 31, 2008

		Debit	Credit	
1	Cash			1
2	Supplies			2
3	Prepaid Insurance			3
4	Land			4
5	Lodge			5
6	Accum. Depreciation - Lodge			6
7	Furniture			7
8	Accum. Depreciation - Furniture			8
9	Accounts Payable			9
10	Unearned Rent			10
11	Salaries Payable			11
12	Interest Payable			12
13	Mortgage Payable			13
14	Mary Lerner, Capital			14
15	Rent Revenue			15
16	Advertising Expense			16
17	Depr. Expense - Lodge			17
18	Depr. Expense - Furniture			18
19	Supplies Expense			19
20	Interest Expense			20
21	Insurance Expense			21
22	Salaries Expense			22
23	Utilities Expense			23
24	Totals			24
25				25
26				26
27				27

Name | Problem 3-2B Continued

Section

Date | Elston Motel

(d)

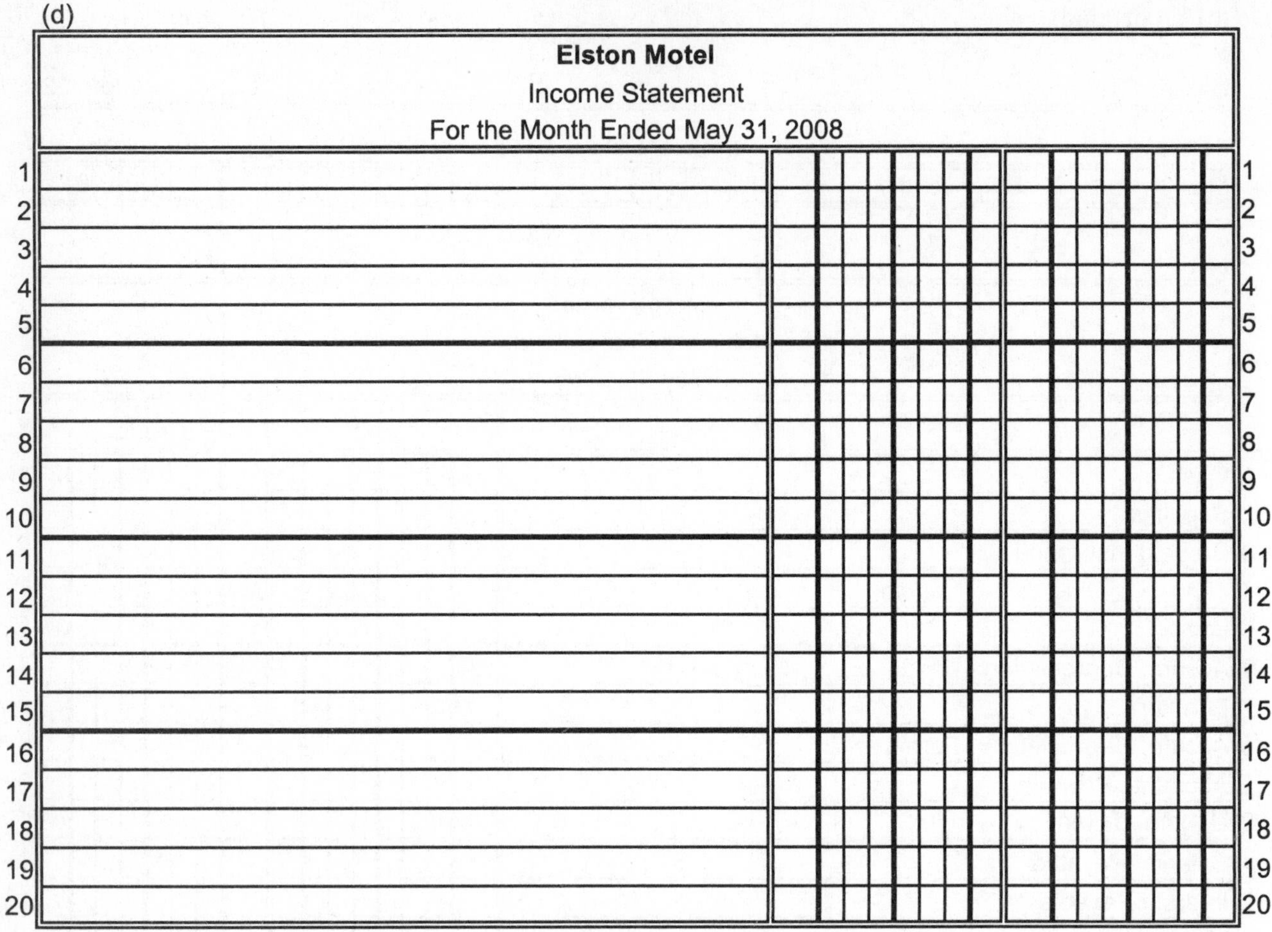

Elston Motel

Income Statement

For the Month Ended May 31, 2008

Elston Motel

Owner's Equity Statement

For the Month Ended May 31, 2008

(d) (Continued)

Elston Motel
Balance Sheet
May 31, 2008

Assets

Liabilities and Owner's Equity

Name

Section

Date

Problem 3-3B

Orterga Co.

(a)

Date	Accounts Titles	Debit	Credit
Sept. 30			
30			
30			
30			
30			
30			
30			

(b)

Ortega Co.

Income Statement

For the Quarter Ended September 30, 2008

Revenues:		
Expenses:		

(b) (Continued)

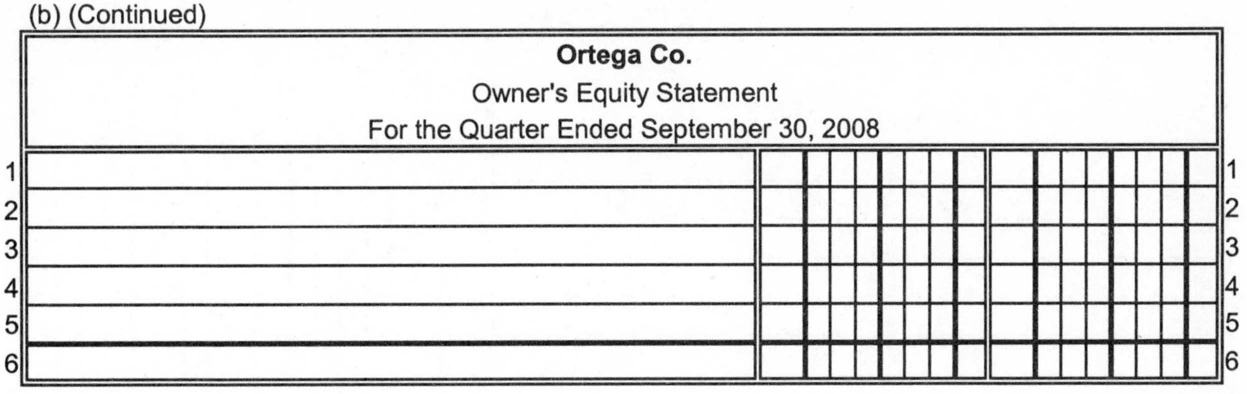

Ortega Co.
Owner's Equity Statement
For the Quarter Ended September 30, 2008

Ortega Co.
Balance Sheet
September 30, 2008

Assets

Liabilities and Owner's Equity

(c)

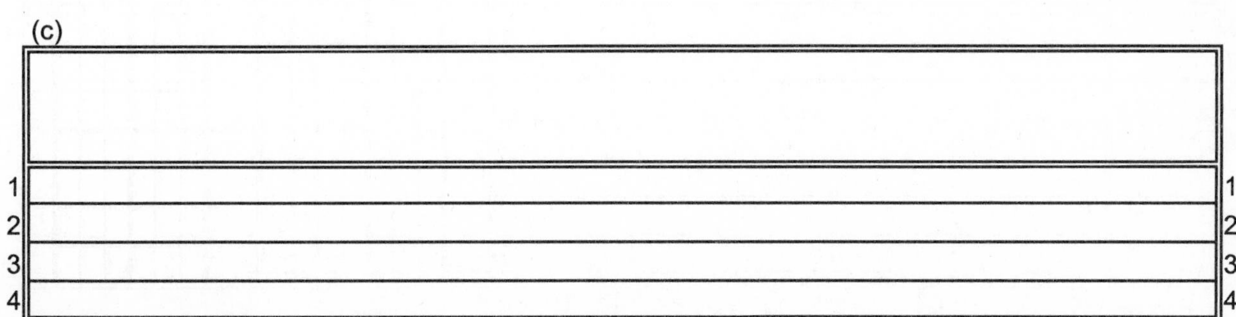

Name | Problem 3-4B
Section
Date | Yoda Company

General Journal

Date	Accounts Titles	Debit	Credit
1.			
Dec. 31			
2.			
Dec. 31			
3.			
Dec. 31			
4.			
Dec. 31			

Name | Problem 3-5B

Section

Date | Rondeli Equipment Repair

(a), (c) and (e)

Cash — No. 101

Date	Explanation	Ref.	Debit	Credit	Balance
Nov. 1	Balance	√			2790

Accounts Receivable — No. 112

Date	Explanation	Ref.	Debit	Credit	Balance
Nov. 1	Balance	√			2510

Supplies — No. 126

Date	Explanation	Ref.	Debit	Credit	Balance
Nov. 1	Balance	√			2000

Store Equipment — No. 153

Date	Explanation	Ref.	Debit	Credit	Balance
Nov. 1	Balance	√			10000

Accumulated Depreciation - Store Equipment — No. 154

Date	Explanation	Ref.	Debit	Credit	Balance
Nov. 1	Balance	√			500

Accounts Payable — No. 201

Date	Explanation	Ref.	Debit	Credit	Balance
Nov. 1	Balance	√			2100

Name
Section
Date

Problem 3-5B Continued

Rondeli Equipment Repair

(a), (c) and (e) (Continued)

Unearned Service Revenue — No. 209

Date	Explanation	Ref.	Debit	Credit	Balance
Nov. 1	Balance	√			1400

Salaries Payable — No. 212

Date	Explanation	Ref.	Debit	Credit	Balance
Nov. 1	Balance	√			500

P. Rondeli, Capital — No. 301

Date	Explanation	Ref.	Debit	Credit	Balance
Nov. 1	Balance	√			12800

Service Revenue — No. 407

Date	Explanation	Ref.	Debit	Credit	Balance

Depreciation Expense — No. 615

Date	Explanation	Ref.	Debit	Credit	Balance

Supplies Expense — No. 631

Date	Explanation	Ref.	Debit	Credit	Balance

Salaries Expense — No. 726

Date	Explanation	Ref.	Debit	Credit	Balance

Rent Expense — No. 729

Date	Explanation	Ref.	Debit	Credit	Balance

Name | Problem 3-5B Continued

Section

Date | Rondeli Equipment Repair

(b) General Journal J1

	Date	Account Titles	Ref	Debit	Credit	
1	Nov. 8					1
2						2
3						3
4						4
5	10					5
6						6
7						7
8	12					8
9						9
10						10
11	15					11
12						12
13						13
14	17					14
15						15
16						16
17	20					17
18						18
19						19
20	22					20
21						21
22						22
23	25					23
24						24
25						25
26	27					26
27						27
28						28
29	29					29
30						30
31						31
32						32
33						33
34						34
35						35

Name

Section

Date

Problem 3-5B Continued

Rondeli Equipment Repair

(d) & (f)

Rondeli Equipment Repair Trial Balances November 30, 2008				
	Before Adjustment		After Adjustment	
	Dr.	Cr.	Dr.	Cr.
Cash				
Accounts Receivable				
Supplies				
Equipment				
Accumulated Depreciation				
Accounts Payable				
Unearned Service Revenue				
Salaries Payable				
P. Rondeli, Capital				
Service Revenue				
Depreciation Expense				
Supplies Expense				
Salaries Expense				
Rent Expense				
Totals				

Name

Section

Date

Problem 3-5B Continued

Rondeli Equipment Repair

(e)

General Journal

J1

Date	Account Titles	Ref	Debit	Credit
1.				
Nov. 30				
2.				
Nov. 30				
3.				
Nov. 30				
4.				
Nov. 30				

Name Problem 3-5B Continued

Section

Date Rondeli Equipment Repair

(g)

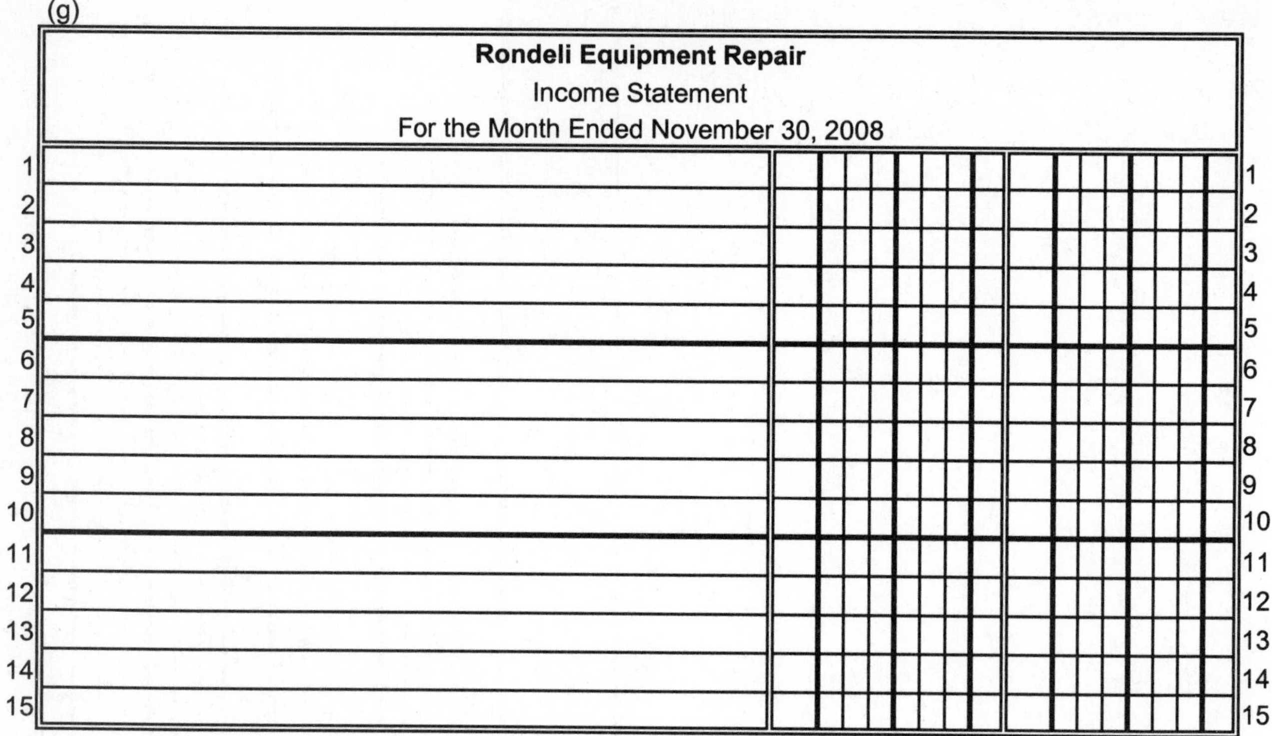

Rondeli Equipment Repair

Income Statement

For the Month Ended November 30, 2008

Rondeli Equipment Repair

Owner's Equity Statement

For the Month Ended November 30, 2008

(g) (Continued)

Rondeli Equipment Repair
Balance Sheet
November 30, 2008

Assets

Liabilities and Owner's Equity

Name

Section

Date

Chapter 3 Comparative Analysis Problem

PepsiCo, Inc. versus Coca-Cola Company

	PepsiCo	Coca-Cola
Increase (decrease) from 2004 to 2005 in:		
(a) Property, plant, and equipment, net		
(b) Selling, general, and administrative expenses		
(c) Long-term debt (obligations)		
(d) Net income		
(e) Cash and cash equivalents		

Name

Section

Date

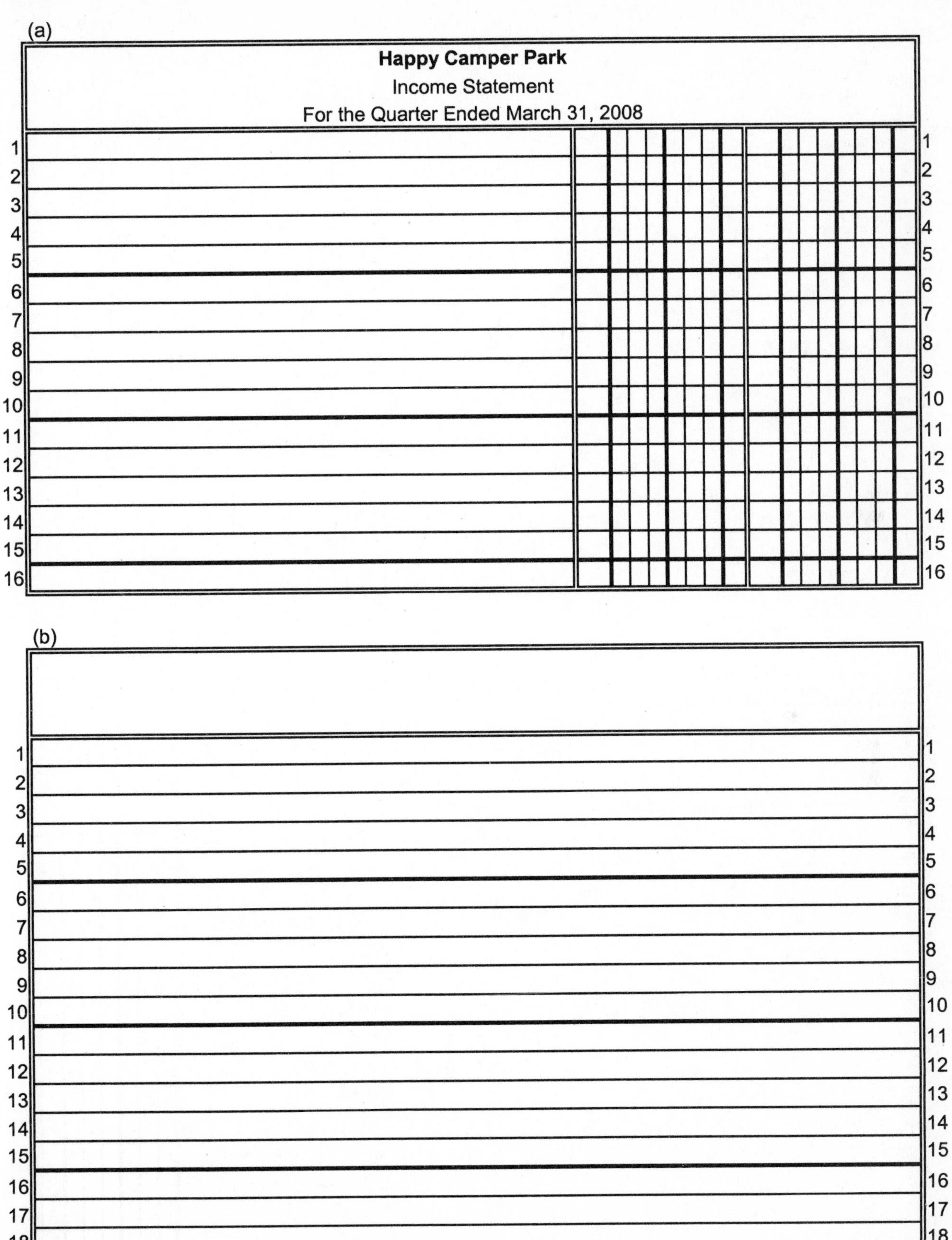

Name

Section

Date

BE4-1

BE4-2 is on the next page

BE4-3

Account	Income Statement Debit	Income Statement Credit	Balance Sheet Debit	Balance Sheet Credit
Accum. Depreciation				
Depreciation Expense				
N. Batan, Capital				
N. Batan, Drawing				
Service Revenue				
Supplies				
Accounts Payable				

BE4-4

Date	Account Titles	Debit	Credit
Dec. 31			
31			
31			
31			

Brief Exercise 4-2

Ley Company

See Appendix

Name

Section

Date

BE4-5

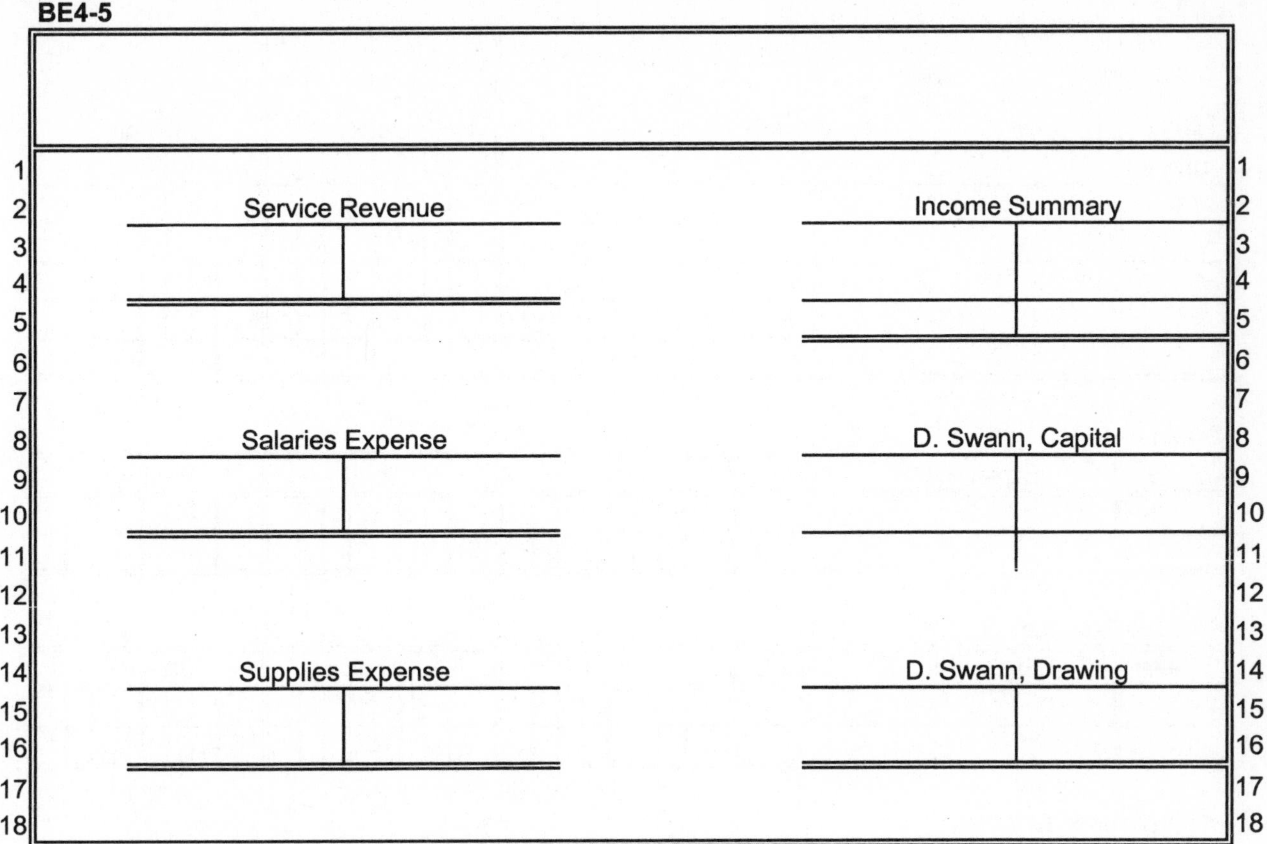

Section

Date

BE4-6

Date	Account Titles	Debit	Credit
July 31			
31			

Green Fee Revenue

Date	Explanation	Ref.	Debit	Credit	Balance

Salaries Expense

Date	Explanation	Ref.	Debit	Credit	Balance

Maintenenace Expense

Date	Explanation	Ref.	Debit	Credit	Balance

Name

Section

Date

BE4-9

	Account Titles	Debit	Credit
1.			
2.			

BE4-10

Diaz Company

Partial Balance Sheet

Current assets		

BE4-11

	Accounts payable
	Accounts receivable
	Accumulated depreciation
	Building
	Cash
	Copyrights
	Income tax payable
	Investment in long-term bonds
	Land
	Merchandise inventory
	Patent
	Supplies

***BE4-12**

Date	Account Titles	Debit	Credit
Nov. 1			

Exercise 4-1

Briscoe Company

See Appendix

Name Exercise 4-2

Section

Date Goode Company

Goode Company
(Partial) Worksheet
For the Month Ended April 30, 2008

	Account Titles	Adjusted Trial Balance Dr.	Adjusted Trial Balance Cr.	Income Statement Dr.	Income Statement Cr.	Balance Sheet Dr.	Balance Sheet Cr.	
1	Cash	13752						1
2	Accounts Receivable	7840						2
3	Prepaid Rent	2280						3
4	Equipment	23050						4
5	Accumulated Depreciation		4921					5
6	Notes Payable		5700					6
7	Accounts Payable		5672					7
8	T. Goode, Capital		30960					8
9	T. Goode, Drawing	3650						9
10	Service Revenue		15590					10
11	Salaries Expense	10840						11
12	Rent Expense	760						12
13	Depreciation Expense	671						13
14	Interest Expense	57						14
15	Interest Payable		57					15
16	Totals	62900	62900					16
17	Net Income							17
18	Totals							18
19								19
20								20

Goode Company
Income Statement
For the Month Ended April 30, 2008

Goode Company
Owner's Equity Statement
For the Month Ended April 30, 2008

(Continued)

Goode Company
Balance Sheet
April 30, 2008

Assets

Liabilities and Owner's Equity

Name Exercise 4-4

Section

Date Goode Company

(a)

Date	Account Titles	Debit	Credit
Apr. 30			
30			
30			
30			

(b)

INCOME SUMMARY

T. GOODE, CAPITAL

(c)

Goode Company

Post-Closing Trial Balance

April 30, 2008

	Debit	Credit

Name | Exercise 4-5
Section
Date | Mears Company

(a)

	Account Titles	Debit	Credit	
1				1
2				2
3				3
4				4
5				5
6				6
7				7
8				8
9				9
10				10
11				11
12				12

(b)

		Income Statement		Balance Sheet		
		Debit	Credit	Debit	Credit	
1	Accounts Receivable					1
2	Prepaid Insurance					2
3	Accum. Depreciation					3
4	Salaries Payable					4
5	Service Revenue					5
6	Salaries Expense					6
7	Insurance Expense					7
8	Depr. Expense					8
9						9

Name

Section

Date

Exercise 4-6

Nicholson Company

(a)

	Account Titles	Trial Balance Debit	Trial Balance Credit	Adjustments Debit	Adjustments Credit	Adjusted Trial Balance Debit	Adjusted Trial Balance Credit	
1	Accounts Receivable					34000		1
2	Prepaid Insurance	26000				20000		2
3	Supplies	7000						3
4	Accumulated Depreciation		12000					4
5	Salaries Payable						5000	5
6	Service Revenue		88000				97000	6
7	Insurance Expense							7
8	Depreciation Expense					10000		8
9	Supplies Expense					4000		9
10	Salaries Expense					49000		10

(b)

	Account Titles	Debit	Credit	
1				1
2				2
3				3
4				4
5				5
6				6
7				7
8				8
9				9
10				10
11				11
12				12
13				13
14				14

Name

Section

Date

Exercise 4-7

Emil Skoda Company

(a)

Account Titles	Debit	Credit

(b)

Emil Skoda Company

Post-Closing Trial Balance

For the Month Ended June 30, 2008

Account Titles	Debit	Credit

Name

Section

Date

Exercise 4-8

Apachi Company

(a)

General Journal J15

Date	Account Titles	Ref.	Debit	Credit
July 31				
31				
31				
31				

(b)

B. J. Apachi, Capital No. 301

Date	Explanation	Ref.	Debit	Credit	Balance

Income Summary No. 350

Date	Explanation	Ref.	Debit	Credit	Balance

(c)

Apachi Company

Post-Closing Trial Balance

July 31, 2008

	Debit	Credit

Name | Exercise 4-9

Section

Date | Apachi Company

(a)

Apachi Company

Income Statement

For The Year Ended July 31, 2008

Apachi Company

Owner's Equity Statement

For the Year Ended July 31, 2008

Name

Section

Date

(b) (Continued)

Apachi Company

Balance Sheet

July 31, 2008

Assets

Liabilities and Owner's Equity

Name

Section

Date

E4-11

	Date	Account Titles	Debit	Credit	
1	(a)				1
2	June 30				2
3					3
4					4
5	30				5
6					6
7					7
8					8
9					9
10	30				10
11					11
12					12
13	30				13
14					14

(b)

INCOME SUMMARY

E4-13

	Date	Account Titles	Debit	Credit	
1	1.				1
2					2
3					3
4	2.				4
5					5
6					6
7					7
8	3.				8
9					9
10					10

Name

Section

Date

Exercise 4-12

Max Weinberg Company

Account Titles	Debit	Credit
(a)		
1.		
2.		
3.		
(b)		
1.		
2.		
3.		

Name | Exercise 4-14

Section

Date | Karr Bowling Alley

(a)

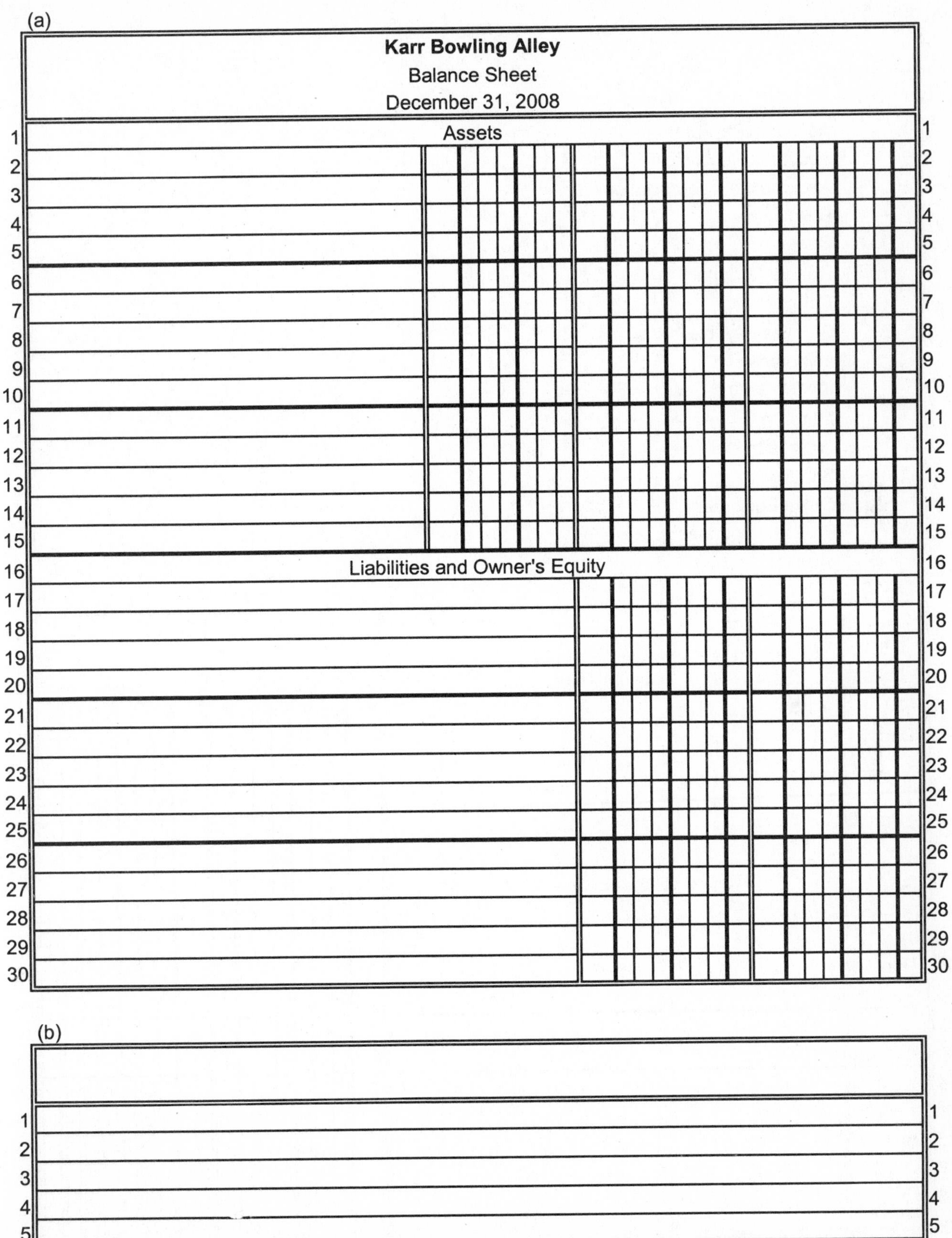

Karr Bowling Alley

Balance Sheet

December 31, 2008

Assets

Liabilities and Owner's Equity

(b)

Name

Section

Date

E4-15

	Accounts Payable
	Accounts Receivable
	Accumulated Depreciation
	Buildings
	Cash
	Roberts, Capital
	Patents
	Salaries Payable
	Inventories
	Investments
	Land
	Long-term Debt
	Supplies
	Office Equipment
	Prepaid Expenses

***E4-18**

Date	Account Titles	Debit	Credit
(a)			
Dec. 31			
Jan. 6			
(b)			
Dec. 31			
Jan. 1			
6			

Name Exercise 4-16

Section

Date R. Stevens Company

R. Stevens Company

Balance Sheet

December 31, 2008

(in thousands)

Assets

Liabilities and Owner's Equity

Name

Section

Date

Exercise 4-17

B. Snyder Company

(a)

B. Snyder Company

Income Statement

For The Year Ended July 31, 2008

1	Revenues:			1
2				2
3				3
4				4
5				5
6	Expenses:			6
7				7
8				8
9				9
10				10
11				11
12				12
13				13
14				14
15				15

B. Snyder Company

Owner's Equity Statement

For the Year Ended July 31, 2008

1				1
2				2
3				3
4				4
5				5

(b) (Continued)

B. Snyder Company
Balance Sheet
July 31, 2008

Assets

Liabilities and Owner's Equity

Name

Section

Date

*Exercise 4-19

Oslo Employment Agency

(a) & (b)

Date	Account Titles	Debit	Credit
Dec. 31			
31			
Jan. 1			
1			

(c) & (e)

ACCOUNTS RECEIVABLE

Dec 31 Bal 19,800	

COMMISSION REVENUE

	Dec 31 Bal 87,500

INTEREST PAYABLE

INTEREST EXPENSE

Dec 31 Bal 6,300	

(d)

Date	Account Titles		Debit	Credit
	(1)			
Jan. 10				
	(2)			
15				

Problem 4-1A

Thomas Magnum, P.I.

See Appendix

Name

Section

Date

Problem 4-1A Continued

Thomas Magnum, P.I.

(b)

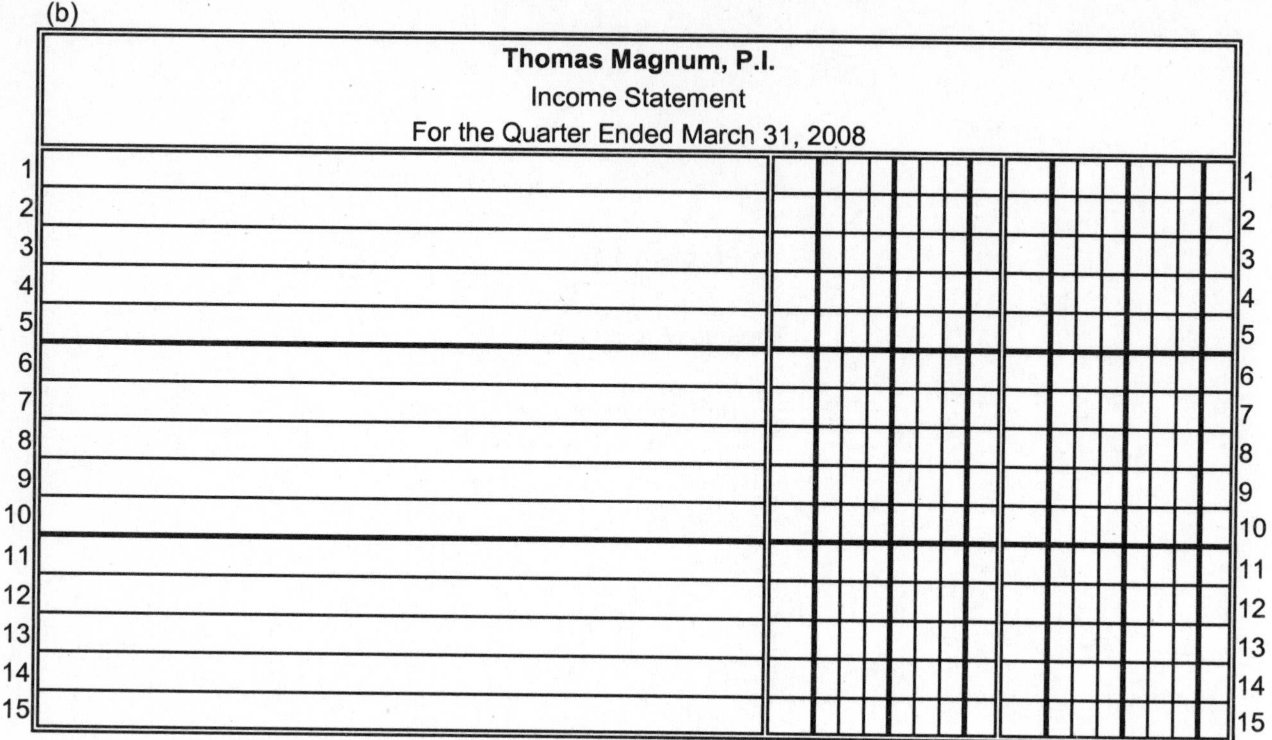

Thomas Magnum, P.I.
Income Statement
For the Quarter Ended March 31, 2008

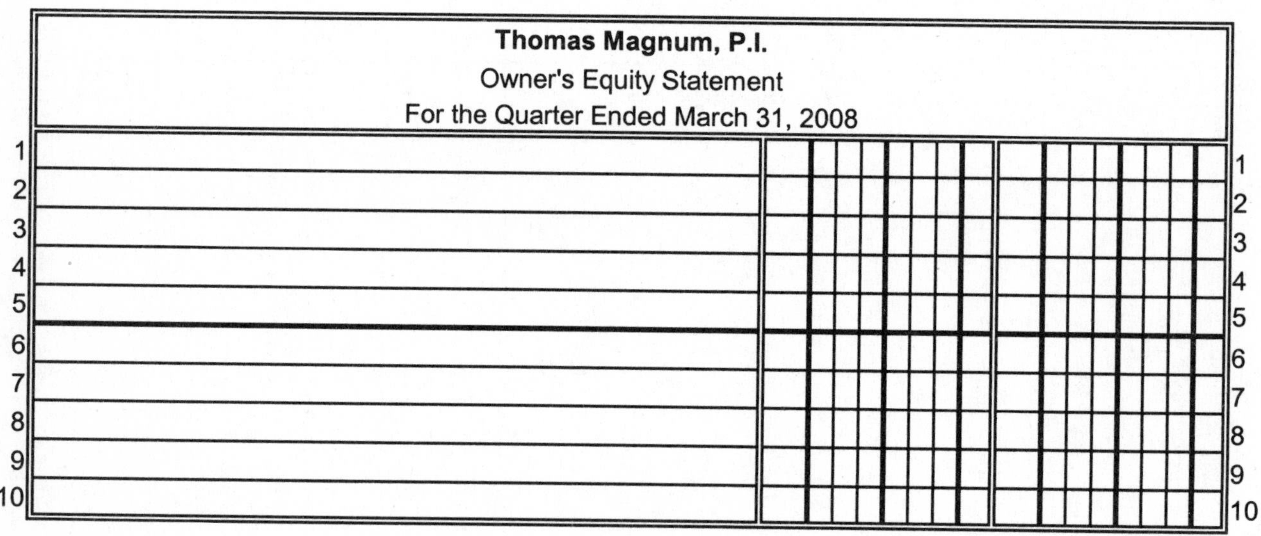

Thomas Magnum, P.I.
Owner's Equity Statement
For the Quarter Ended March 31, 2008

(b) (Continued)

Thomas Magnum, P.I.
Balance Sheet
March 31, 2008

Assets

Liabilities and Owner's Equity

Name | Problem 4-1A Concluded

Section

Date | Thomas Magnum, P.I.

(c)

General Journal

Date	Account Titles	Debit	Credit
	Adjusting Entries		
Mar. 31			
31			
31			
31			
31			

(d)

General Journal

Date	Account Titles	Debit	Credit
	Closing Entries		
Mar. 31			
31			
31			
31			

Name

Section

Date

Problem 4-2A

Porter Company

(a)

Porter Company

Worksheet (Partial)

For the Year Ended December 31, 2008

Account No.	Account Titles	Adjusted Trial Balance Dr.	Adjusted Trial Balance Cr.	Income Statement Dr.	Income Statement Cr.	Balance Sheet Dr.	Balance Sheet Cr.
101	Cash	18800					
112	Accounts Receivable	16200					
126	Supplies	2300					
130	Prepaid Insurance	4400					
151	Office Equipment	44000					
152	Accum. Depr. - Office Equip.		20000				
200	Notes Payable		20000				
201	Accounts Payable		8000				
212	Salaries Payable		2600				
230	Interest Payable		1000				
301	B. Porter, Capital		36000				
306	B. Porter, Drawing	12000					
400	Service Revenue		77800				
610	Advertising Expense	12000					
631	Supplies Expense	3700					
711	Depreciation Expense	8000					
722	Insurance Expense	4000					
726	Salaries Expense	39000					
905	Interest Expense	1000					
	Totals	165400	165400				
	Net Income						
	Totals						

Name

Section

Date

(b)

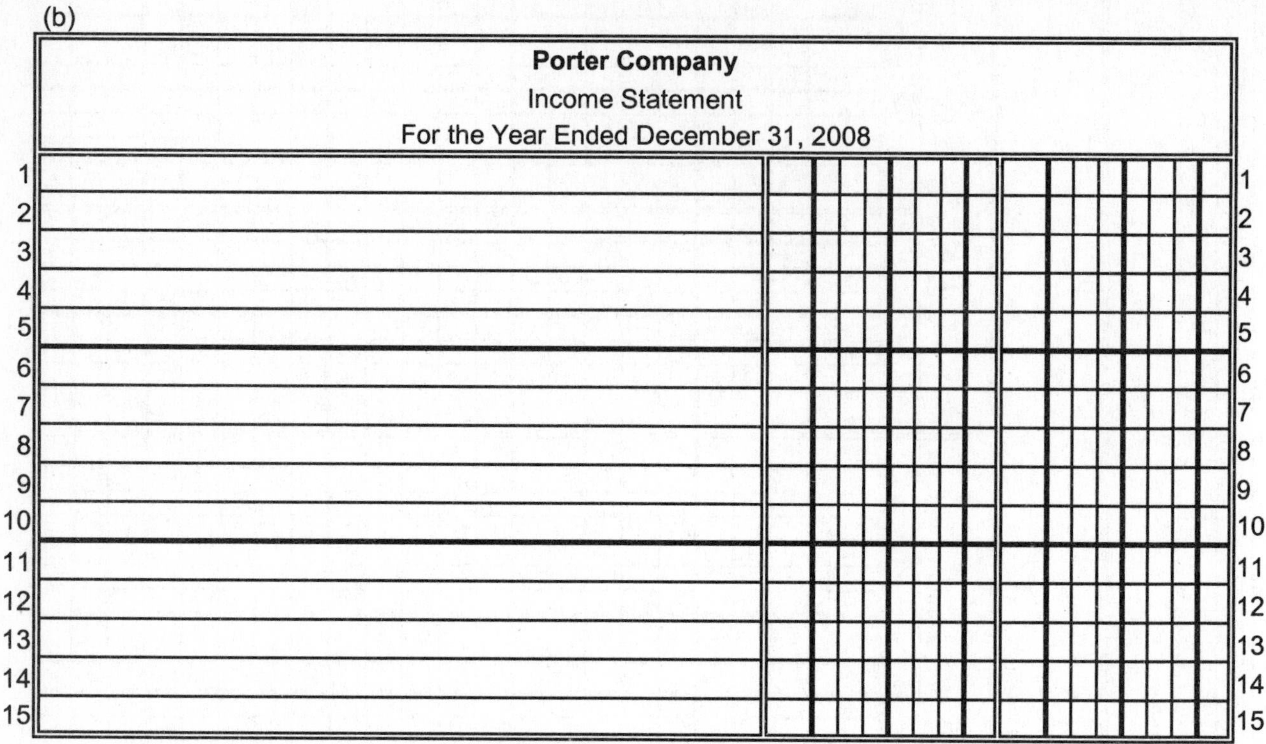

Porter Company

Income Statement

For the Year Ended December 31, 2008

Porter Company

Owner's Equity Statement

For the Year Ended December 31, 2008

(b) (Continued)

Porter Company

Balance Sheet

December 31, 2008

Assets

Liabilities and Owner's Equity

Name

Section

Date

Problem 4-2A Continued

Porter Company

(c)

General Journal J14

Date	Account Titles	Ref.	Debit	Credit
Dec. 31				
31				
31				
31				

(d)

B. Porter, Capital No.301

Date	Explanation	Ref.	Debit	Credit	Balance
Dec 31	Balance	√			36000

B. Porter, Drawing No. 306

Date	Explanation	Ref.	Debit	Credit	Balance
Dec 31	Balance	√			12000

Income Summary No. 350

Date	Explanation	Ref.	Debit	Credit	Balance

(d) (Continued)

Service Revenue — No. 400

Date	Explanation	Ref.	Debit	Credit	Balance
Dec 31	Balance	√			77800

Advertising Expense — No. 610

Date	Explanation	Ref.	Debit	Credit	Balance
Dec 31	Balance	√			12000

Supplies Expense — No. 631

Date	Explanation	Ref.	Debit	Credit	Balance
Dec 31	Balance	√			3700

Depreciation Expense — No. 711

Date	Explanation	Ref.	Debit	Credit	Balance
Dec 31	Balance	√			8000

Insurance Expense — No. 722

Date	Explanation	Ref.	Debit	Credit	Balance
Dec 31	Balance	√			4000

Salaries Expense — No. 726

Date	Explanation	Ref.	Debit	Credit	Balance
Dec 31	Balance	√			39000

Interest Expense — No. 905

Date	Explanation	Ref.	Debit	Credit	Balance
Dec 31	Balance	√			1000

Name
Section
Date

(e)

Porter Company
Post-Closing Trial Balance
December 31, 2008

	Debit	Credit

Name Problem 4-3A

Section

Date Woods Company

(a)

Woods Company

Income Statement

For the Year Ended December 31, 2008

Woods Company

Owner's Equity Statement

For the Year Ended December 31, 2008

(a) (Continued)

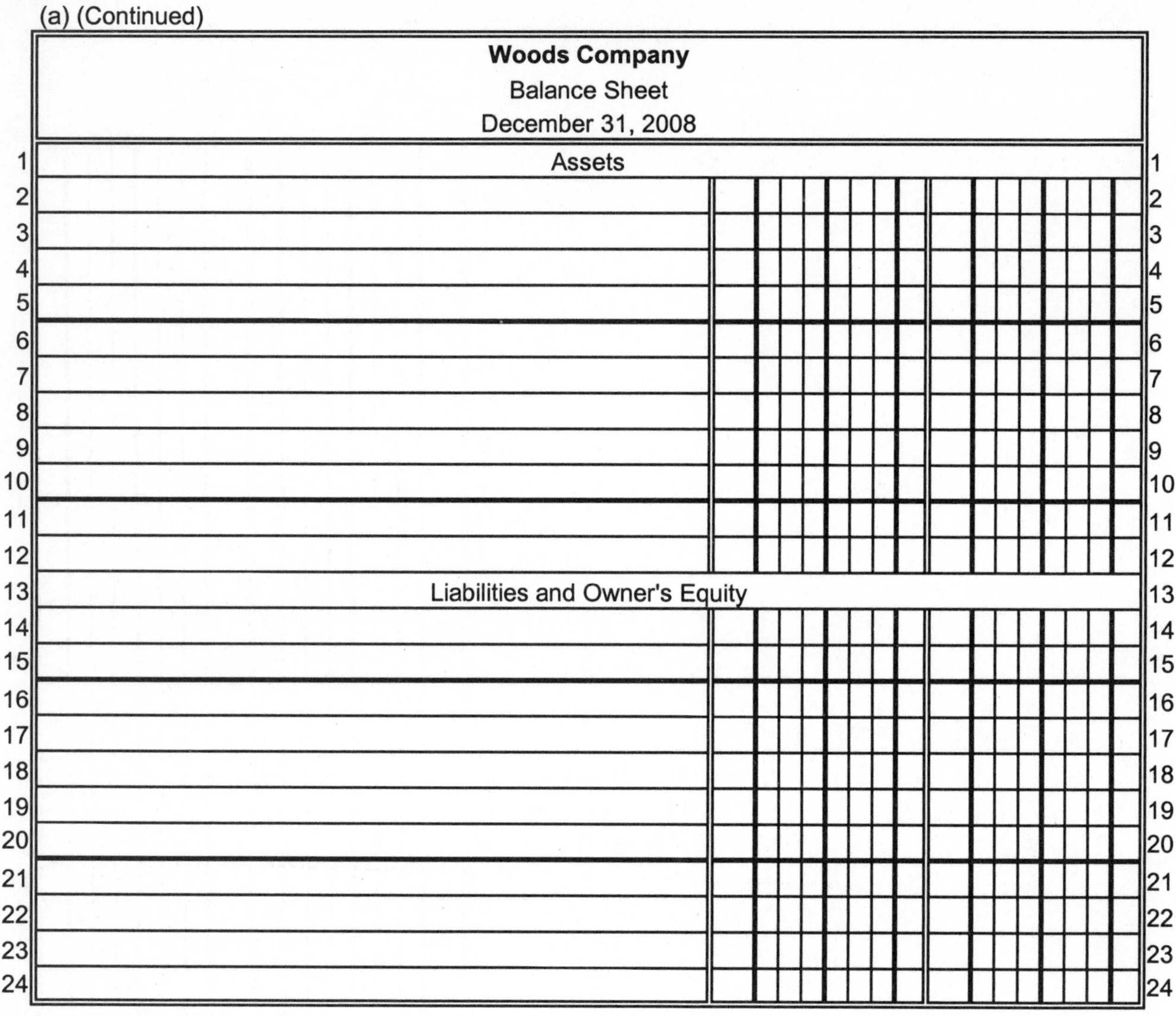

Woods Company
Balance Sheet
December 31, 2008

Assets

Liabilities and Owner's Equity

Name Problem 4-3A Continued

Section

Date Woods Company

(b) General Journal

Date	Accounts Titles	Ref.	Debit	Credit
	Closing Entries			
Dec. 31				
31				
31				
31				

(c)

S. Woods, Capital No. 301	
	12/31 Bal 34,000

S. Woods, Drawing No.306	
12/31 Bal 7,200	

Income Summary No. 350	

Service Revenue No. 400	
	12/31 Bal 44,000

Repair Expense No. 622	
12/31 Bal 5,400	

Depreciation Expense No. 711	
12/31 Bal 2,800	

Insurance Expense No. 722	
12/31 Bal 1,200	

Salaries Expense No. 726	
12/31 Bal 35,200	

Utilities Expense No. 732	
12/31 Bal 4,000	

(d)

Woods Company
Post-Closing Trial Balance
December 31, 2008

		Debit	Credit	
1				1
2				2
3				3
4				4
5				5
6				6
7				7
8				8
9				9
10				10

Problem 4-4A

Disney Amusement Park

See Appendix

(b)

Disney Amusement Park

Balance Sheet

September 30, 2008

Assets

Liabilities and Owner's Equity

Name | Problem 4-4A Continued

Section

Date | Disney Amusement Park

(c) & (d)

Date	Accounts Titles	Debit	Credit
(c)	Adjusting Entries		
Sept. 30			
30			
30			
30			
30			
30			
(d)	Closing Entries		
Sept. 30			
30			
30			
30			

(e)

Disney Amusement Park

Post-Closing Trial Balance

September 30, 2008

	Debit	Credit

Name | Problem 4-5A

Section

Date | Eddy's Carpet Cleaners

(a) General Journal J1

Date	Accounts Titles	Ref.	Debit	Credit
Mar. 1				
1				
3				
5				
14				
18				
20				
21				
28				
31				
31				

Problem 4-5A

Eddy's Carpet Cleaners

See Appendix

Name Problem 4-5A Continued

Section

Date Eddy's Carpet Cleaners

(a), (e) and (f)

Cash No. 101

Date	Explanation	Ref.	Debit	Credit	Balance

Accounts Receivabl No. 112

Date	Explanation	Ref.	Debit	Credit	Balance

Cleaning Supplies No. 128

Date	Explanation	Ref.	Debit	Credit	Balance

Prepaid Insurance No. 130

Date	Explanation	Ref.	Debit	Credit	Balance

Equipment No. 157

Date	Explanation	Ref.	Debit	Credit	Balance

(a), (e) and (f) (Continued)

Accumulated Depreciation - Equipment — No. 158

Date	Explanation	Ref.	Debit	Credit	Balance

Accounts Payable — No. 201

Date	Explanation	Ref.	Debit	Credit	Balance

Salaries Payable — No. 212

Date	Explanation	Ref.	Debit	Credit	Balance
			Debit	Credit	Balance

L. Eddy, Capital — No. 301

Date	Explanation	Ref.	Debit	Credit	Balance

L. Eddy, Drawing — No. 306

Date	Explanation	Ref.	Debit	Credit	Balance

Income Summary — No. 350

Date	Explanation	Ref.	Debit	Credit	Balance

Service Revenue — No. 400

Date	Explanation	Ref.	Debit	Credit	Balance

(a), (e) and (f) (Continued)

Gas & Oil Expense No. 633

Date	Explanation	Ref.	Debit	Credit	Balance

Cleaning Supplies E No. 634

Date	Explanation	Ref.	Debit	Credit	Balance

Depreciation Expens No. 711

Date	Explanation	Ref.	Debit	Credit	Balance

Insurance Expense No. 722

Date	Explanation	Ref.	Debit	Credit	Balance

Salaries Expense No. 726

Date	Explanation	Ref.	Debit	Credit	Balance

(d)

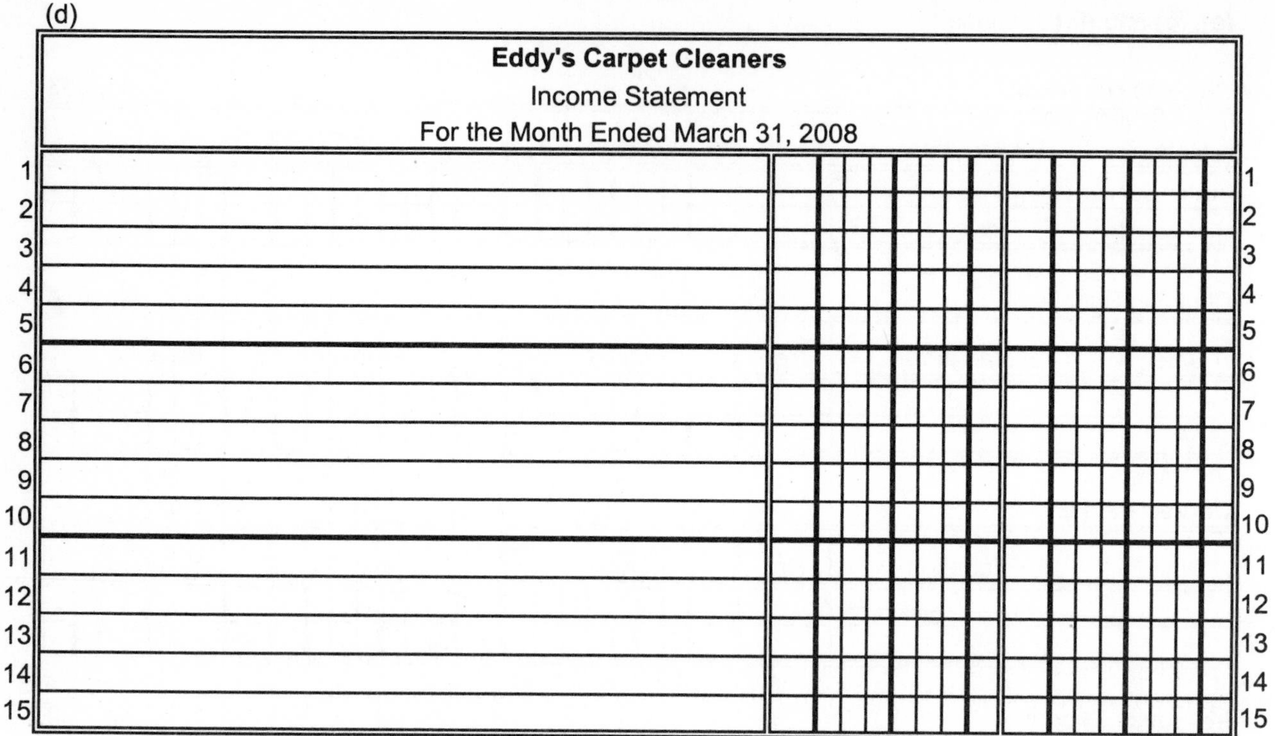

Eddy's Carpet Cleaners

Owner's Equity Statement

For the Month Ended March 31, 2008

(d) (Continued)

Eddy's Carpet Cleaners
Balance Sheet
March 31, 2008

Assets

Liabilities and Owner's Equity

Name

Section

Date

Problem 4-5A Continued

Eddy's Carpet Cleaners

(e) General Journal J2

Date	Accounts Titles	Ref.	Debit	Credit
	Adjusting Entries			
Mar. 31				
31				
31				
31				
31				

(f) General Journal J3

Date	Account Titles	Ref.	Debit	Credit
	Closing Entries			
Mar. 31				
31				
31				
31				

(g)

Eddy's Carpet Cleaners
Post-Closing Trial Balance
March 31, 2008

		Debit	Credit	
1				
2				1
3				2
4				3
5				4
6				5
7				6
8				7
9				8
10				9
11				10
12				11
				12

Problem 4-6A

Fox Cable

See Appendix

(b)

Fox Cable
Trial Balance
April 30, 2008

		Debit	Credit	
1	Cash			1
2	Accounts Receivable			2
3	Supplies			3
4	Equipment			4
5	Accumulated Depreciation			5
6	Accounts Payable			6
7	Salaries Payable			7
8	Unearned Revenue			8
9	A. Manion, Capital			9
11	Service Revenue			11
12	Salaries Expense			12
13	Advertising Expense			13
14	Miscellaneous Expense			14
15	Repair Expense			15
16	Depreciation Expense			16
17				17
18				18
19				19
20				20
21				21
22				22
23				23
24				24
25				25
26				26
27				27
28				28
29				29
30				30

Problem 4-1B

Everlast Roofing

See Appendix

(b)

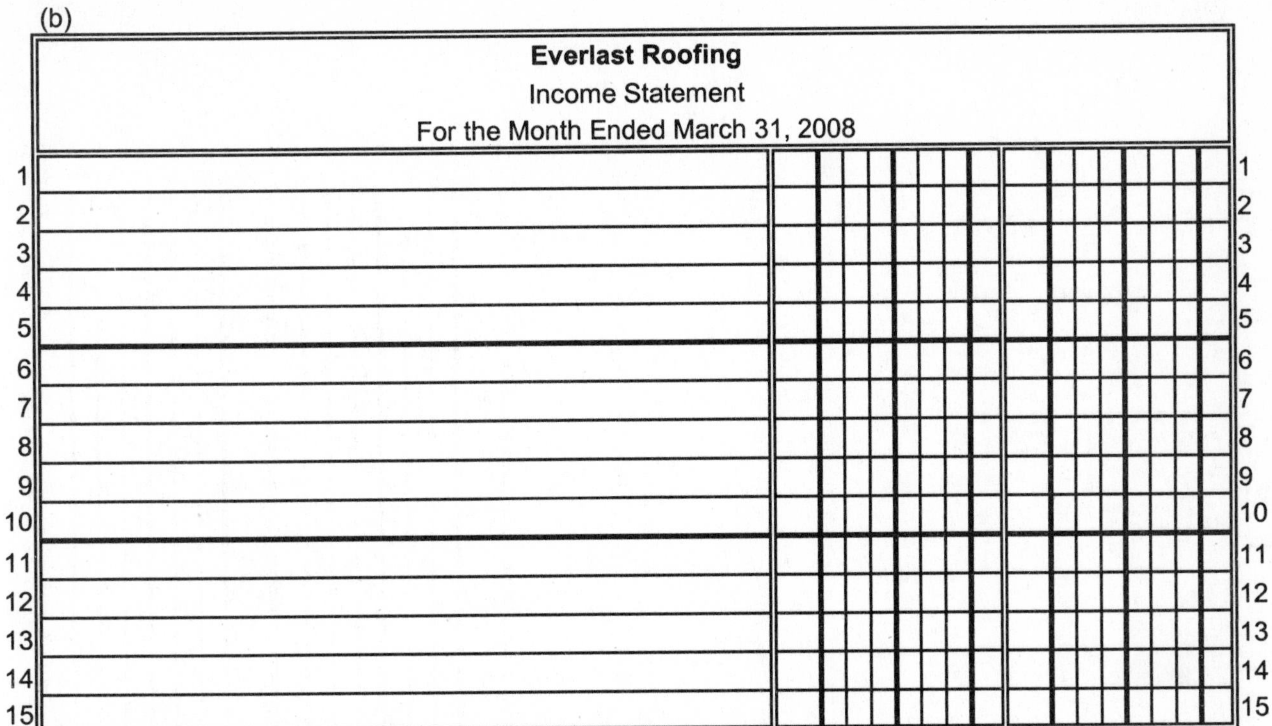

Everlast Roofing

Income Statement

For the Month Ended March 31, 2008

Everlast Roofing

Owner's Equity Statement

For the Month Ended March 31, 2008

Name
Section
Date

Problem 4-1B Continued

Everlast Roofing

(b) (Continued)

Everlast Roofing
Balance Sheet
March 31, 2008

Assets

Liabilities and Owner's Equity

(c)

General Journal

Date	Account Titles	Debit	Credit
	Adjusting Entries		
Mar. 31			
31			
31			
31			

(d)

General Journal

Date	Account Titles	Debit	Credit
	Closing Entries		
Mar. 31			
31			
31			
31			

Name

Section

Date

Problem 4-2B

Sparks Company

(a)

Sparks Company
Partial Worksheet
For the Year Ended December 31, 2008

Account No.	Account Titles	Adjusted Trial Balance Dr.	Adjusted Trial Balance Cr.	Income Statement Dr.	Income Statement Cr.	Balance Sheet Dr.	Balance Sheet Cr.
101	Cash	11600					
112	Accounts Receivable	15400					
126	Supplies	2000					
130	Prepaid Insurance	2800					
151	Office Equipment	34000					
152	Accum. Depr. - Office Equip.		8000				
200	Notes Payable		20000				
201	Accounts Payable		9000				
212	Salaries Payable		3500				
230	Interest Payable		800				
301	B. Sparks, Capital		25000				
306	B. Sparks, Drawing	10000					
400	Service Revenue		85000				
610	Advertising Expense	12000					
631	Supplies Expense	5700					
711	Depreciation Expense	8000					
722	Insurance Expense	5000					
726	Salaries Expense	44000					
905	Interest Expense	800					
	Totals	151300	151300				
	Net Income						
	Totals						

(b)

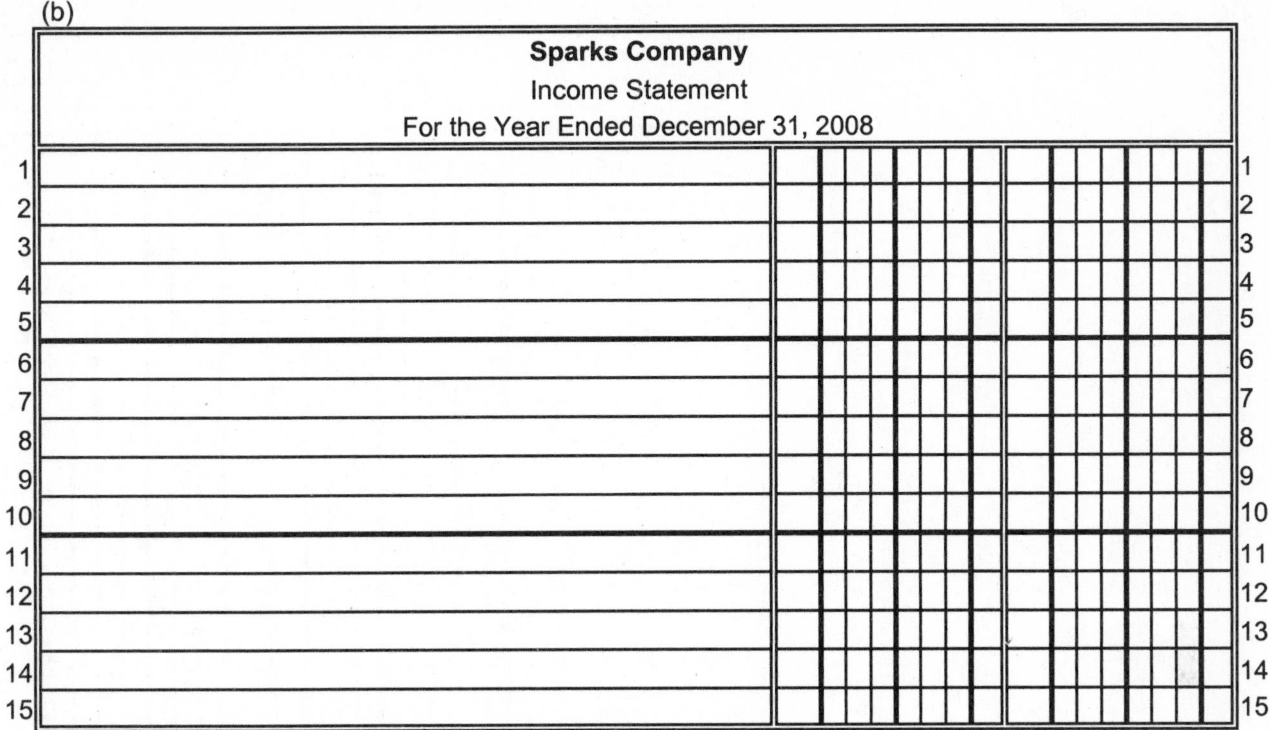

Sparks Company
Income Statement
For the Year Ended December 31, 2008

Sparks Company
Owner's Equity Statement
For the Year Ended December 31, 2008

Name

Section

Date

Problem 4-2B Continued

Sparks Company

(b) (Continued)

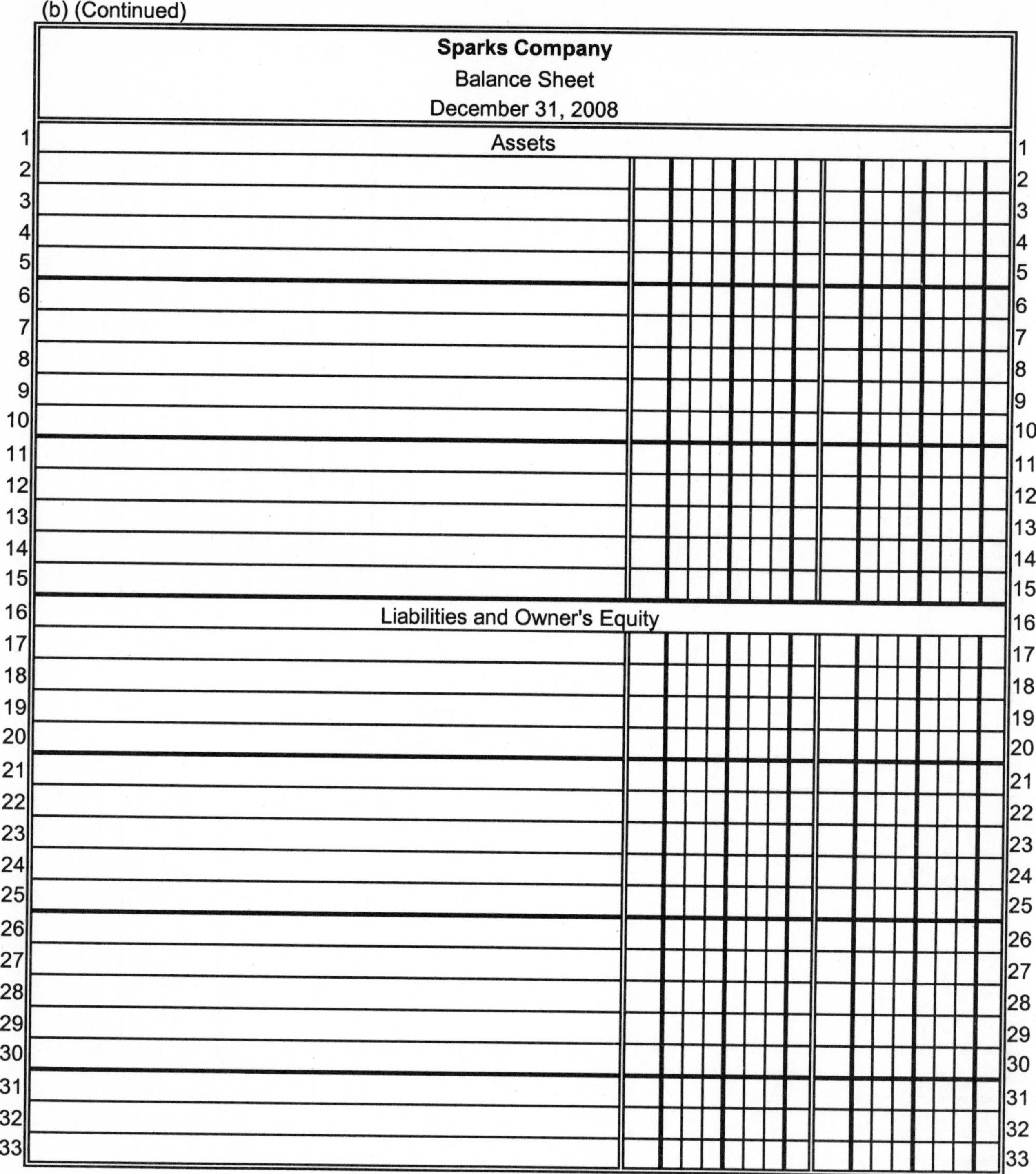

Sparks Company

Balance Sheet

December 31, 2008

Assets

Liabilities and Owner's Equity

Name | Problem 4-2B Continued

Section

Date | Sparks Company

(c)

General Journal | J14

	Date	Account Titles	Ref.	Debit	Credit	
1	Dec. 31					1
2						2
3						3
4	31					4
5						5
6						6
7						7
8						8
9						9
10						10
11						11
12	31					12
13						13
14						14
15	31					15
16						16
17						17
18						18

(d)

B. Sparks, Capital | No. 301

Date	Explanation	Ref.	Debit	Credit	Balance
Jan 1	Balance	√			25000

B. Sparks, Drawing | No. 306

Date	Explanation	Ref.	Debit	Credit	Balance
Dec 31	Balance	√			10000

Income Summary | No. 350

Date	Explanation	Ref.	Debit	Credit	Balance

Name

Section

Date

Problem 4-2B Continued

Sparks Company

(d) (Continued)

Service Revenue — No. 400

Date	Explanation	Ref.	Debit	Credit	Balance
Dec 31	Balance	√			85000

Advertising Expense — No. 610

Date	Explanation	Ref.	Debit	Credit	Balance
Dec 31	Balance	√			12000

Supplies Expense — No. 631

Date	Explanation	Ref.	Debit	Credit	Balance
Dec 31	Balance	√			5700

Depreciation Expense — No. 711

Date	Explanation	Ref.	Debit	Credit	Balance
Dec 31	Balance	√			8000

Insurance Expense — No. 722

Date	Explanation	Ref.	Debit	Credit	Balance
Dec 31	Balance	√			5000

Salaries Expense — No. 726

Date	Explanation	Ref.	Debit	Credit	Balance
Dec 31	Balance	√			44000

Interest Expense — No. 905

Date	Explanation	Ref.	Debit	Credit	Balance
Dec 31	Balance	√			800

(e)

Sparks Company
Post-Closing Trial Balance
December 31, 2008

	Debit	Credit

Name

Section

Date

Problem 4-3B

Molinda Company

(a)

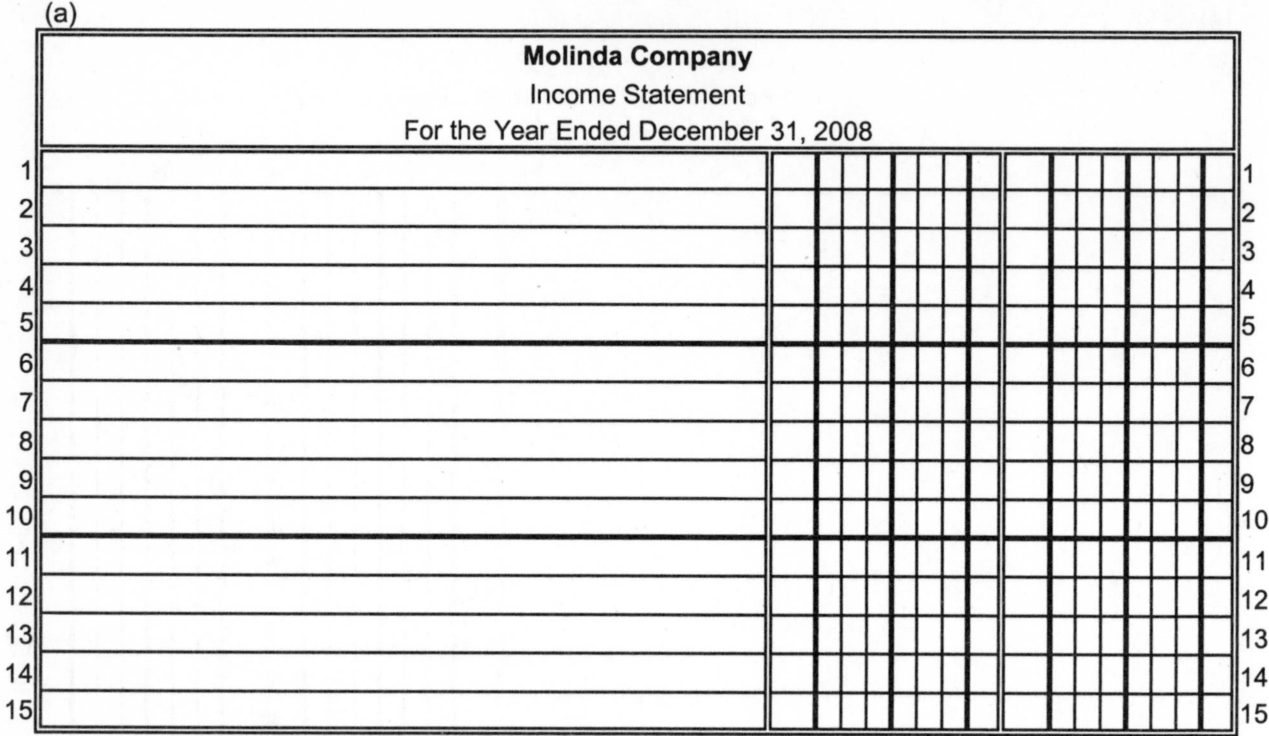

Molinda Company

Income Statement

For the Year Ended December 31, 2008

Molinda Company

Owner's Equity Statement

For the Year Ended December 31, 2008

(a) (Continued)

Molinda Company

Balance Sheet

December 31, 2008

Assets

Liabilities and Owner's Equity

Name | Problem 4-3B Continued
Section
Date | Molinda Company

(b) General Journal

Date	Accounts Titles	Ref.	Debit	Credit
	Closing Entries			
Dec. 31				
31				
31				
31				

(c)

Ann Molinda, Capital	No. 301
	1/1 Bal 36,000

Ann Molinda, Drawing	No.306
12/31 Bal 14,000	

Income Summary	No. 350

Service Revenue	No. 400

Repair Expense	No. 622

Depreciation Expense	No. 711

Insurance Expense	No. 722

Salaries Expense	No. 726

Utilities Expense	No. 732

(d)

Molinda Company
Post-Closing Trial Balance
December 31, 2008

		Debit	Credit	
1				1
2				2
3				3
4				4
5				5
6				6
7				7
8				8
9				9
10				10

Problem 4-4B

Pettengill Management Services

See Appendix

(b)

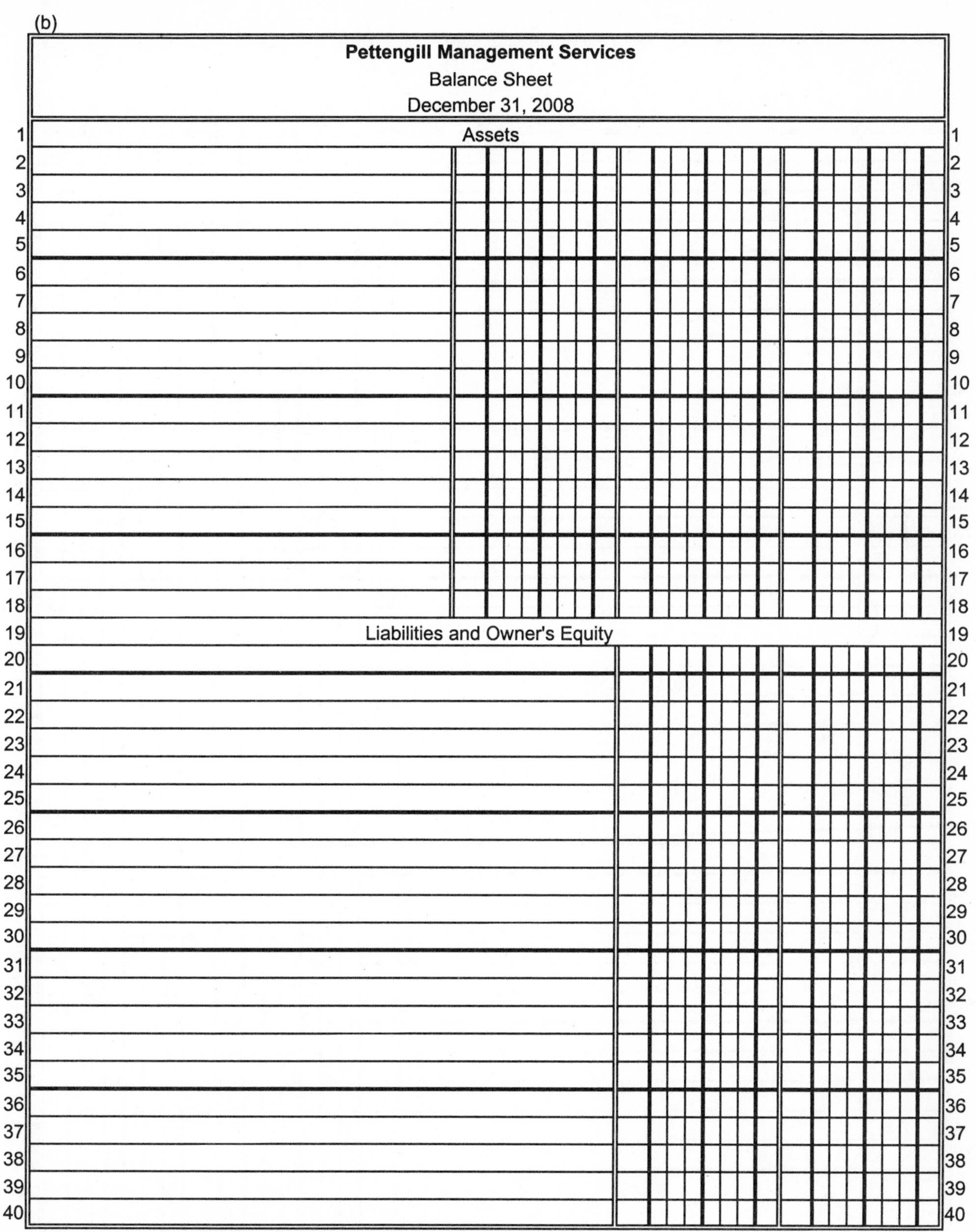

Pettengill Management Services

Balance Sheet

December 31, 2008

Assets

Liabilities and Owner's Equity

Name

Section

Date

Problem 4-4B Continued

Pettengill Management Services

Date	Accounts Titles	Debit	Credit
(c)	Adjusting Entries		
Dec. 31			
31			
31			
31			
31			
(d)	Closing Entries		
Dec. 31			
31			
31			
31			

(e)

Pettengill Management Services
Post-Closing Trial Balance
December 31, 2008

	Debit	Credit

Name Problem 4-5B

Section

Date Choi's Window Washing

(a) General Journal J1

Date	Accounts Titles	Ref.	Debit	Credit
July 1				
1				
3				
5				
12				
18				
20				
21				
25				
31				
31				

Problem 4-5B

Choi's Window Washing

See Appendix

(a), (e) and (f)

Cash No. 101

Date	Explanation	Ref.	Debit	Credit	Balance

Accounts Receivable No. 112

Date	Explanation	Ref.	Debit	Credit	Balance

Cleaning Supplies No. 128

Date	Explanation	Ref.	Debit	Credit	Balance

Prepaid Insurance No. 130

Date	Explanation	Ref.	Debit	Credit	Balance

Equipment No. 157

Date	Explanation	Ref.	Debit	Credit	Balance

(a), (e) and (f) (Continued)

Accumulated Depreciation - Equipment — No. 158

Date	Explanation	Ref.	Debit	Credit	Balance

Accounts Payable — No. 201

Date	Explanation	Ref.	Debit	Credit	Balance

Salaries Payable — No. 212

Date	Explanation	Ref.	Debit	Credit	Balance

Lee Choi, Capital — No. 301

Date	Explanation	Ref.	Debit	Credit	Balance

Lee Choi, Drawing — No. 306

Date	Explanation	Ref.	Debit	Credit	Balance

Income Summary — No. 350

Date	Explanation	Ref.	Debit	Credit	Balance

Service Revenue — No. 400

Date	Explanation	Ref.	Debit	Credit	Balance

(a), (e) and (f) (Continued)

Gas & Oil Expense No. 633

Date	Explanation	Ref.	Debit	Credit	Balance

Cleaning Supplies Expense No. 634

Date	Explanation	Ref.	Debit	Credit	Balance

Depreciation Expense No. 711

Date	Explanation	Ref.	Debit	Credit	Balance

Insurance Expense No. 722

Date	Explanation	Ref.	Debit	Credit	Balance

Salaries Expense No. 726

Date	Explanation	Ref.	Debit	Credit	Balance

(d)

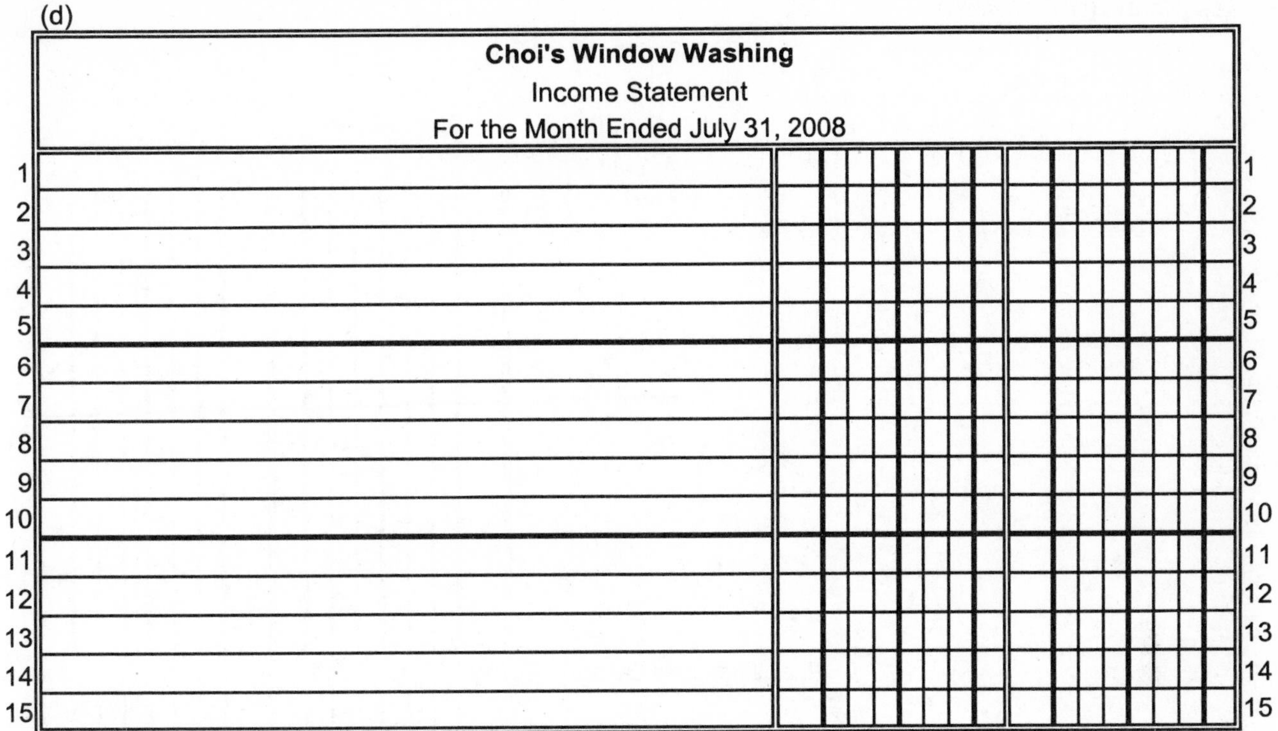

Choi's Window Washing
Income Statement
For the Month Ended July 31, 2008

Choi's Window Washing
Owner's Equity Statement
For the Month Ended July 31, 2008

(d) (Continued)

Choi's Window Washing
Balance Sheet
July 31, 2008

Assets

Liabilities and Owner's Equity

Name

Section

Date

Problem 4-5B Continued

Choi's Window Washing

(e) General Journal J2

	Date	Accounts Titles	Ref.	Debit	Credit	
1		Adjusting Entries				1
2	July 31					2
3						3
4						4
5	31					5
6						6
7						7
8	31					8
9						9
10						10
11	31					11
12						12
13						13
14	31					14
15						15
16						16

(f) General Journal J3

	Date	Account Titles	Ref.	Debit	Credit	
1		Closing Entries				1
2	July 31					2
3						3
4						4
5	31					5
6						6
7						7
8						8
9						9
10						10
11						11
12	31					12
13						13
14						14
15	31					15
16						16
17						17
18						18
19						19

(g)

Choi's Window Washing

Post-Closing Trial Balance

July 31, 2008

	Debit	Credit

Name

Section

Date

Julie's Maids Cleaning Service

(a) General Journal J1

Date	Accounts Titles	Ref.	Debit	Credit
July 1				
1				
3				
5				
12				
18				
20				
21				
25				
31				
31				

Comprehensive Problem Ch 2 - 4

Julie's Maids Cleaning Service

See Appendix

Name

Section

Date

Comprehensive Problem: Chapters 2 to 4

Julie's Maids Cleaning Service

(a), (e) and (f)

Cash — No. 101

Date	Explanation	Ref.	Debit	Credit	Balance

Accounts Receivabl — No. 112

Date	Explanation	Ref.	Debit	Credit	Balance

Cleaning Supplies — No. 128

Date	Explanation	Ref.	Debit	Credit	Balance

Prepaid Insurance — No. 130

Date	Explanation	Ref.	Debit	Credit	Balance

Equipment — No. 157

Date	Explanation	Ref.	Debit	Credit	Balance

Accumulated Depreciation - Equip — No. 158

Date	Explanation	Ref.	Debit	Credit	Balance

(a), (e) and (f) (Continued)

Accounts Payable No. 201

Date	Explanation	Ref.	Debit	Credit	Balance

Salaries Payable No. 212

Date	Explanation	Ref.	Debit	Credit	Balance

Julie Molony, Capital No. 301

Date	Explanation	Ref.	Debit	Credit	Balance

Julie Molony, Drawing No. 306

Date	Explanation	Ref.	Debit	Credit	Balance

Income Summary No. 350

Date	Explanation	Ref.	Debit	Credit	Balance

Service Revenue No. 400

Date	Explanation	Ref.	Debit	Credit	Balance

(a), (e) and (f) (Continued)

Gas & Oil Expense No. 633

Date	Explanation	Ref.	Debit	Credit	Balance

Cleaning Supplies Expense No. 634

Date	Explanation	Ref.	Debit	Credit	Balance

Depreciation Expense No. 711

Date	Explanation	Ref.	Debit	Credit	Balance

Insurance Expense No. 722

Date	Explanation	Ref.	Debit	Credit	Balance

Salaries Expense No. 726

Date	Explanation	Ref.	Debit	Credit	Balance

(d)

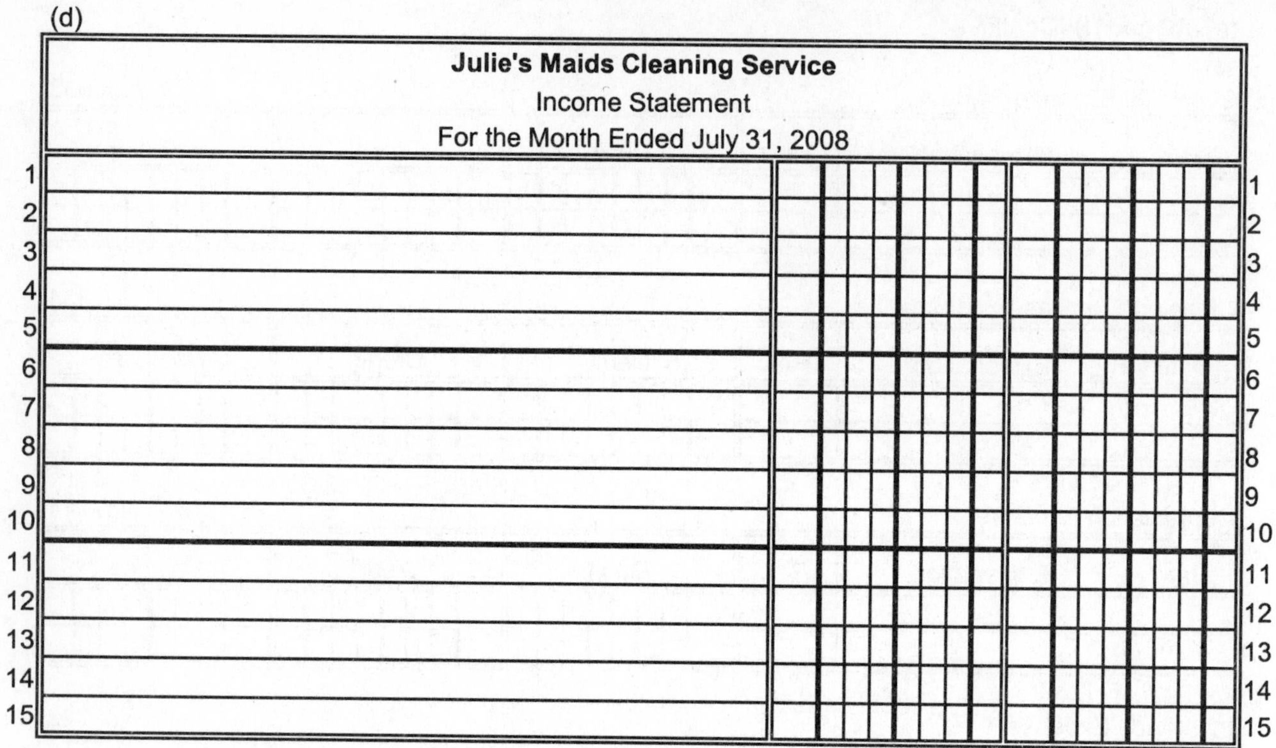

Julie's Maids Cleaning Service
Income Statement
For the Month Ended July 31, 2008

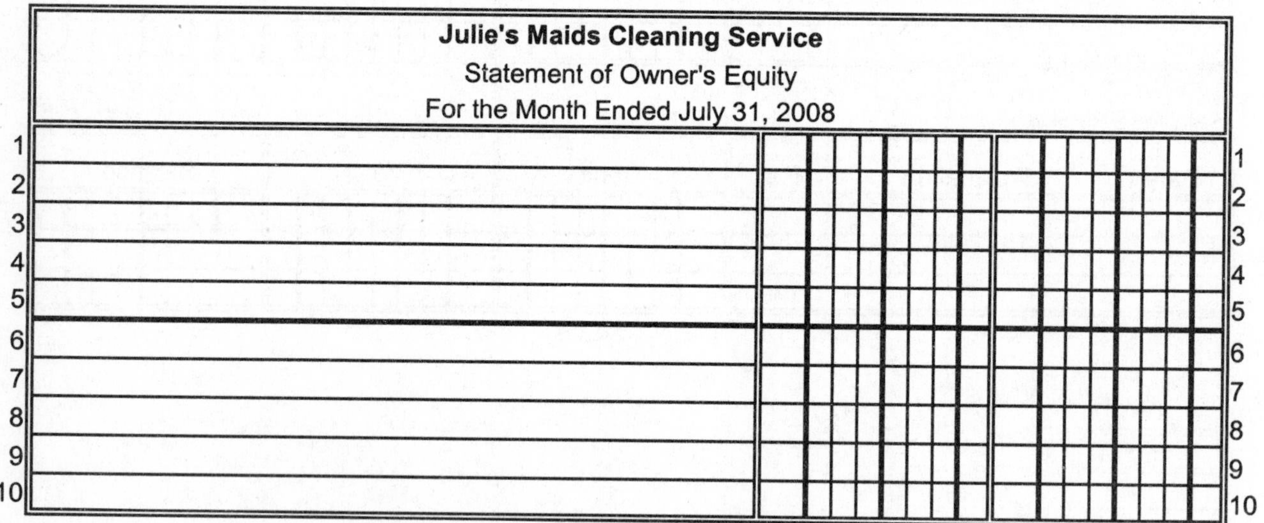

Julie's Maids Cleaning Service
Statement of Owner's Equity
For the Month Ended July 31, 2008

(d) (Continued)

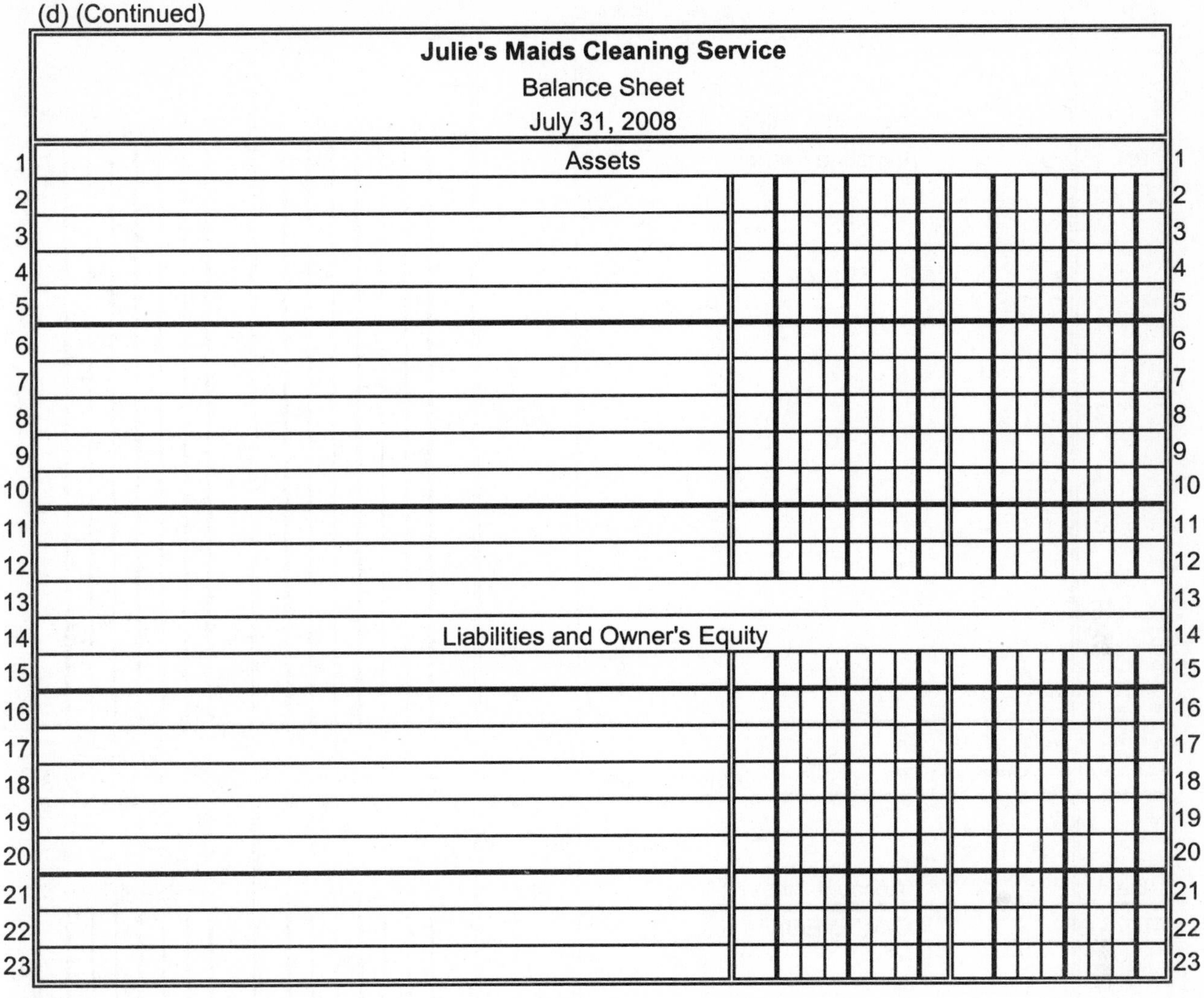

Julie's Maids Cleaning Service
Balance Sheet
July 31, 2008

Assets

Liabilities and Owner's Equity

(g)

Julie's Maids Cleaning Service
Post-Closing Trial Balance
July 31, 2008

	Debit	Credit

General Journal

J2

Date	Accounts Titles	Ref.	Debit	Credit
(e)	Adjusting Entries			
July 31				
31				
31				
31				
31				

General Journal

J3

Date	Account Titles	Ref.	Debit	Credit
(f)	Closing Entries			
July 31				
31				
31				
31				

	PepsiCo	Coca-Cola
(a) (in millions)		
1. Total current assets		
2. Net property, plant, and equipment		
3. Total current liabilities		
4. Total stockholders' (shareholders') equity		

(b)

Name

Section

Date

(a)

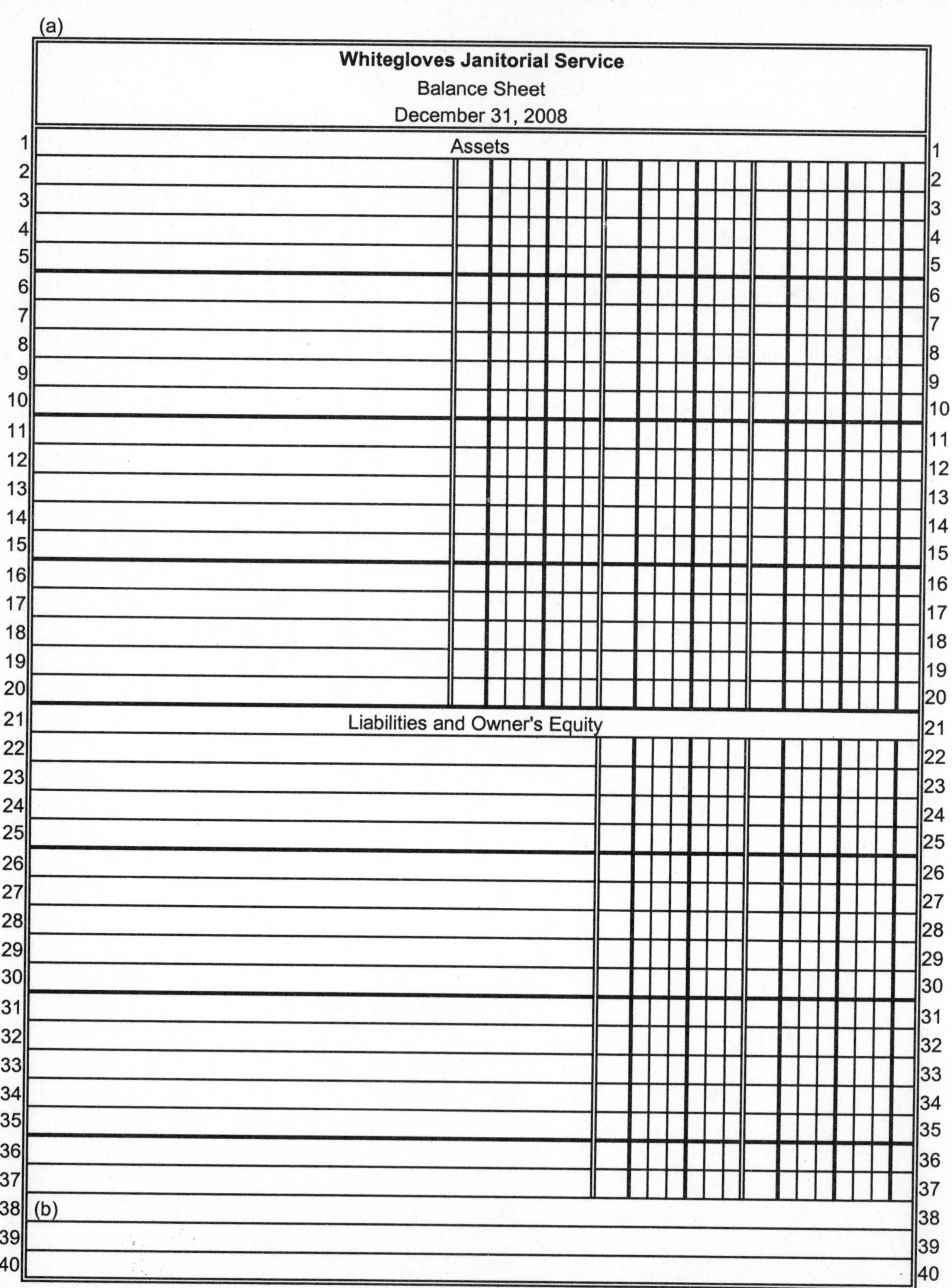

Whitegloves Janitorial Service

Balance Sheet

December 31, 2008

Assets

Liabilities and Owner's Equity

(b)

Whitegloves Janitorial Service
Capital Account Detail
December 31, 2008

Capital account balance as reported		

(b)

Name

Section

Date

Personal Balance Sheet

Assets

Liabilities and Owner's Equity

Name

Section

Date

BE5-1

	Sales	Cost of Goods Sold	Gross Profit	Operating Expenses	Net Income
(a)	$ 75000		$ 30000		$ 10800
(b)	108000	70000			29500
(c)		71900	79600	39500	

BE5-2 Account Titles	Debit	Credit
Hollins Company		
Gordon Company		

BE5-3 Account Titles	Debit	Credit
(a)		
(b)		
(c)		

Name

Section

Date

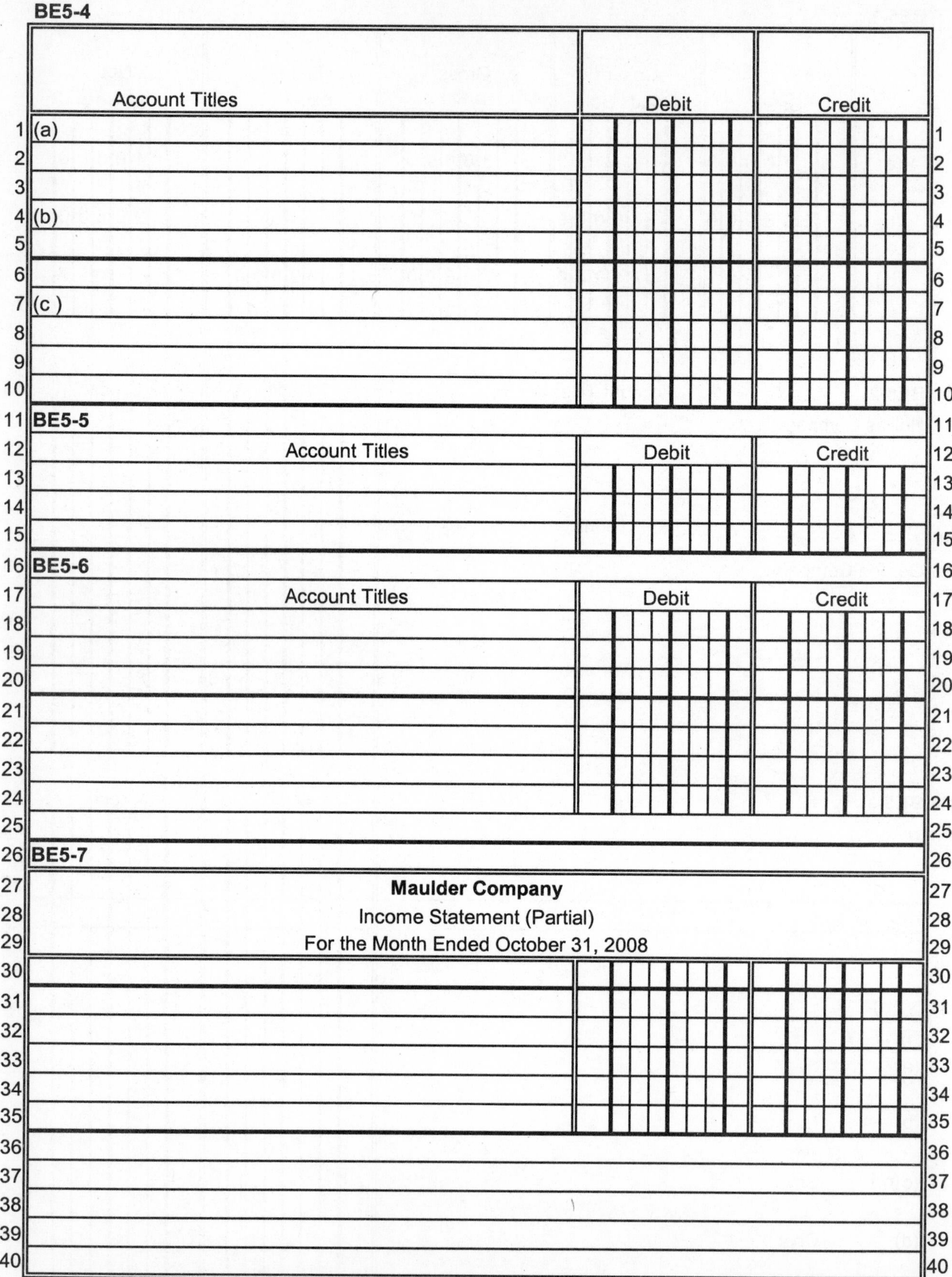

BE5-4

Account Titles	Debit	Credit
(a)		
(b)		
(c)		

BE5-5

Account Titles	Debit	Credit

BE5-6

Account Titles	Debit	Credit

BE5-7

Maulder Company

Income Statement (Partial)

For the Month Ended October 31, 2008

Name

Section

Date

BE5-10

BE5-11

BE5-12 Account Titles	Debit	Credit
(a)		
(b)		
(c)		

BE5-13

(a) Cash:

(b) Merchandise Inventory:

(c) Sales:

(d) Cost of Goods Sold

Name

Section

Date

E5-2

General Journal

Date	Account Titles	Debit	Credit
(a)			
Apr. 5			
6			
7			
8			
15			
(b)			
May 4			

E5-3

Date	Account Titles	Debit	Credit
Sept. 6			
9			
10			
12			

Name

Section

Date

E5-3 (Continued) General Journal

Date	Account Titles	Debit	Credit
Sept. 14			
20			

E5-4

Date	Account Titles	Debit	Credit
(a)			
June 10			
11			
12			
19			
(b)			
June 10			

Name

Section

Date

E5-4 (Continued) General Journal

Date	Account Titles	Debit	Credit
June 12			
19			

E5-5

Date	Account Titles	Debit	Credit
(a)			
Dec. 3			
8			
13			
(b)			

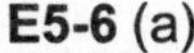

Section

Date

E5-6 (a)

Zambrana Company
Income Statement (Partial)
For the Year Ended October 31, 2008

1				1
2				2
3				3
4				4
5				5
6				6

(b)

	Date	Account Titles	Debit	Credit	
1	Oct. 31				1
2					2
3					3
4	31				4
5					5
6					6
7					7

E5-7

	Account Titles	Debit	Credit	
1	(a)			1
2				2
3				3
4	(b)			4
5				5
6				6
7				7
8				8
9				9
10				10
11				11
12				12
13				13
14				14
15				15
16				16
17				17

Name Exercise 5-8

Section

Date Rogers Co.

Account Titles	Debit	Credit
(a)		
(b)		

Name Exercise 5-9

Section

Date Pele Company

(a)

Pele Company

Income Statement

For the Year Ended December 31, 2008

(b)

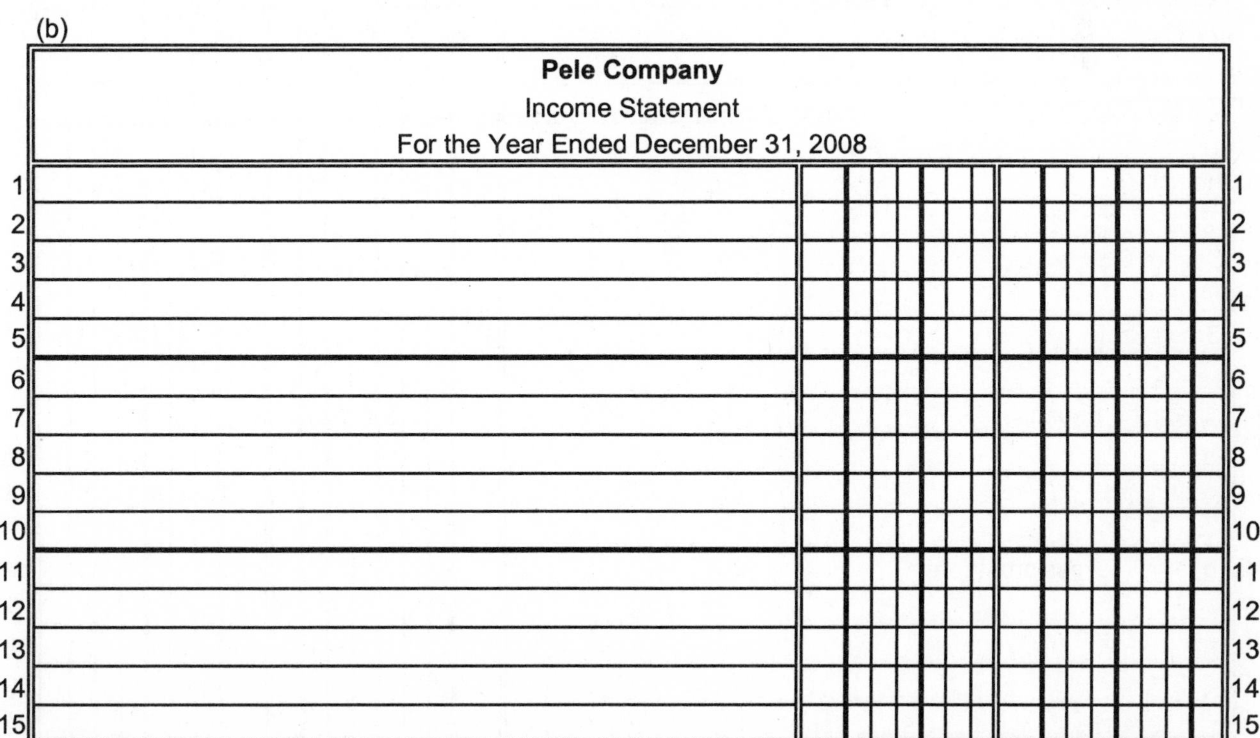

E5-10

Account Titles	Debit	Credit
1.		
2.		
3.		
4.		

E5-12

(a)	Nam Company	Mayo Company
Sales	$ 90000	$
Sales Returns		5000
Net Sales	84000	100000
Cost of Goods Sold	56000	
Gross Profit		41000
Operating Expenses	15000	
Net Income	$	$ 15000
(b) Gross profit rate		

Section

Date

E5-13

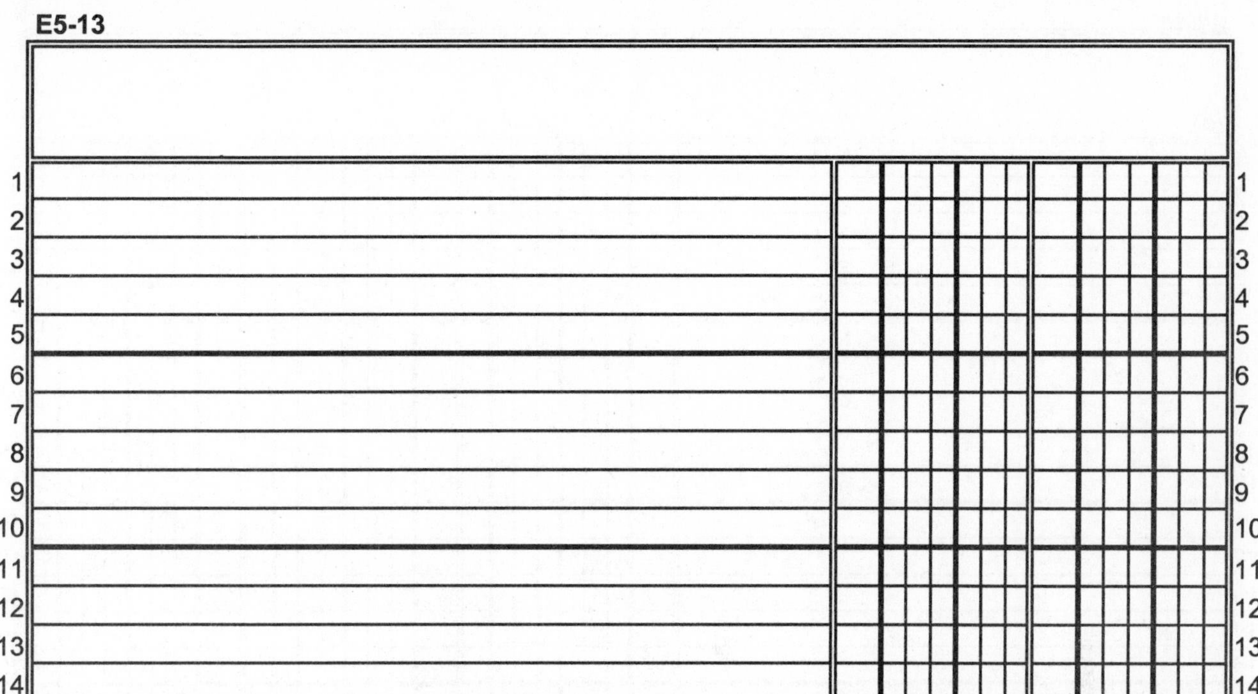

E5-15

	B	F	L	R
Beginning inventory	$ 150	$ 70	$ 1000	$
Purchases	1600	1080		43950
Purchase returns and allowances	40		290	
Net purchases		1030	6210	41090
Freight-in	110			2240
Cost of goods purchased		1280	7940	
Cost of goods available for sale	1820	1350		49530
Ending inventory	310		1450	6230
Cost of goods sold		1230	7490	43300

Name Exercise 5-14

Section

Date Rachael Ray Corporation

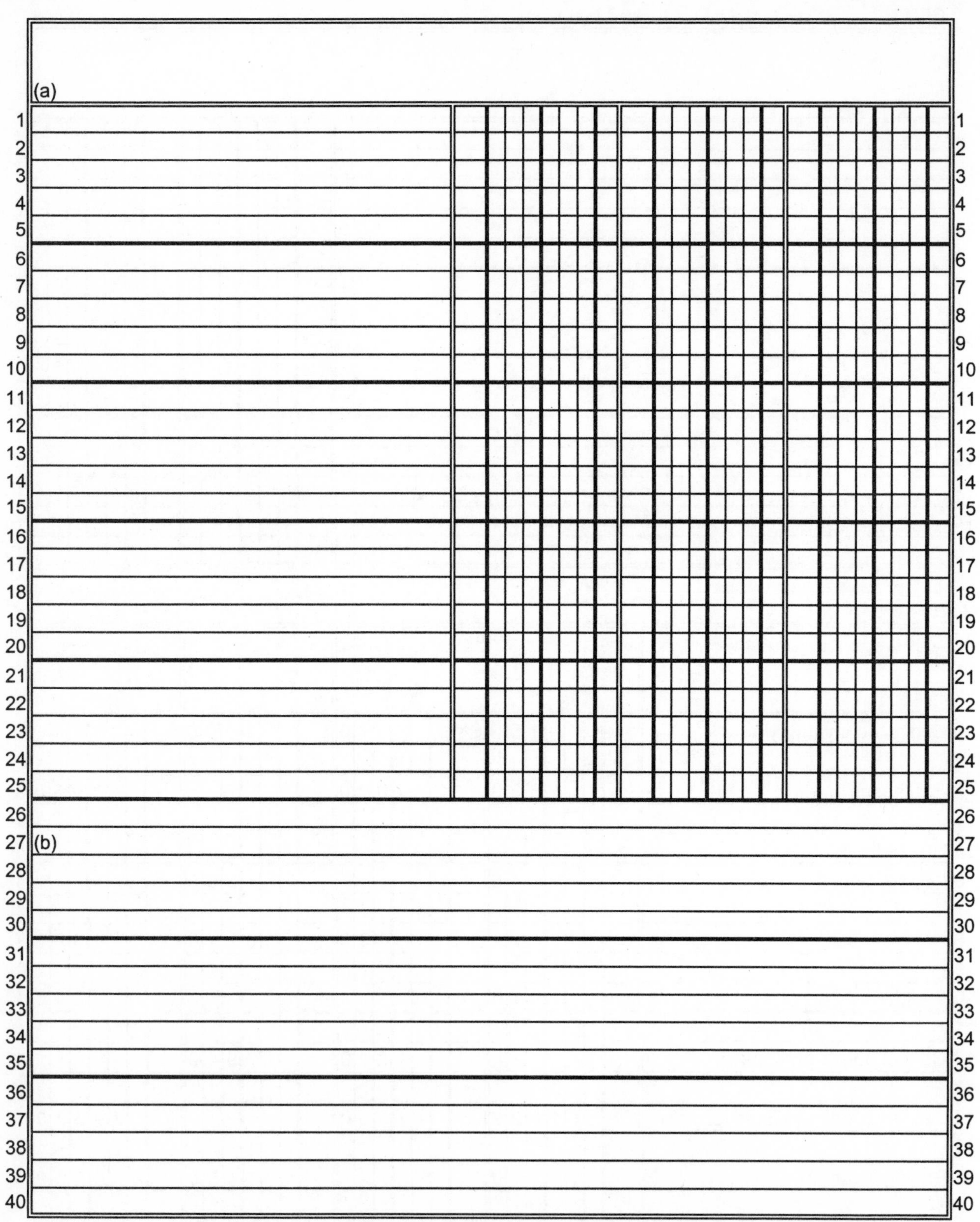

Name *Exercise 5-16

Section

Date Martinez Co.

Date	Account Titles	Debit	Credit
(a)			
Apr. 5			
6			
7			
8			
15			
(b)			
May 4			

Name *Exercise 5-17

Section

Date Chevalier Co.

Date	Account Titles	Debit	Credit
(a)			
Apr. 5			
6			
7			
8			
15			
(b)			
May 4			

Name *Exercise 5-18

Section

Date Carpenter Company

Carpenter Company
Worksheet (Partial)
For the Period Ended May 31, 2008

	Account Titles	Adjusted Trial Balance		Income Statement		Balance Sheet		
		Dr.	Cr.	Dr.	Cr.	Dr.	Cr.	
1	Cash	9000						1
2	Merchandise Inventory	76000						2
3	Sales		450000					3
4	Sales Returns and Allowances	10000						4
5	Sales Discounts	9000						5
6	Cost of Goods Sold	300000						6
7								7
8								8
9								9
10								10
11								11
12								12
13								13
14								14
15								15

Exercise 5-19

Green Company

See Appendix

Name
Section
Date

Problem 5-1A

Sansomite Co.

General Journal

Date	Account Titles	Debit	Credit
July 1			
3			
9			
12			
17			
18			
20			
21			

Name

Section

Date

Problem 5-1A Concluded

Sansomite Co.

General Journal

Date	Account Titles	Debit	Credit
July 22			
30			
31			

Name Problem 5-2A

Section

Date Olaf Distributing Company

(a) General Journal J1

Date	Account Titles	Ref.	Debit	Credit
Apr. 2				
4				
5				
6				
11				
13				
14				
16				
18				
20				
23				

(a) (Continued)

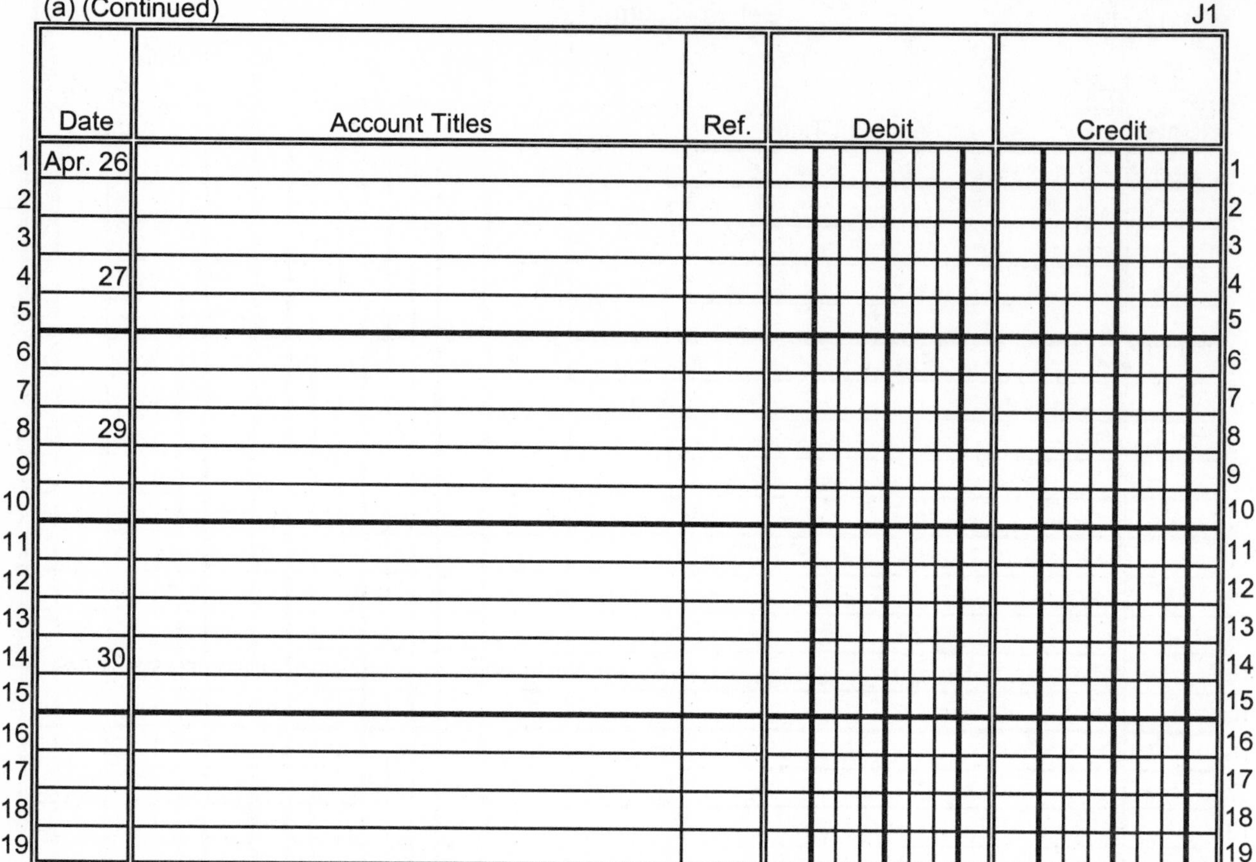

J1

	Date	Account Titles	Ref.	Debit	Credit	
1	Apr. 26					1
2						2
3						3
4	27					4
5						5
6						6
7						7
8	29					8
9						9
10						10
11						11
12						12
13						13
14	30					14
15						15
16						16
17						17
18						18
19						19

(b)

Cash No. 101

Date	Explanation	Ref.	Debit	Credit	Balance
Apr. 1	Balance	√			9000

Accounts Receivable No. 112

Date	Explanation	Ref.	Debit	Credit	Balance

(b) (Continued)

Merchandise Invento

No. 120

Date	Explanation	Ref.	Debit	Credit	Balance

Accounts Payable

No. 201

Date	Explanation	Ref.	Debit	Credit	Balance

M. Olaf, Capital

No. 301

Date	Explanation	Ref.	Debit	Credit	Balance
Apr. 1	Balance	√			9000

Sales

No. 401

Date	Explanation	Ref.	Debit	Credit	Balance

Sales Returns and Allowances

No. 412

Date	Explanation	Ref.	Debit	Credit	Balance

(b) (Continued)

Sales Discounts

No. 414

Date	Explanation	Ref.	Debit	Credit	Balance

Cost of Goods Sold

No. 505

Date	Explanation	Ref.	Debit	Credit	Balance

Freight-out

No. 644

Date	Explanation	Ref.	Debit	Credit	Balance

(c)

Olaf Distributing Company

Income Statement (Partial)

For the Month Ended April 30, 2008

Name Problem 5-3A

Section

Date Maine Department Store

(a)

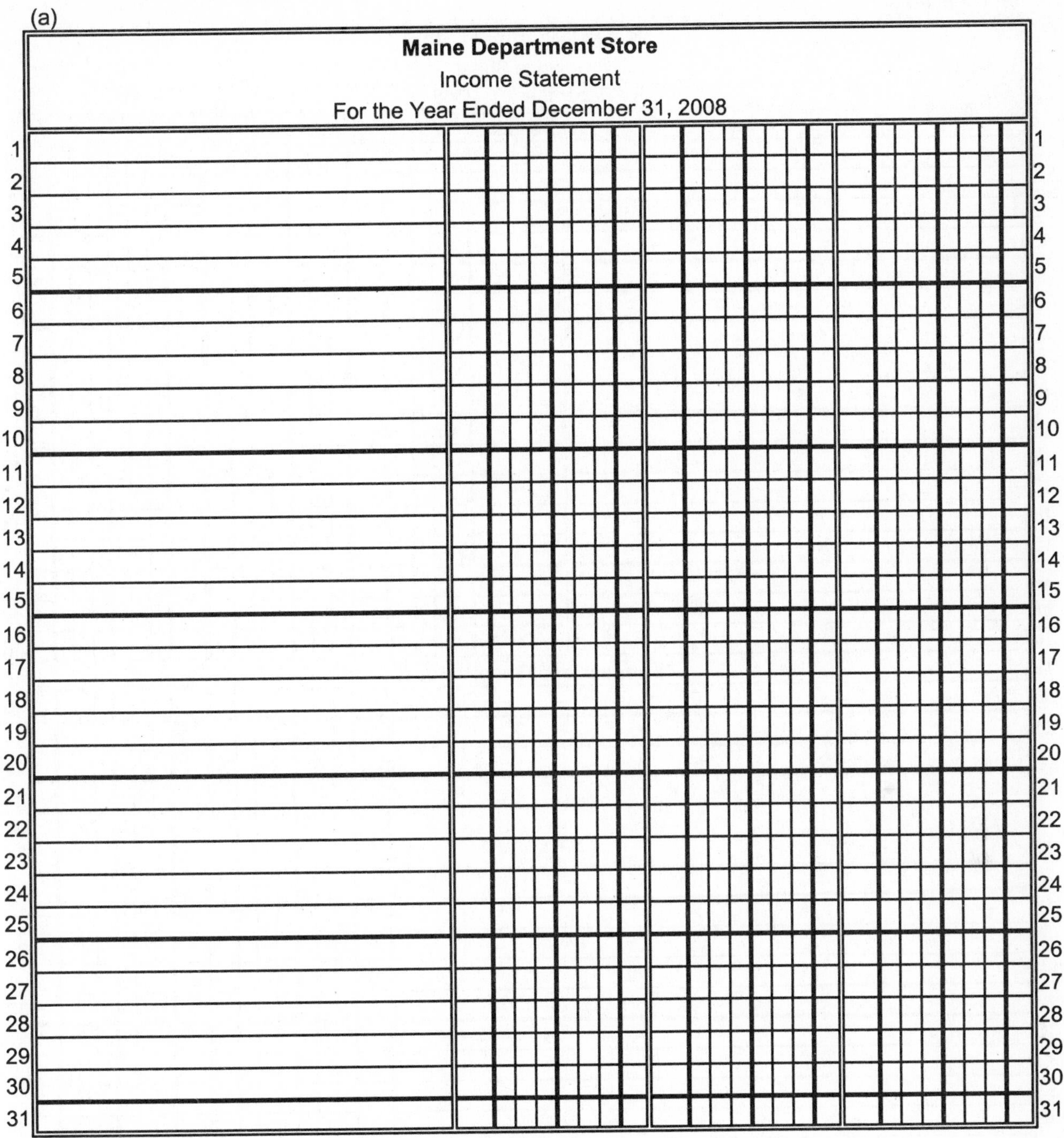

Maine Department Store

Income Statement

For the Year Ended December 31, 2008

Maine Department Store

Owner's Equity Statement

For the Year Ended December 31, 2008

(a) (Continued)

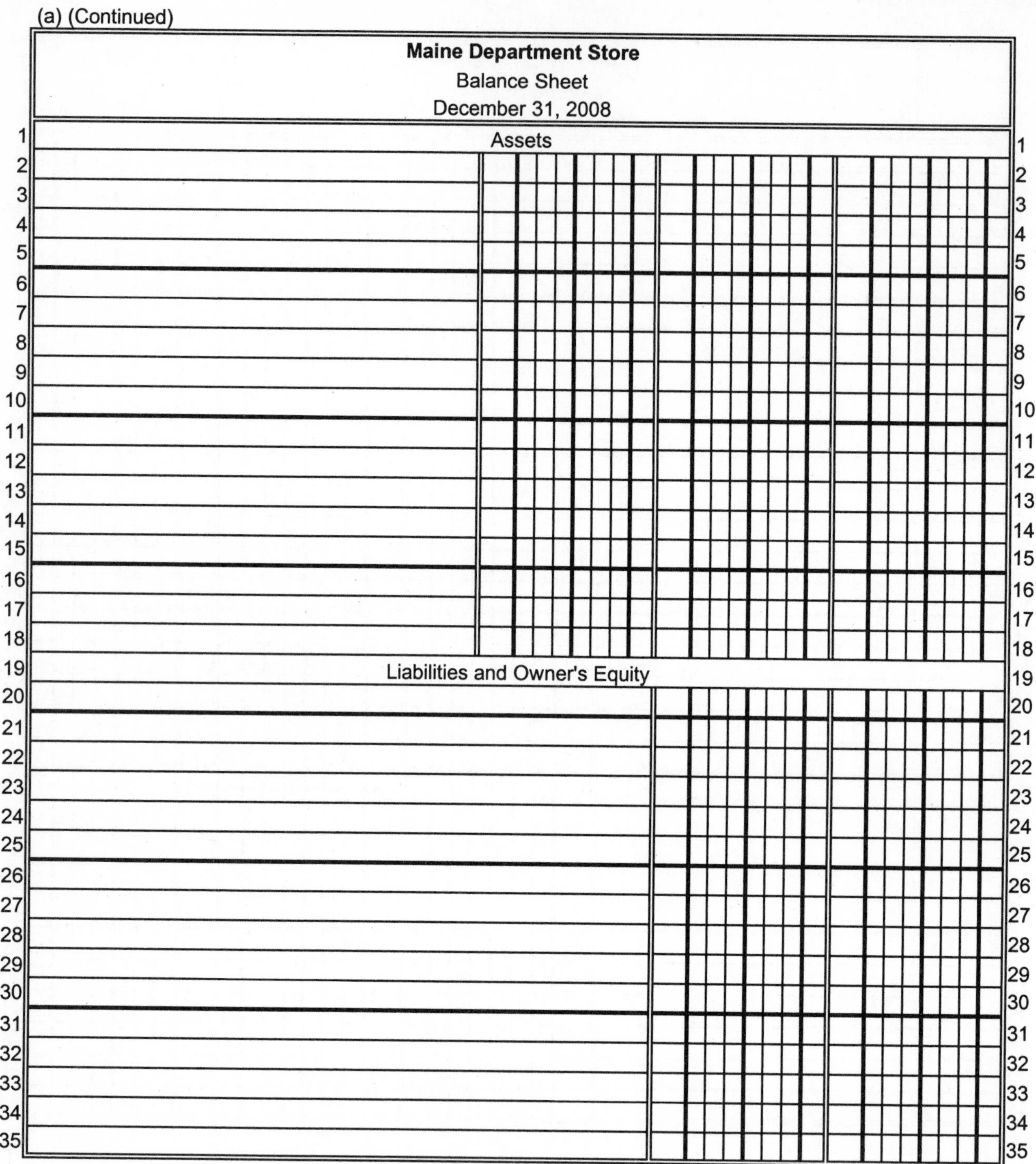

Maine Department Store

Balance Sheet

December 31, 2008

Assets

Liabilities and Owner's Equity

(b) General Journal

Date	Account Titles	Debit	Credit
	Adjusting Entries		
Dec. 31			
31			
31			
31			
31			
31			
31			

Name

Section

Date

Problem 5-3A Concluded

Maine Department Store

(c) General Journal

Date	Account Titles	Debit	Credit
	Closing Entries		
Dec. 31			
31			
31			
31			

Name Problem 5-4A

Section

Date Hafner's Tennis Shop

(a) General Journal J1

Date	Account Titles	Ref.	Debit	Credit
Apr. 4				
6				
8				
10				
11				
13				
14				
15				
17				
18				

(a) (Continued) General Journal J1

Date	Account Titles	Ref.	Debit	Credit
Apr. 20				
21				
27				
30				

(b)

Cash No. 101

Date	Explanation	Ref.	Debit	Credit	Balance
Apr 1	Balance	√			2500

Accounts Receivable No. 112

Date	Explanation	Ref.	Debit	Credit	Balance

Merchandise Inventory No. 120

Date	Explanation	Ref.	Debit	Credit	Balance
Apr 1	Balance	√			1700

Accounts Payable No. 201

Date	Explanation	Ref.	Debit	Credit	Balance

(b) (Continued)

J. Hafner, Capital — No. 301

Date	Explanation	Ref.	Debit	Credit	Balance
Apr 1	Balance	√			4200

Sales — No. 401

Date	Explanation	Ref.	Debit	Credit	Balance

Sales Returns and Allowances — No. 412

Date	Explanation	Ref.	Debit	Credit	Balance

Cost of Goods Sold — No. 505

Date	Explanation	Ref.	Debit	Credit	Balance

(c)

Hafner's Tennis Shop
Trial Balance
April 30, 2008

		Debit	Credit	
1				1
2				2
3				3
4				4
5				5
6				6
7				7
8				8
9				9
10				10

Name Problem 5-5A

Section

Date Gordman Department Store

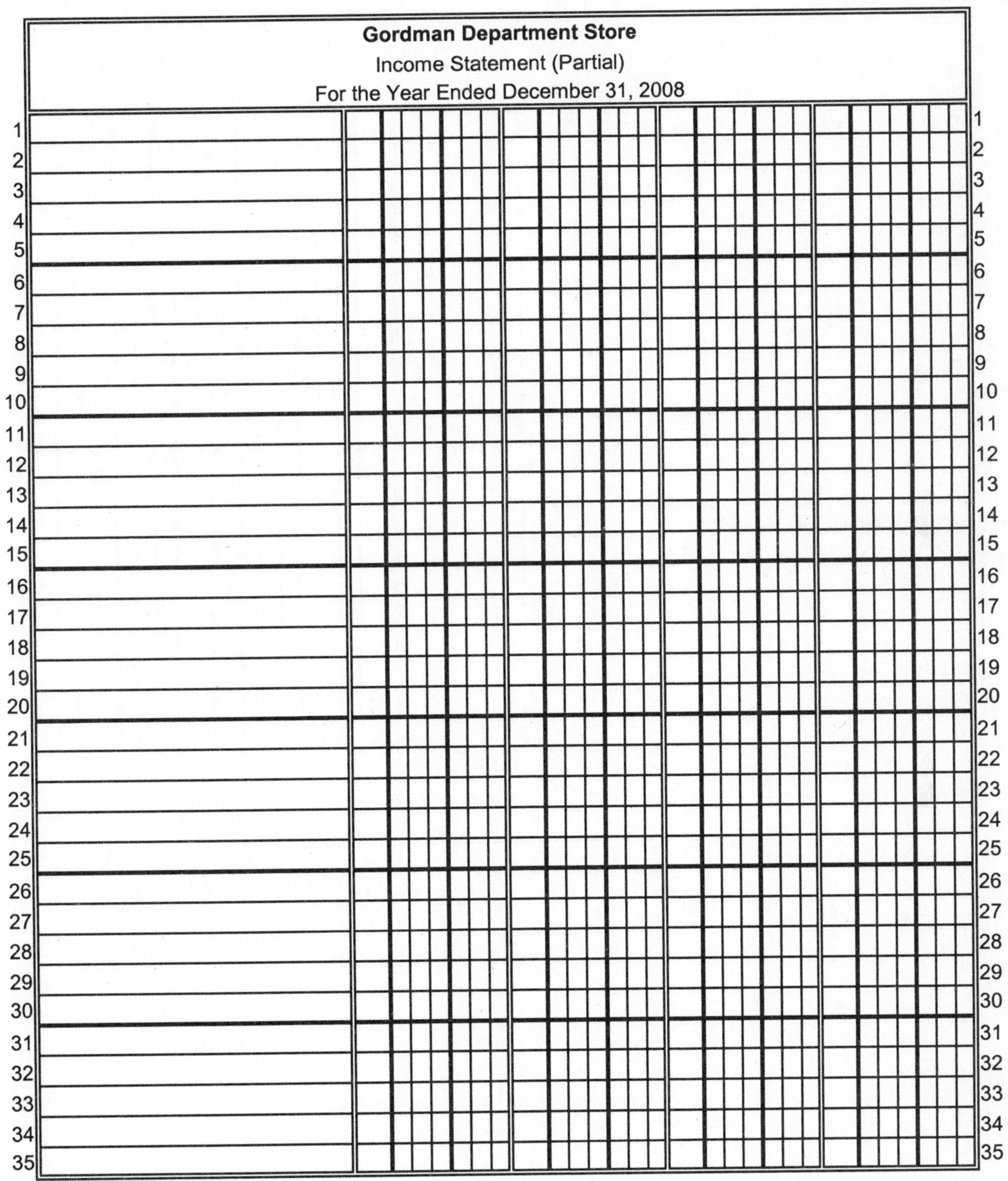

Gordman Department Store

Income Statement (Partial)

For the Year Ended December 31, 2008

Name

Section

Date

Problem 5-6A

Kristen Montana

(a)	2006	2007	2008
Cost of goods sold:			
(b)			
Sales			
(c)			
Beginning accounts payable			
(d)			
Gross profit rate			

Name *Problem 5-7A

Section

Date Village Tennis Shop

(a)

General Journal

Date	Account Titles	Debit	Credit
Apr. 4			
6			
8			
10			
11			
13			
14			
15			
17			
18			

Name

Section

Date

*Problem 5-7A Continued

Village Tennis Shop

(a) (Continued)

General Journal

Date	Account Titles	Debit	Credit
Apr. 20			
21			
27			
30			

(b)

Cash	
4/1 Bal. 2,500	

Accounts Receivable	

Merchandise Inventory	
4/1/ Bal. 1,700	

Accounts Payable	

Angie Wilbert, Capital	
	4/1/ Bal. 4,200

Sales	

Sales Returns and Allowances	

Purchases	

Purchase Returns and Allowances	

Purchase Discount	

Freight-in	

(c)

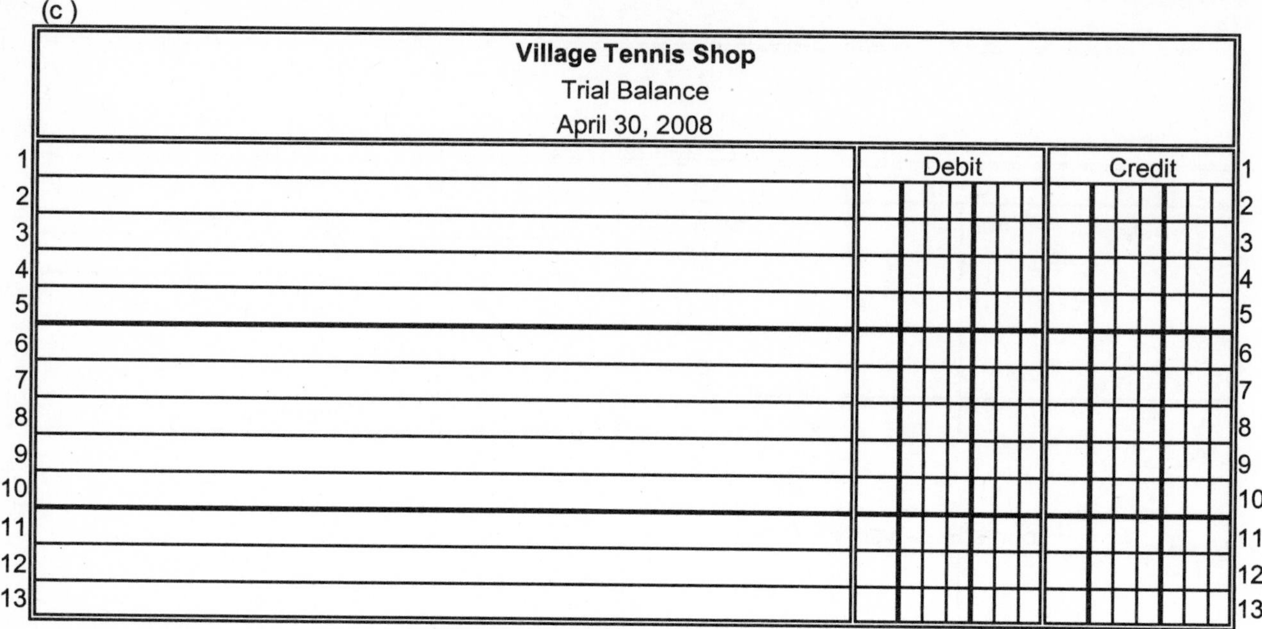

Village Tennis Shop
Trial Balance
April 30, 2008

		Debit	Credit	
1				1
2				2
3				3
4				4
5				5
6				6
7				7
8				8
9				9
10				10
11				11
12				12
13				13

Village Tennis Shop
Income Statement (Partial)
For the Month Ended April 30, 2008

1						1
2						2
3						3
4						4
5						5
6						6
7						7
8						8
9						9
10						10
11						11
12						12
13						13
14						14
15						15
16						16
17						17
18						18
19						19
20						20
21						21
22						22

Problem 5-8A

Terry Manning Fashion Center

See Appendix

(b)

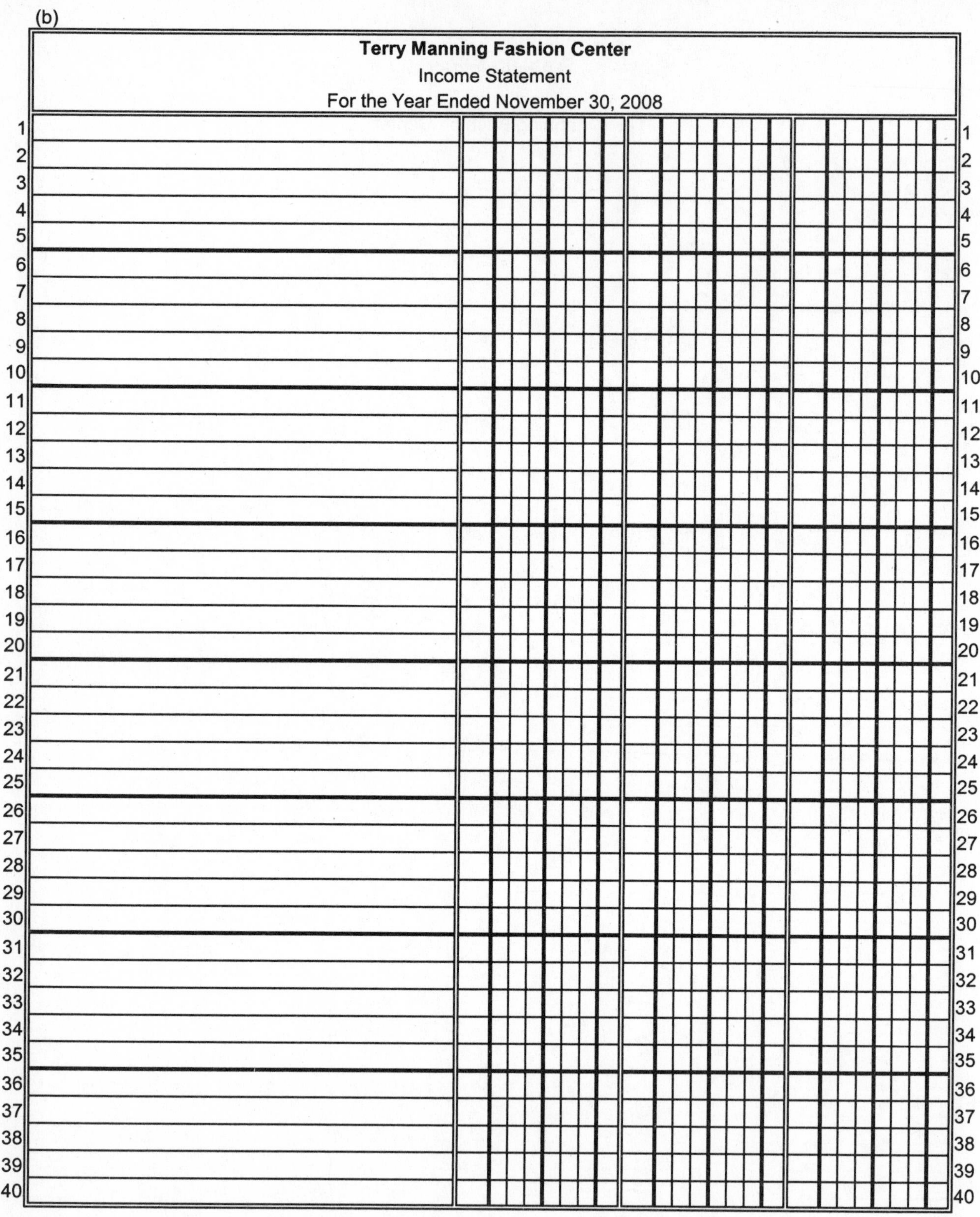
Terry Manning Fashion Center
Income Statement
For the Year Ended November 30, 2008

Name

Section

Date

(b) (Continued)

Terry Manning Fashion Center

Owner's Equity Statement

For the Year Ended November 30, 2008

Terry Manning Fashion Center

Balance Sheet

November 30, 2008

Assets

Liabilities and Owner's Equity

(c) General Journal

Date	Account Titles	Debit	Credit
	Adjusting Entries		
Nov. 30			
30			
30			
30			
30			

(d)

Date	Account Titles	Debit	Credit
	Closing Entries		
Nov. 30			
30			
30			
30			

(e)

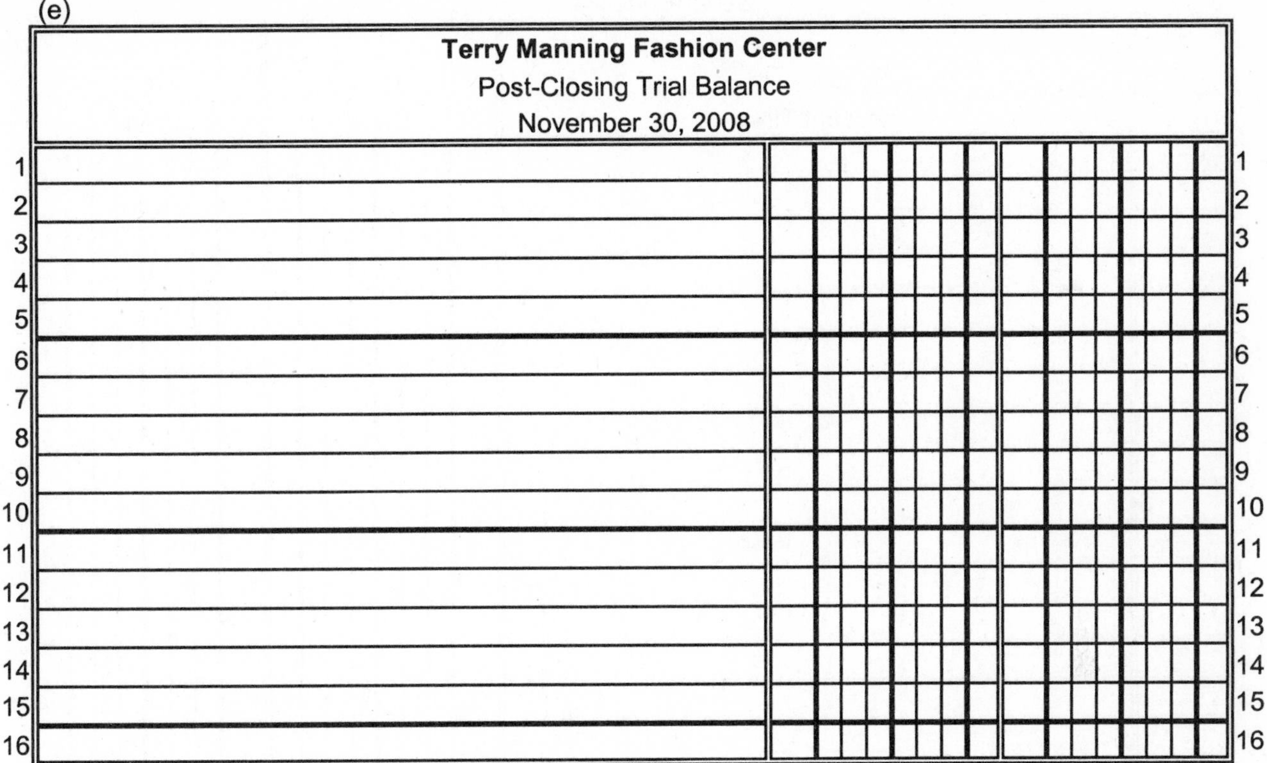

Terry Manning Fashion Center
Post-Closing Trial Balance
November 30, 2008

Name | Problem 5-1B

Section

Date | Sorvino Book Warehouse

General Journal

Date	Account Titles	Debit	Credit
June 1			
3			
6			
9			
15			
17			
20			
24			
26			

Name Problem 5-1B Concluded

Section

Date Sorvino Book Warehouse

General Journal

Date	Account Titles	Debit	Credit
June 28			
30			

Name | Problem 5-2B

Section

Date | Newson Hardware Store

(a) General Journal J1

Date	Account Titles	Ref.	Debit	Credit
May 1				
2				
5				
9				
10				
11				
12				
15				
17				
19				
24				

Name | Problem 5-2B Continued
Section
Date | Newson Hardware Store

(a) (Continued) J1

Date	Account Titles	Ref.	Debit	Credit
May 25				
27				
29				
31				

(b)

Cash No. 101

Date	Explanation	Ref.	Debit	Credit	Balance
May 1	Balance	√			10000

Accounts Receivabl No. 112

Date	Explanation	Ref.	Debit	Credit	Balance

(b) (Continued)

Merchandise Inventory No. 120

Date	Explanation	Ref.	Debit	Credit	Balance

Supplies No. 126

Date	Explanation	Ref.	Debit	Credit	Balance

Accounts Payable No. 201

Date	Explanation	Ref.	Debit	Credit	Balance

J. Newson, Capital No. 400

Date	Explanation	Ref.	Debit	Credit	Balance
May 1	Balance	√			10000

Sales No. 401

Date	Explanation	Ref.	Debit	Credit	Balance

(b) (Continued)

Sales Returns and Allowances — No. 412

Date	Explanation	Ref.	Debit	Credit	Balance

Sales Discounts — No. 414

Date	Explanation	Ref.	Debit	Credit	Balance

Cost of Goods Sold — No. 505

Date	Explanation	Ref.	Debit	Credit	Balance

(c)

Newson Hardware Store
Income Statement (Partial)
For the Month Ended May 31, 2008

1				1
2				2
3				3
4				4
5				5
6				6
7				7
8				8
9				9
10				10

Name Problem 5-3B

Section

Date Huffman Department Store

(a)

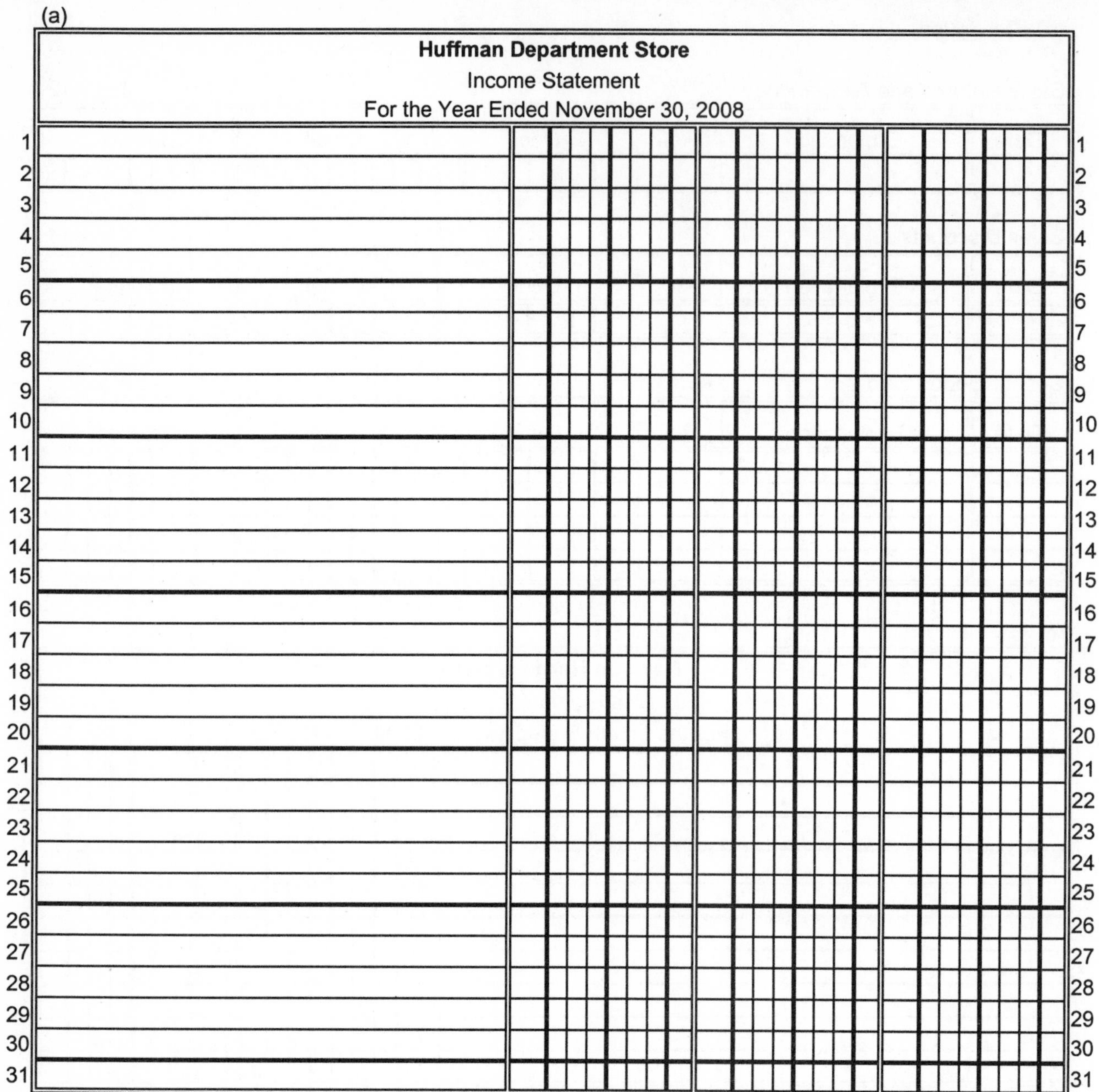

Huffman Department Store

Income Statement

For the Year Ended November 30, 2008

Huffman Department Store

Owner's Equity Statement

For the Year Ended November 30, 2008

(a) (Continued)

Huffman Department Store
Balance Sheet
November 30, 2008

Assets

Liabilities and Owner's Equity

(b)

General Journal

	Date	Account Titles	Debit	Credit	
1		Adjusting Entries			1
2	Nov. 30				2
3					3
4					4
5	30				5
6					6
7					7
8	30				8
9					9
10					10
11	30				11
12					12
13					13
14	30				14
15					15
16					16
17					17
18					18
19					19
20					20
21					21
22					22
23					23
24					24
25					25

Name Problem 5-3B Concluded

Section

Date Huffman Department Store

(c)

General Journal

	Date	Account Titles	Debit	Credit	
1		Closing Entries			1
2	Nov. 30				2
3					3
4					4
5					5
6	30				6
7					7
8					8
9					9
10					10
11					11
12					12
13					13
14					14
15					15
16					16
17					17
18					18
19					19
20	30				20
21					21
22					22
23	30				23
24					24
25					25
26					26
27					27
28					28
29					29
30					30
31					31
32					32
33					33
34					34
35					35

Name

Section

Date

Problem 5-4B

Mike's Pro Shop

(a)

General Journal

J1

Date	Account Titles	Ref.	Debit	Credit
Apr. 5				
7				
9				
10				
12				
14				
17				
20				
21				
27				
30				

(b)

Cash — No. 101

Date	Explanation	Ref.	Debit	Credit	Balance
Apr 1	Balance	√			2500

Accounts Receivable — No. 112

Date	Explanation	Ref.	Debit	Credit	Balance

Merchandise Inventory — No. 120

Date	Explanation	Ref.	Debit	Credit	Balance
Apr 1	Balance	√			3500

Accounts Payable — No. 201

Date	Explanation	Ref.	Debit	Credit	Balance

(b) (Continued)

M. Palmer, Capital — No. 301

Date	Explanation	Ref.	Debit	Credit	Balance
Apr 1	Balance	√			6000

Sales — No. 401

Date	Explanation	Ref.	Debit	Credit	Balance

Sales Returns and Allowances — No. 412

Date	Explanation	Ref.	Debit	Credit	Balance

Cost of Goods Sold — No. 505

Date	Explanation	Ref.	Debit	Credit	Balance

(c)

Mike's Pro Shop
Trial Balance
April 30, 2008

		Debit	Credit	
1				1
2				2
3				3
4				4
5				5
6				6
7				7
8				8
9				9
10				10

Name

Section

Date

Problem 5-5B

Duckwall Department Store

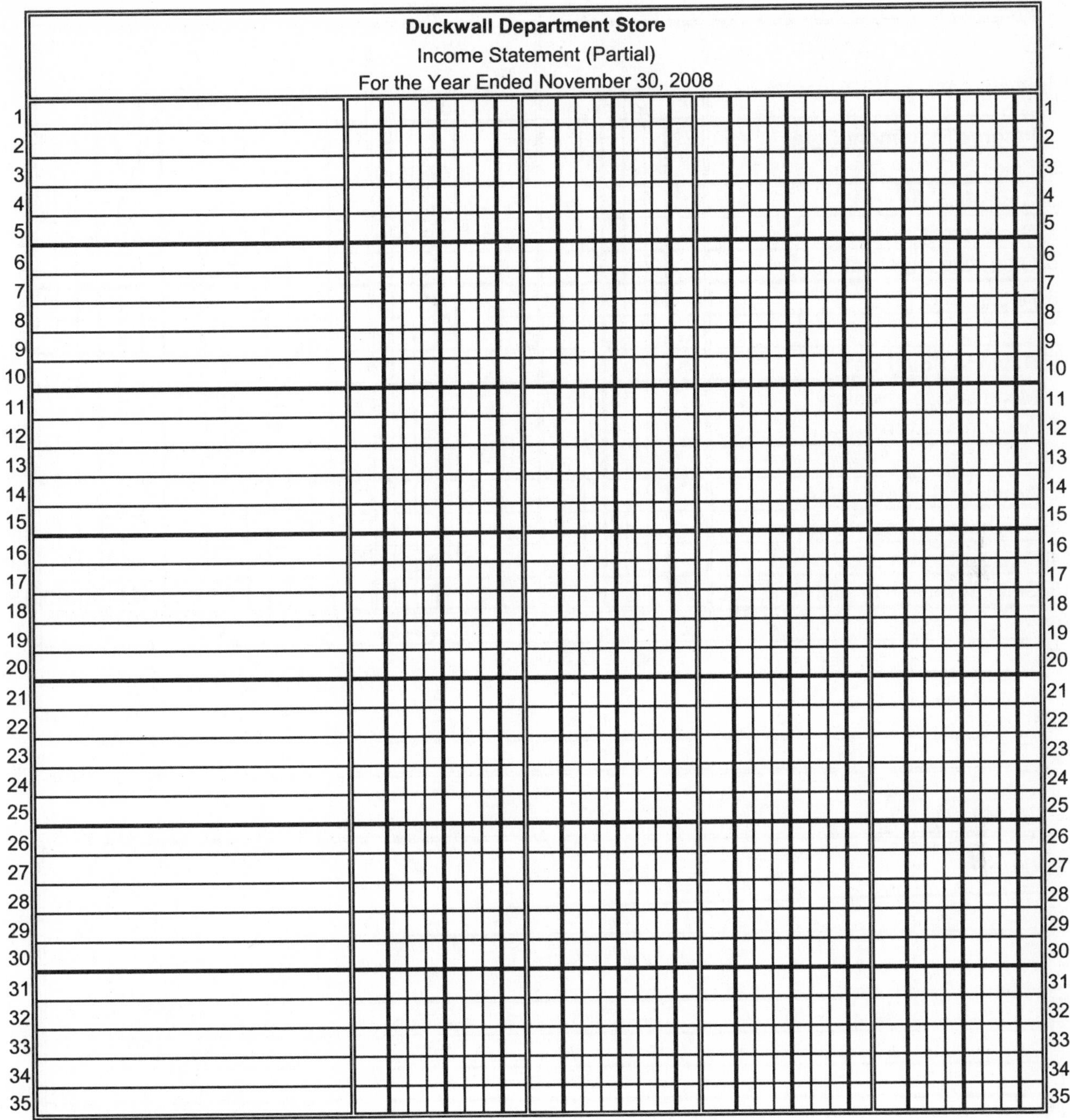

Duckwall Department Store

Income Statement (Partial)

For the Year Ended November 30, 2008

Name

Section

Date

Problem 5-6B

Howitt Inc.

(a)

	2005	2006	2007	2008
Income Statement Data				
Sales		$ 96850		$ 82220
Cost of goods sold			25140	25990
Gross profit		63500		52060
Operating expenses			4570	
Net income				
Balance Sheet Data				
Merchandise inventory	$ 13000		$ 14700	
Accounts payable	5800	6500	4600	
Additional Information				
Purchases of merchandise inventory on account		25890		24050
Cash payments to suppliers				24650

(b)

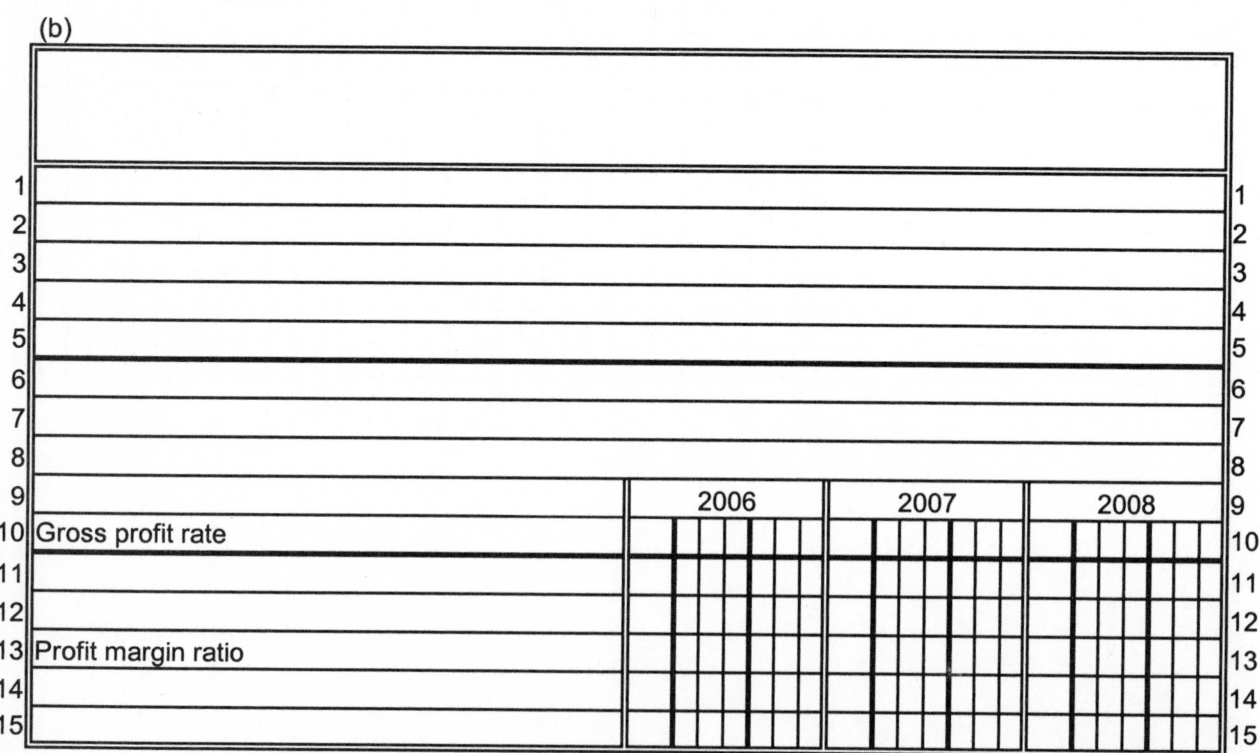

	2006	2007	2008
Gross profit rate			
Profit margin ratio			

Name *Problem 5-7B

Section

Date Four Oaks Pro Shop

(a) General Journal

Date	Account Titles	Debit	Credit
Apr. 5			
7			
9			
10			
12			
14			
17			
20			
21			
27			
30			

Name

Section

Date

*Problem 5-7B Continued

Four Oaks Pro Shop

(b)

Cash	
4/1 Bal. 2,500	

Phil Mickel, Capital	
	4/1 Bal. 6,000

Sales	

Accounts Receivable	

Sales Returns and Allowances	

Merchandise Inventory	
4/1 Bal. 3,500	

Purchases	

Accounts Payable	

Freight-in	

Purchase Returns and Allowances	

Purchase Discounts	

(c)

Four Oaks Pro Shop
Trial Balance
April 30, 2008

	Debit	Credit

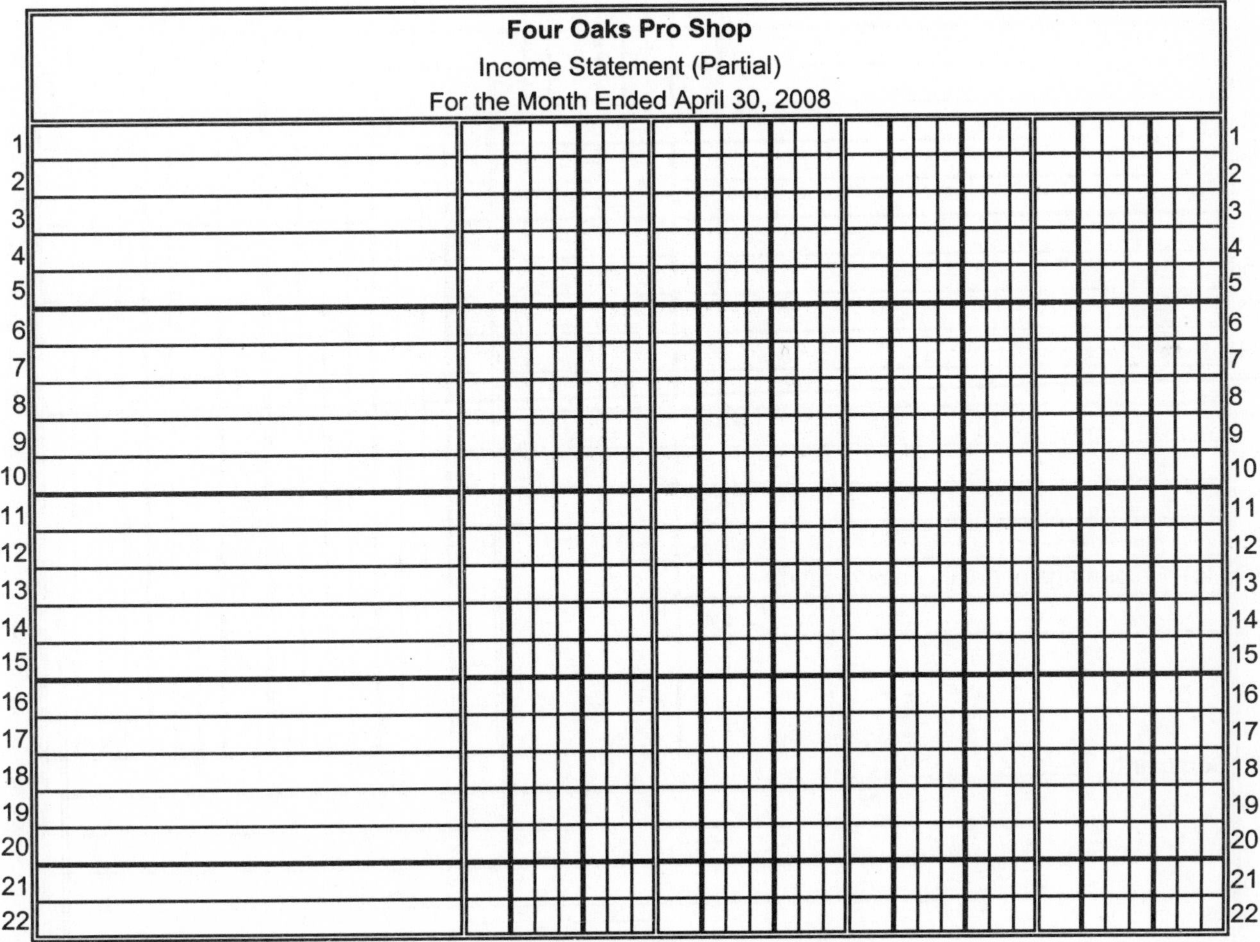

Name
Section
Date

PepsiCo, Inc.

	2004		2005
(a) (1) Percentage change in sales:			
(2) Percentage change in net income:			

	2003	2004	2005
(b) Gross profit rate:			
(c) Percentage of net income to sales:			

Comment:

	PepsiCo		Coca-Cola
(a)			
(1) 2005 Gross profit			
(2) 2005 Gross profit rate			
(3) 2005 Operating Income			
(4) Percentage change in operating income, 2004 to 2005			

(b)

(a) (1)

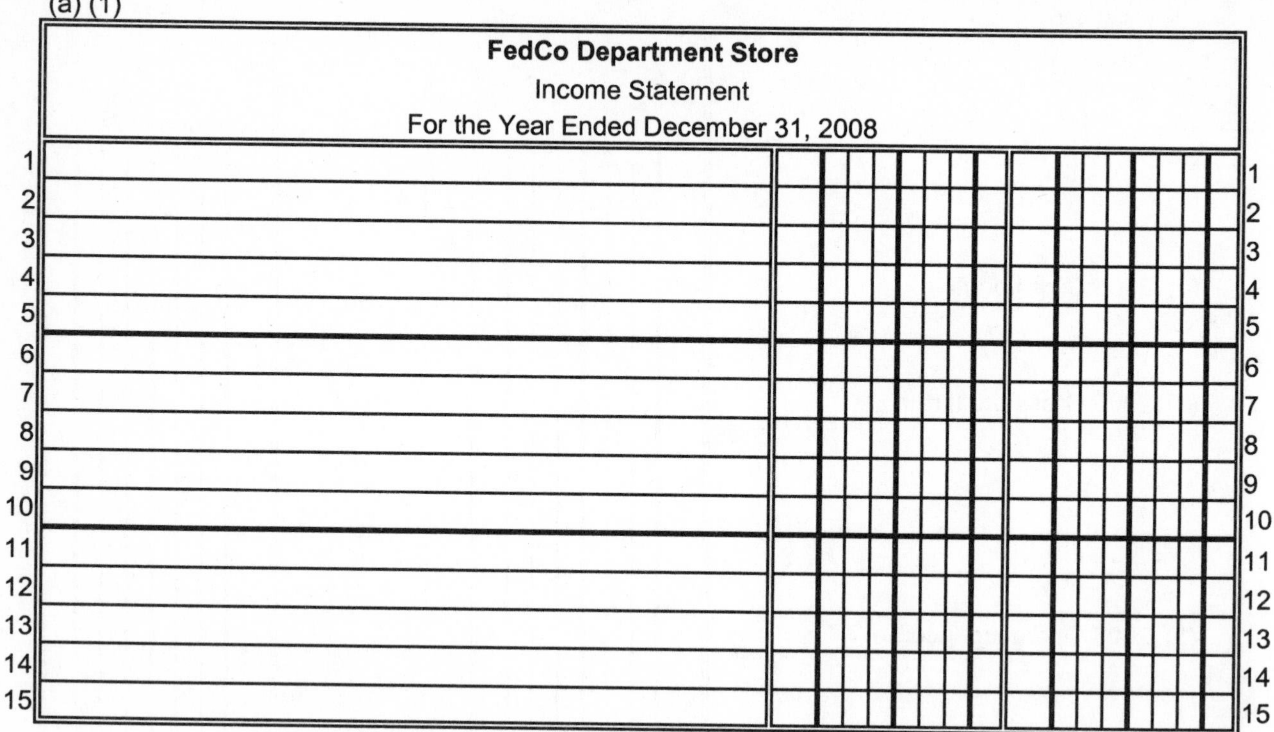

FedCo Department Store
Income Statement
For the Year Ended December 31, 2008

(2)

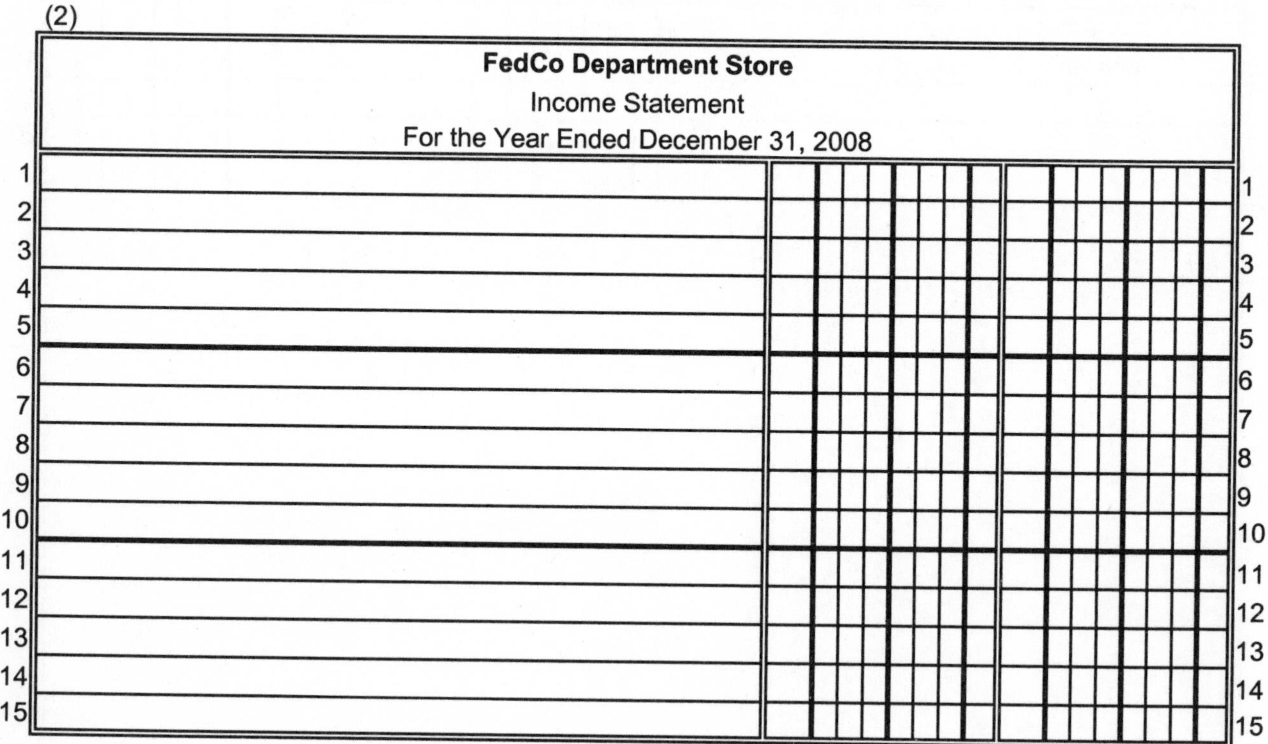

FedCo Department Store
Income Statement
For the Year Ended December 31, 2008

(b)

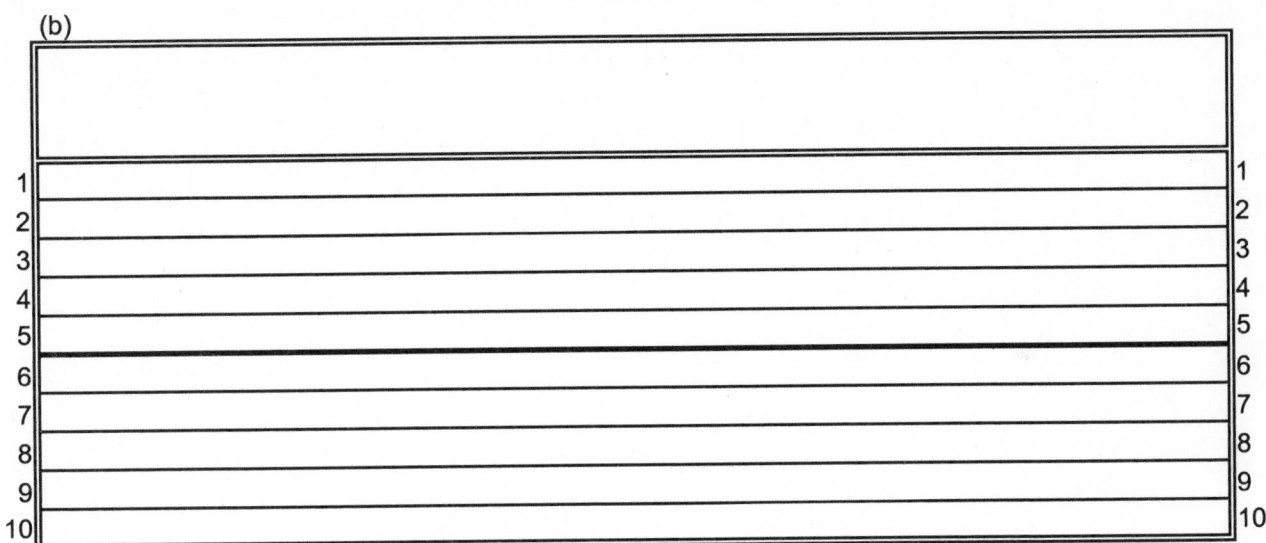

(c)

FedCo Department Store

Income Statement

For the Year Ended December 31, 2008

Name

Section

Date

BE6-1

(a)

(b)

(c)

(d)

BE6-2

BE6-3	(a) FIFO			(b) LIFO		
	Units	Unit Cost	Total	Units	Unit Cost	Total
Ending inventory				Ending inventory		

BE6-4	Units	Unit Cost	Total

Average cost per unit

Ending inventory

Name

Section

Date

BE6-5

(a)

(b)

(c)

(d)

BE6-6 Cost of goods sold under:

	LIFO	FIFO
Purchases		
Cost of goods available for sale		
Less: Ending inventory		
Cost of goods sold		

BE6-7

Inventory categories:	Cost	Market	LCM
Cameras			
Camcorders			
VCRs			
Total valuation			

BE6-8

Name

Section

Date

BE6-9

Inventory turnover:

Days in inventory:

***BE6-10** See next page

***BE6-11**

(1)

(2)

***BE6-12**	At Cost	At Retail

Cost-to-retail ratio:

Estimated cost of ending inventory:

Name

Section

Date

***BE6-10**

Product E2-D2			
(1) FIFO Method			
Date	Purchases	Cost of Goods Sold	Balance
(2) LIFO Method			
Date	Purchases	Cost of Goods Sold	Balance
(3) Average-Cost			
Date	Purchases	Cost of Goods Sold	Balance

Name

Section

Date

E6-1

Ending Inventory - physical count	$	297000

E6-2

Ending inventory - as reported	$	740000

Name

Section

Date

Exercise 6-3

Bargain Electronics Ltd.

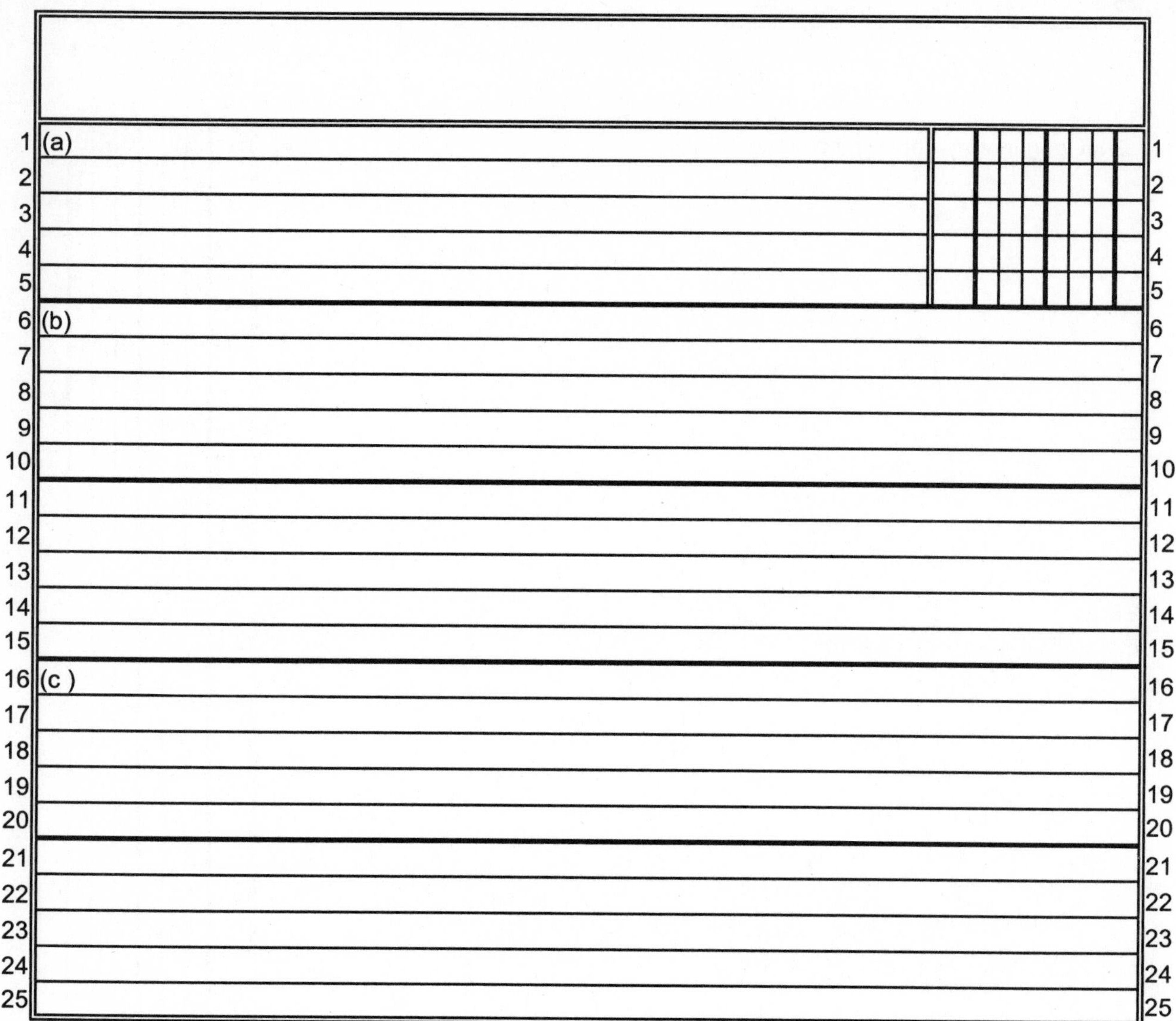

Name

Section

Date

Exercise 6-4

Xpert

(a)

FIFO

Proof:

	Date	Units	Unit Cost	Total Cost

LIFO

Proof:

	Date	Units	Unit Cost	Total Cost

(b)

Name | Exercise 6-5
Section
Date | Catlet Co.

FIFO

Proof:

	Date	Units	Unit Cost	Total Cost

LIFO

Proof:

	Date	Units	Unit Cost	Total Cost

Name

Section

Date

Exercise 6-6

Yount Company

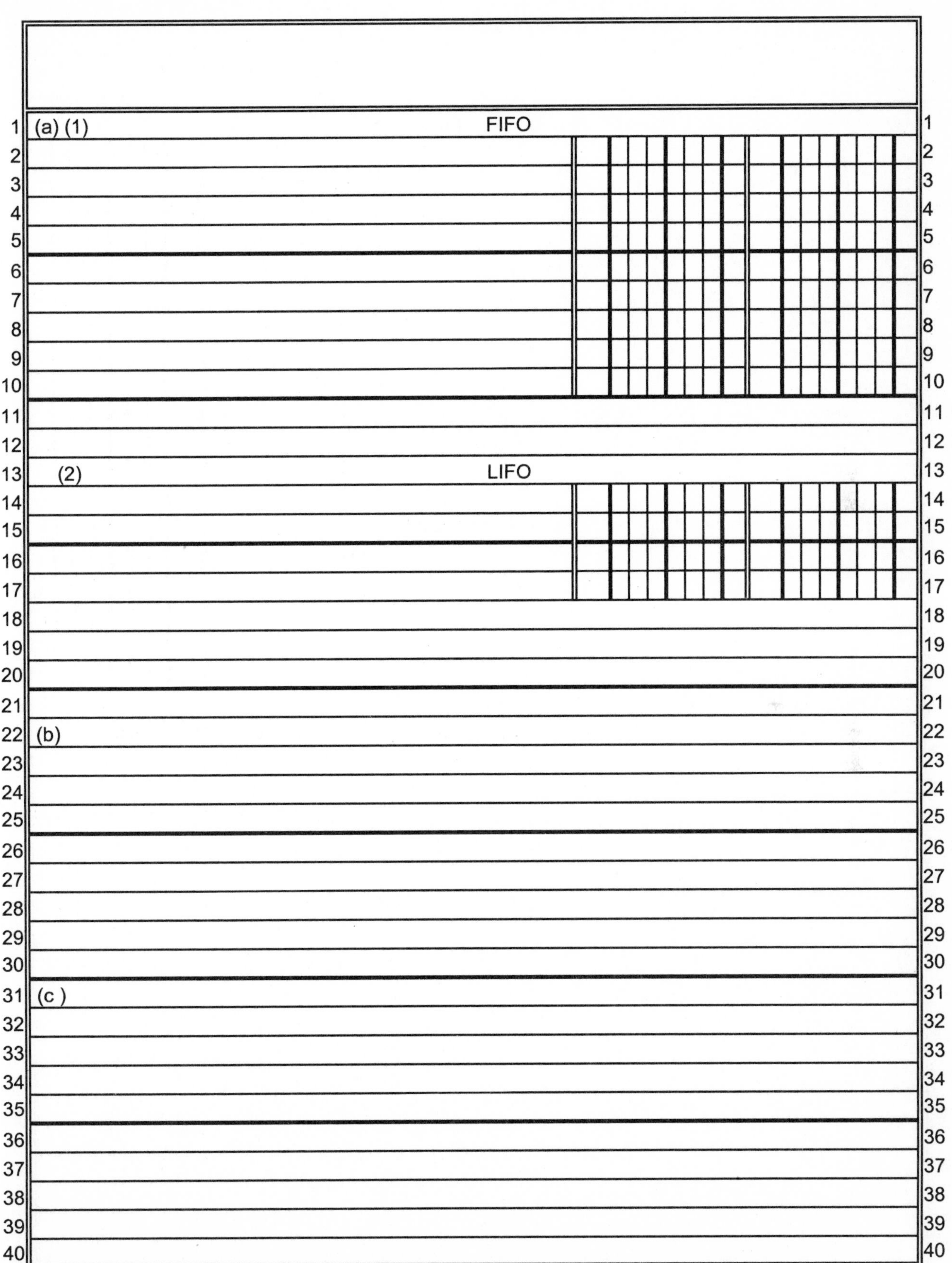

(a) (1) FIFO

(2) LIFO

(b)

(c)

Name

Section

Date

Exercise 6-7

Jones Company

(a) (1) FIFO

(2) LIFO

(3) AVERAGE

(b)

(c)

(d)

Name

Section

Date

Exercises 6-8 to 6-10

E6-8

Cost of Goods Available for Sale	÷	Total Units Avaialable for Sale	=	Weighted Average Unit Cost
(a)				
Ending inventory				
Cost of goods sold				
(b)				
(c)				

E6-9

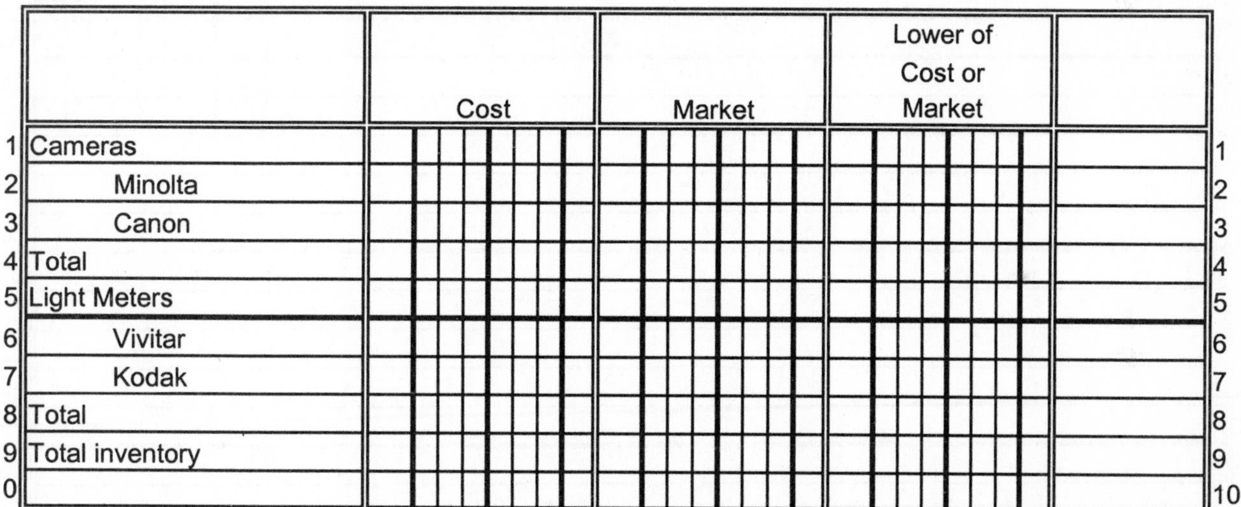

	Cost	Market	Lower of Cost or Market	
Cameras				
Minolta				
Canon				
Total				
Light Meters				
Vivitar				
Kodak				
Total				
Total inventory				

E6-10

	Cost	Market	Lower of Cost or Market	
VCRs				
DVD players				
Ipods				
Total inventory				

Name Exercise 6-12

Section

Date Staley Watch Company

(a)	2008	2009

(b)

(c)

Name

Section

Date

Exercise 6-11

	2008	2009	
Beginning inventory			
Cost of goods purchased			
Cost of goods available for sale			
Corrected ending inventory			
Cost of goods sold			

Name

Section

Date

*Exercise 6-15

Klugman Appliance

(1)

FIFO

Date	Purchases	Cost of Goods Sold	Balance
Jan. 1			
8			
10			
15			

(2)

LIFO

Date	Purchases	Cost of Goods Sold	Balance
Jan. 1			
8			
10			
15			

(3)

AVERAGE-COST

Date	Purchases	Cost of Goods Sold	Balance
Jan. 1			
8			
10			
15			

Name

Section

Date

*Exercise 6-16

Yount Company

(a)

Cost of goods available for sale:

FIFO

Date	Purchases	Cost of goods sold	Balance
June 1			
12			
15			
23			
27			

Ending inventory = Cost of goods sold =

Name
Section
Date

*Exercise 6-16 Continued

Yount Company

(a) (Continued)

LIFO

Date	Purchases	Cost of goods sold	Balance
June 1			
12			
15			
23			
27			

Ending inventory =

Cost of goods sold =

MOVING-AVERAGE

Date	Purchases	Cost of goods sold	Balance
June 1			
12			
15			
23			
27			

Ending inventory =

Cost of goods sold =

(b)

(c)

Name

Section

Date

*Exercise 6-17

Boarders

(a)

FIFO			
Date	Purchases	Cost of Goods Sold	Balance
9/1			
9/5			
9/12			
9/16			
9/19			
9/26			
9/29			

LIFO			
Date	Purchases	Cost of Goods Sold	Balance
9/1			
9/5			
9/12			
9/16			
9/19			
9/26			
9/29			

Name

Section

Date

Xpert

(a) (Continued)

AVERAGE-COST

Date	Purchases		Cost of Goods Sold		Balance	
9/1						
9/5						
9/12						
9/16						
9/19						
9/26						
9/29						

(b)

	Periodic		Perpetual
Ending inventory FIFO			
Ending inventory LIFO			

(c)

Name

Section

Date

*Exercise 6-18

Doc Gibbs Company

(a)

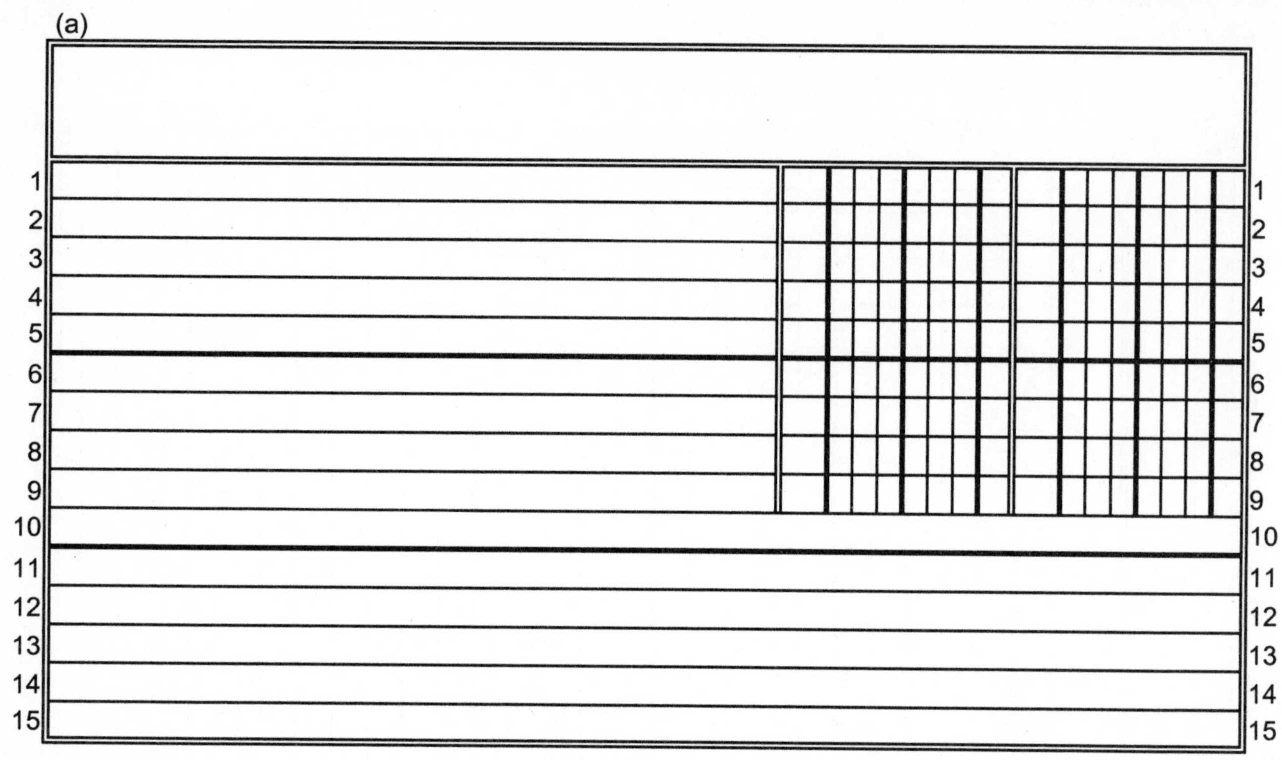

(b)

Name *Exercises 6-19 and 6-20

Section

Date

***E6-19**

(a)

(b)

***E6-20**

	Women's Department		Men's Department	
	Cost	Retail	Cost	Retail
Beginning inventory				
Goods purchased				
Goods avail. for sale				
Net sales				
Ending inv. at retail				
Cost/retail ratio				
Estimated cost of ending inventory				

Name

Section

Date

Problem 6-2A

Glanville Distribution

(a)

COST OF GOODS AVAILABLE FOR SALE

Date	Explanation	Units	Unit Cost	Total Cost
March 1				
5				
13				
21				
26				

(b)

FIFO

(1) Ending Inventory

Date		Units	Unit Cost	Total Cost

(2) Cost of Goods Sold

Proof of Cost of Goods Sold

Date		Units	Unit Cost	Total Cost

(b) (Continued)

LIFO

(1) Ending Inventory

Date		Units	Unit Cost	Total Cost

(2) Cost of Goods Sold

Proof of Cost of Goods Sold

Date		Units	Unit Cost	Total Cost

Average Cost

(1) Ending Inventory

Average Cost Per Unit	Units	Unit Cost	Total Cost

(2) Cost of Goods Sold

(c)

(1)

(2)

Name

Section

Date

Problem 6-3A

Eddings Company

(a)

COST OF GOODS AVAILABLE FOR SALE

Date	Explanation	Units	Unit Cost	Total Cost
2/1				
2/20				
5/5				
8/12				
12/8				

(b)

FIFO

(1)

Ending Inventory

Date		Units	Unit Cost	Total Cost

(2)

Cost of Goods Sold

Proof of Cost of Goods Sold

Date		Units	Unit Cost	Total Cost

Name

Section

Date

Problem 6-3A Concluded

Eddings Company

(b) (Continued)

LIFO

(1) Ending Inventory

Date		Units	Unit Cost	Total Cost

(2) Cost of Goods Sold

Proof of Cost of Goods Sold

Date		Units	Unit Cost	Total Cost

Average Cost

(1) Ending Inventory

Average Cost Per Unit	Units	Unit Cost	Total Cost

(2) Cost of Goods Sold

Proof of Cost of Goods Sold

(c)

(1)

(2)

Name

Section

Date

Problem 6-4A

Morales Co.

(a)

Morales Co. Condensed Income Statements For the Year Ended December 31, 2008		
	FIFO	LIFO

(b)

Name | Problem 6-5A

Section

Date | Pavey Inc.

(a)

Cost of Goods Available For Sale

Date	Explanation	Units	Unit Cost	Total Cost
Oct. 1				
9				
17				
25				

Ending Inventory in Units

Sales Revenue

Date		Units	Unit Price	Total Sales
Oct. 11				
22				
29				

(1) **LIFO**

(i) Ending Inventory

Date		Units	Unit Cost	Total Cost

(ii) Cost of Goods Sold

(iii) Gross Profit

(iv) Gross Profit Rate

(a) (Continued)

(2)

FIFO

(i) Ending Inventory

Date		Units	Unit Cost	Total Cost

(ii) Cost of Goods Sold

(iii) Gross Profit

(iv) Gross Profit Rate

(3)

Average Cost

Weighted Average Cost Per Unit

(i) Ending Inventory

(ii) Cost of Goods Sold

(iii) Gross Profit

(a) (Continued)

Average Cost

(iv) Gross Profit Rate

(b)

Name

Section

Date

Problem 6-6A

Bernelli Diamonds

(a)

Specific Identification

(1) To maximize gross profit

Sales Revenue

Date		Units	Unit Price	Sales Revenue
Mar. 5				
25				

Cost of Goods Sold

Date		Units	Unit Cost	Total Cost
Mar. 5				
25				

Sales Revenue	
Cost of Goods Sold	
Gross profit	

(2) To minimize gross profit

Sales Revenue

Date		Units	Unit Price	Sales Revenue
Mar. 5				
25				

Cost of Goods Sold

Date		Units	Unit Cost	Total Cost
Mar. 5				
25				

Sales Revenue	
Cost of Goods Sold	
Gross profit	

Name

Section

Date

(b)

FIFO

Cost of Goods Available for Sale

Date		Units	Unit Cost	Total Cost
Mar. 1				
3				
10				

	Units	Unit Cost	Total Cost
Goods available for sale			
Units sold			
Ending inventory			

Goods available for sale	
Ending inventory	
Cost of goods sold	

Sales revenue	
Cost of goods sold	
Gross profit	

(c)

LIFO

Cost of Goods Available for Sale	
Ending inventory	
Cost of goods sold	

Sales revenue	
Cost of goods sold	
Gross profit	

(d)

Name

Section

Date

Problem 6-7A

Utley Inc.

(a)

Utley Inc.
Condensed Income Statement
For the Year Ended December 31, 2008

	FIFO	LIFO

(b)

Name | Problem 6-8A

Section

Date | Vasquez Ltd.

(a)

Cost of Goods Available for Sale

	Units	Unit Cost	Total Cost
Inventory			
Purchases:			
January 2			
January 9			
January 10 return			
Januarty 23			

Sales:

	Units	Unit Cost	Total Cost
January 6			
January 9 return			
January 10			
January 30			

Name

Section

Date

Problem 6-8A Continued

Vasquez Ltd.

(a) (Continued)

(1) Date	LIFO Purchases		Cost of Goods Sold		Balance	
Jan. 1					(150 units @ $17)	2550
2						
6						
9						
9						
10						
10						
23						
30						

(i) Cost of goods sold =

(ii) Ending inventory =

(iii) Gross profit =

Name

Section

Date

Problem 6-8A Continued

Vasquez Ltd.

(a) (Continued)

(2) Date	FIFO					
	Purchases		Cost of Goods Sold		Balance	
Jan. 1					(150 units @ $17)	2550
2						
6						
9						
9						
10						
10						
23						
30						

(i) Cost of goods sold =

(ii) Ending inventory =

(iii) Gross profit =

Name

Section

Date

Problem 6-8A Continued

Vasquez Ltd.

(a) (Continued)

(3) Date	Moving Average					
	Purchases		Cost of Goods Sold		Balance	
Jan. 1					(150 units @ $17)	2550
2						
6						
9						
9						
10						
10						
23						
30						

(i) Cost of goods sold =

(ii) Ending inventory =

(iii) Gross profit =

(b)

	LIFO	FIFO	Moving Average

Name

Section

Date

Problem 6-9A

Sandoval Appliance Mart

(a)

(1)

Date	FIFO		
	Purchases	Cost of Goods Sold	Balance
May 1			
4			
8			
12			
15			
20			
25			

(2)

Date	Moving Average Cost		
	Purchases	Cost of Goods Sold	Balance
May 1			
4			
8			
12			
15			
20			
25			

Name

Section

Date

Problem 6-9A Concluded

Sandoval Appliance Mart

(a) (Continued)

(3) Date	LIFO Purchases		LIFO Cost of Goods Sold		LIFO Balance	
May 1						
4						
8						
12						
15						
20						
25						

(b)

Name

Section

Date

*Problem 6-10A

Saffordville Company

(a)

February

Net sales

Gross profit rate

(b)

Net sales

Name | *Problem 6-11A
Section
Date | Neer Department Store

(a)	Sporting Goods		Jewelry and Cosmetics	
	Cost	Retail	Cost	Retail
Beginning inventory				
Purchases				
Purchase returns				
Purchase discounts				
Freight-in				
Goods available for sale				
Net sales				
Ending inventory at retail				

Cost-to-retail ratio:

Sporting goods:

Jewelry and cosmetics:

Estimated ending inventory at cost:

Sporting goods:

Jewelry and cosmetics:

(b) Sporting goods:

Jewelry and cosmetics:

Name

Section

Date

Problem 6-2B

Carrington Distribution

(a)

COST OF GOODS AVAILABLE FOR SALE

Date	Explanation	Units	Unit Cost	Total Cost
Oct. 1				
3				
9				
19				
25				

(b) **FIFO**

(1) Ending Inventory

Date		Units	Unit Cost	Total Cost

(2) Cost of Goods Sold

Proof of Cost of Goods Sold

Date		Units	Unit Cost	Total Cost

(b) (Continued)

LIFO

(1) Date	Ending Inventory	Units	Unit Cost	Total Cost

(2) Cost of Goods Sold

Proof of Cost of Goods Sold

Date		Units	Unit Cost	Total Cost

Average Cost

(1) Ending Inventory

Average Cost Per Unit	Units	Unit Cost	Total Cost

(2) Cost of Goods Sold

(c)

(1)

(2)

Name Problem 6-3B

Section

Date Shellankamp Company

(a)

COST OF GOODS AVAILABLE FOR SALE

Date	Explanation	Units	Unit Cost	Total Cost
1/1				
3/15				
7/20				
9/4				
12/2				

(b) **FIFO**

(1) Ending Inventory

Date		Units	Unit Cost	Total Cost

(2) Cost of Goods Sold

Proof of Cost of Goods Sold

Date		Units	Unit Cost	Total Cost

(b) (Continued)

LIFO

(1) Ending Inventory

Date		Units	Unit Cost	Total Cost

(2) Cost of Goods Sold

Proof of Cost of Goods Sold

Date		Units	Unit Cost	Total Cost

Average Cost

(1) Ending Inventory

Average Cost Per Unit	Units	Unit Cost	Total Cost

(2) Cost of Goods Sold

Proof of Cost of Goods Sold

(c)

Name Problem 6-4B

Section

Date Groneman Inc.

(a)

Groneman Inc.

Condensed Income Statements

For the Year Ended December 31, 2008

	FIFO	LIFO

(b)

Name Problem 6-5B

Section

Date Charlote Inc.

(a)

Cost of Goods Available For Sale

Date	Explanation	Units	Unit Cost	Total Cost
June 1				
4				
18				
18				
28				

Ending Inventory in Units

Sales Revenue

Date		Units	Unit Price	Total Sales
June 10				
11				
25				

(1) **LIFO**

(i) Ending Inventory

Date		Units	Unit Cost	Total Cost

(ii) Cost of Goods Sold

(iii) Gross Profit

(iv) Gross Profit Rate

Name

Section

Date

Problem 6-5B Continued

Charlote Inc.

(a) (Continued)

(2)

FIFO

(i) Ending Inventory

Date		Units	Unit Cost	Total Cost

(ii) Cost of Goods Sold

(iii) Gross Profit

(iv) Gross Profit Rate

(3)

Average Cost

Weighted Average Cost Per Unit

(i) Ending Inventory

(ii) Cost of Goods Sold

(iii) Gross Profit

(a) (Continued)

Average Cost

(iv) Gross Profit Rate

(b)

Name | Problem 6-6B
Section
Date | Rondelli Inc.

(a)

Rendelli Inc.
Income Statement (Partial)
For the Year Ended December, 31, 2008

	Specific Identification	FIFO	LIFO

Specific identification ending inventory consists of:

	Units	Unit Cost	Total Cost

FIFO ending inventory consists of:

	Units	Unit Cost	Total Cost

LIFO ending inventory consists of:

	Units	Unit Cost	Total Cost

(b)

Name | Problem 6-7B

Section

Date | Dains Co.

(a)

Dains Co.

Condensed Income Statement

For the Year Ended December 31, 2008

	FIFO	LIFO

(b)

Name

Section

Date

Problem 6-8B

Fechter Inc.

(a)

Cost of Goods Available for Sale

	Units	Unit Cost	Total Cost
Inventory			
Purchases:			
January 5			
January 15			
January 16 return			
January 25			
Sales:			
January 8			
January 10 return			
January 20			

Name

Section

Date

Problem 6-8B Continued

Fechter Inc.

(a) (Continued)

(1) Date	LIFO Purchases		Cost of Goods Sold		Balance	
Jan. 1					(50 units @ $12)	600
5						
8						
10						
15						
16						
20						
25						

(i) Cost of goods sold =

(ii) Ending inventory =

(iii) Gross profit =

Name

Section

Date

Problem 6-8B Continued

Fechter Inc.

(a) (Continued)

(2) Date	FIFO					
	Purchases		Cost of Goods Sold		Balance	
Jan. 1					(50 units @ $12)	600
5						
8						
10						
15						
16						
20						
25						

(i) Cost of goods sold =

(ii) Ending inventory =

(iii) Gross profit =

Name

Section

Date

Problem 6-8B Continued

Fechter Inc.

(a) (Continued)

	(3) Date	Moving Average Purchases		Cost of Goods Sold		Balance		
1	Jan. 1					(50 units @ $12)	600	1
2	5							2
3	8							3
4	10							4
5	15							5
6	16							6
7	20							7
8	25							8
9								9
10	(i) Cost of goods sold =			(ii) Ending inventory =				10
11								11
12	(iii) Gross profit =							12

Name

Section

Date

Fechter Inc.

(b)

	LIFO	FIFO	Moving Average

Name

Section

Date

*Problem 6-9B

Falco Co.

(a)

FIFO

(1) Date	Purchases	Cost of Goods Sold	Balance
July 1			
6			
11			
14			
21			
27			

AVERAGE-COST

(2) Date	Purchases	Cost of Goods Sold	Balance
July 1			
6			
11			
14			
21			
27			

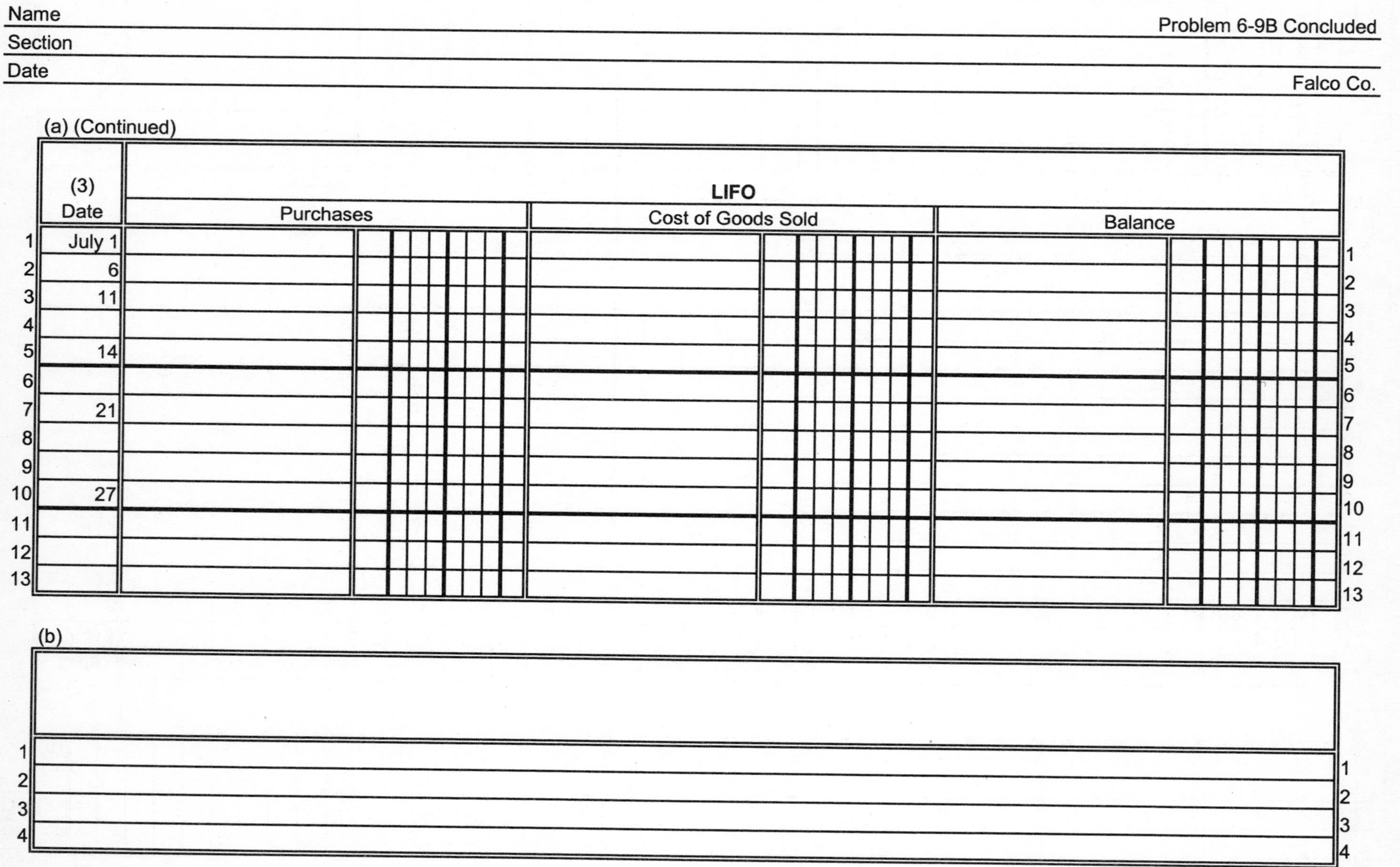

Name

Section

Date

Problem 6-9B Concluded

Falco Co.

(a) (Continued)

(3) Date	LIFO Purchases		LIFO Cost of Goods Sold		LIFO Balance	
July 1						
6						
11						
14						
21						
27						

(b)

Name *Problem 6-10B

Section

Date Hannigan Company

(a) November

Net sales

Gross profit rate

(b)

Net sales

Name

Section

Date

*Problem 6-11B

Frontenac Books

(a)	Hardcovers		Pperbacks	
	Cost	Retail	Cost	Retail
Beginning inventory				
Purchases				
Purchase returns				
Purchase discounts				
Freight-in				
Goods available for sale				
Net sales				
Ending inventory at retail				

Cost-to-retail ratio:

Hardcovers:

Paperbacks:

Estimated ending inventory at cost:

Hardcovers:

Paperbacks:

(b) Hardcovers:

Paperbacks:

Name

Section

Date

	December 31, 2005	December 25, 2004
(a) Inventory (in millions)		

(b) Dollar change in inventories between 2004 and 2005:

Percent change in inventories between 2004 and 2005:

2005 inventory as a percent of current assets:

(c)

(d) PepsiCo (in millions)	2005	2004	2003
Cost of goods sold			

2005 cost of goods sold as a percent of sales:

Name

Section

Date

Chapter 6 Comparative Analysis Problem

PepsiCo, Inc. versus Coca-Cola Company

(a)	PepsiCo	Coca-Cola
Inventory turnover:		
Days in inventory:		

(b)

Name

Section

Date

Inwood Company

(a) (1)

(2)

*(b)

	2007	2006
Net sales		
Gross profit rate		

Average gross profit rate

*(c) Sales

Name

Section

Date

BE7-4

Accounts Receivable Subsidiary Ledger

Agler Co.

Date	Explanation	Ref.	Debit	Credit	Balance

Barto Co.

Date	Explanation	Ref.	Debit	Credit	Balance

Maris Co.

Date	Explanation	Ref.	Debit	Credit	Balance

General Ledger

Accounts Receivable

Date	Explanation	Ref.	Debit	Credit	Balance

Name

Section

Date

Exercise 7-3

Montalvo Company

(a) & (b)

General Ledger

Accounts Receivable

Date	Explanation	Ref.	Debit	Credit	Balance
9/1	Balance	√			1 10960

Accounts Receivable Subsidiary Ledger

Bannister

Date	Explanation	Ref.	Debit	Credit	Balance
9/1	Balance	√			2060

Crampton

Date	Explanation	Ref.	Debit	Credit	Balance
9/1	Balance	√			4820

Iman

Date	Explanation	Ref.	Debit	Credit	Balance

Kingston

Date	Explanation	Ref.	Debit	Credit	Balance
9/1	Balance	√			2640

Ruiz

Date	Explanation	Ref.	Debit	Credit	Balance
9/1	Balance	√			1440

Name

Section

Date

E7-3 (c)

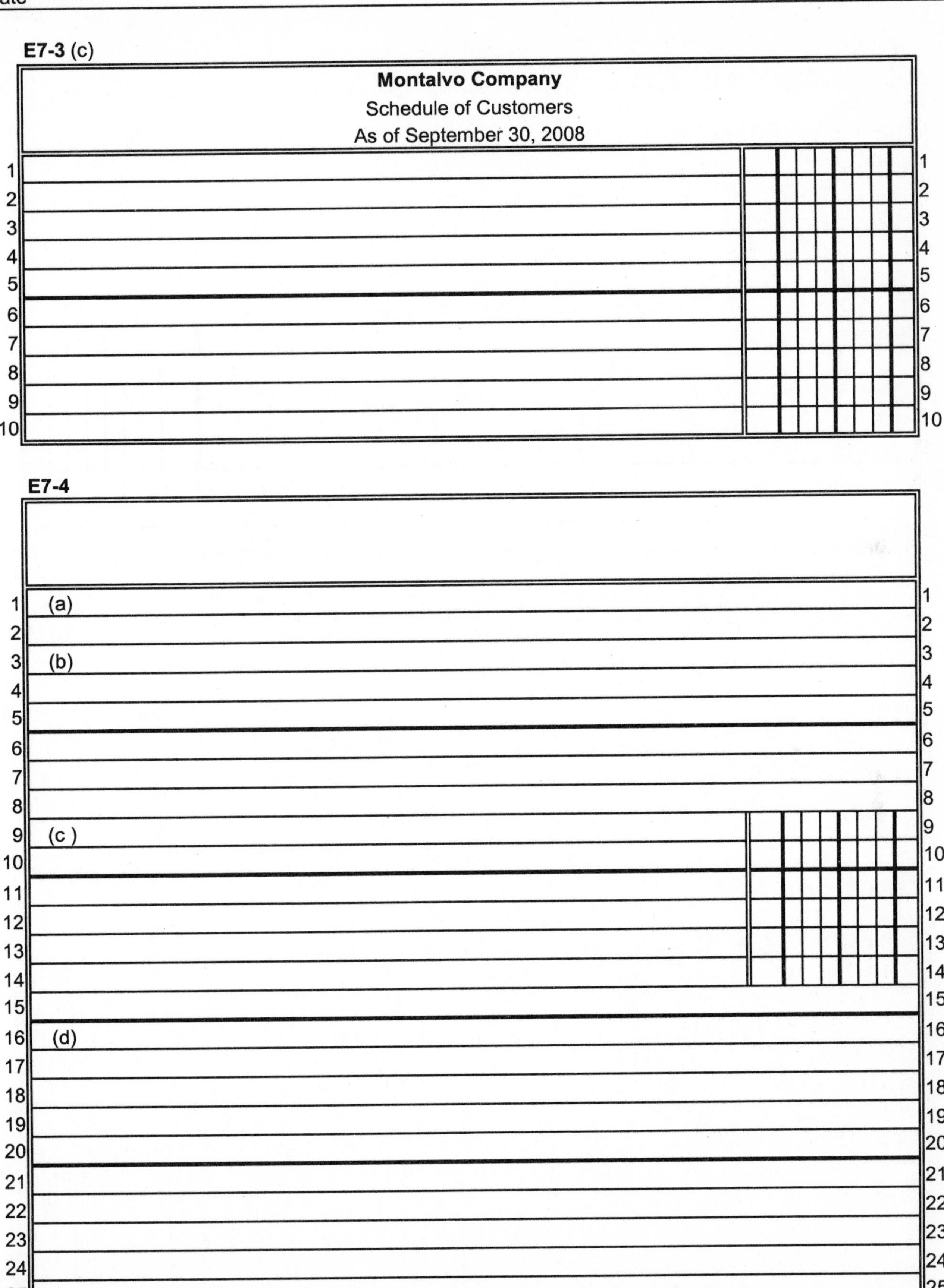

Name
Section
Date

Exercise 7-5

Nobo Uematsu Company

(a)

(b)

(c)

(d)

Name | Exercise 7-6

Section

Date | Montalvo Company

E-6 (a) & (b)

Montalvo Company Sales Journal S1					
Date	Account Debited	Invoice No.	Ref.	Accounts Receiv. Dr. Sales Cr.	COGS Dr. Merchandise Inventory Cr.
2008					

Montalvo Company Purchases Journal P1				
Date	Account Credited	Terms	Ref	Merchandise Inventory (Dr.) Acc. Pay (Cr.)
2008				

Name

Section

Date

Exercise 7-7

Pherigo Co.

#5 (a) & (b)

Pherigo Co.
Cash Receipts Journal

CR1

	Date	Account Credited	Ref.	Cash Dr.	Sales Discounts Dr.	Accounts Receivable Cr.	Sales Cr.	Other Accounts Cr.	COGS Dr. Merch Inv Cr.	
1	2008									1
2										2
3										3
4										4
5										5

Pherigo Co.
Cash Payments Journal

CP1

	Date	Check Number	Account Debited	Ref	Other Accounts Dr.	Accounts Payable Dr.	Cash Cr.	
1	2008							1
2								2
3								3
4								4

Name | Exercise 7-9

Section

Date | Valesquez Company

(a)

Date	Account Titles	Debit	Credit
Mar 2			
5			
7			

(b)

Name

Section

Date

E7-12 (a)

Purchases Journal

P1

Date	Account Credited	Ref.	Merchandise Inventory (Dr.) Acc. Pay. (Cr.)
July 3			
12			
14			
17			
20			
21			
29			

(b)

General Journal

Date	Account Titles	Ref	Debit	Credit
July 1				
15				
18				
25				

E7-13

Name

Section

Date

Exercise 7-14

Matisyahu Company

(a) Accounts Payable

(b) Accounts Receivable

(c) Cash

(d) Inventory

(e) Sales

Name | Problem 7-1A

Section

Date | Grider Company

(a)

Cash Receipts Journal

CR1

	Date	Account Credited	Ref.	Cash Dr.	Sales Discounts Dr.	Accounts Receivable Cr.	Sales Cr.	Other Accounts Cr.	COGS Dr. Merch Inv Cr.	
1										1
2										2
3										3
4										4
5										5
6										6
7										7
8										8
9										9
10										10
11										11
12										12
13										13
14										14
15										15
16										16
17										17

(b)

General Ledger

Accounts Receivable No. 112

Date	Explanation	Ref	Debit	Credit	Balance
Apr. 1	Balance	√			7450

Accounts Receivable Subsidiary Ledger

Ogden

Date	Explanation	Ref	Debit	Credit	Balance
Apr.1	Balance	√			1550

Chelsea

Date	Explanation	Ref	Debit	Credit	Balance
Apr. 1	Balance	√			1200

Eggleston Co.

Date	Explanation	Ref	Debit	Credit	Balance
Apr. 1	Balance	√			2900

Baez

Date	Explanation	Ref	Debit	Credit	Balance
Apr. 1	Balance	√			1800

(c)

1			1
2			2
3			3
4			4
5			5
6			6

Name Problem 7-2A

Section

Date Ming Company

(a)

Cash Payments Journal

CP1

	Date	Ck. No.	Account Debited	Ref.	Other Accounts Dr.	Accounts Payable Dr.	Merchandise Inventory Cr.	Cash Cr.	
1									1
2									2
3									3
4									4
5									5
6									6
7									7
8									8
9									9
10									10
11									11
12									12
13									13
14									14
15									15
16									16
17									17
18									18
19									19
20									20

Name Problem 7-2A Concluded

Section

Date Ming Company

(b)

General Ledger

Accounts Payable No. 201

Date	Explanation	Ref	Debit	Credit	Balance
Oct. 1	Balance	√			10700

Accounts Payable Subsidiary Ledger

Bovary Co.

Date	Explanation	Ref	Debit	Credit	Balance
Oct. 1	Balance	√			2700

Nyman Co.

Date	Explanation	Ref	Debit	Credit	Balance
Oct. 1	Balance	√			2500

Pyron Co.

Date	Explanation	Ref	Debit	Credit	Balance
Oct. 1	Balance	√			1800

Sims Company

Date	Explanation	Ref	Debit	Credit	Balance
Oct. 1	Balance	√			3700

(c)

1			1
2			2
3			3
4			4
5			5
6			6

Name	Problem 7-3A
Section	
Date	Lopez Company

(a)

Purchases Journal

P1

Date	Account Credited (Debited)	Ref.	Other Accounts Dr.	Merchandise Inventory Dr.	Accounts Payable Cr.

Sales Journal

S1

Date	Account Debited	Ref.	Accounts Receiv. Dr. Sales Cr.	COGS Dr. Merchandise Inventory Cr.

Name

Section

Date

Problem 7-3A Continued

Lopez Company

(a) (Continued)

General Journal G1

	Date	Account Titles	Ref.	Debit	Credit	
1	July 8					1
2						2
3						3
4						4
5						5
6	22					6
7						7
8						8
9						9
10						10
11						11
12						12

(b)

General Ledger

Accounts Receivable No. 112

Date	Explanation	Ref.	Debit	Credit	Balance

Merchandise Inventory No. 120

Date	Explanation	Ref.	Debit	Credit	Balance

Supplies No. 126

Date	Explanation	Ref.	Debit	Credit	Balance

Equipment No. 157

Date	Explanation	Ref.	Debit	Credit	Balance

(b)(Continued)

Accounts Payable No. 201

Date	Explanation	Ref.	Debit	Credit	Balance

Sales No. 401

Date	Explanation	Ref.	Debit	Credit	Balance

Sales Returns and Allowances No. 412

Date	Explanation	Ref.	Debit	Credit	Balance

Cost of Goods Sold No. 505

Date	Explanation	Ref.	Debit	Credit	Balance

Advertising Expense No. 610

Date	Explanation	Ref.	Debit	Credit	Balance

(b)(Continued)

Accounts Receivable Subsidiary Ledger

Wayne Bros.

Date	Explanation	Ref.	Debit	Credit	Balance

Pinick Company

Date	Explanation	Ref.	Debit	Credit	Balance

Sager Company

Date	Explanation	Ref.	Debit	Credit	Balance

Haddad Company

Date	Explanation	Ref.	Debit	Credit	Balance

(b)(Continued) *Accounts Payable Subsidiary Ledger*

Cress Supply

Date	Explanation	Ref.	Debit	Credit	Balance

Wayward Shipping

Date	Explanation	Ref.	Debit	Credit	Balance

Fritz Company

Date	Explanation	Ref.	Debit	Credit	Balance

Moon Company

Date	Explanation	Ref.	Debit	Credit	Balance

Lynda Advertisements

Date	Explanation	Ref.	Debit	Credit	Balance

Anton Company

Date	Explanation	Ref.	Debit	Credit	Balance

Name

Section

Date

Lopez Company

(c)

Accounts receivable balance:

Subsidiary account balances:

Accounts payable balance:

Subsidiary account balances:

Name

Section

Date

Problem 7-4A

Boyden Company

(a), (b), & (c)

Sales Journal

S1

Date	Account Debited	Invoice No.	Ref.	Accounts Receivable Dr. Sales Cr.	COGS Dr. Merchandise Inventory Cr.

Purchases Journal

P1

Date	Account Credited	Ref.	Merchandise Inventory (Dr.) Acc. Pay (Cr.)

General Journal

G1

Date	Account Titles	Ref.	Debit	Credit
Jan. 5				
19				

Name

Section

Date

Problem 7-4A Continued

Boyden Company

(a), (b), (c) (Continued)

Cash Receipts Journal

CR1

	Date	Account Credited	Ref.	Cash Dr.	Sales Discounts Dr.	Accounts Receivable Cr.	Sales Cr.	Other Accounts Cr.	COGS Dr. Merch Inv Cr.	
1										1
2										2
3										3
4										4
5										5
6										6
7										7
8										8
9										9
10										10
11										11
12										12
13										13
14										14
15										15

Name

Section

Date

Problem 7-4A Concluded

Boyden Company

(a), (b), (c) (Continued)

Cash Payments Journal

CP1

	Date	Account Debited	Ref.	Other Accounts Dr.	Accounts Payable Dr.	Merchandise Inventory Cr.	Cash Cr.	
1								1
2								2
3								3
4								4
5								5
6								6
7								7
8								8
9								9
10								10
11								11
12								12
13								13
14								14
15								15

Name

Section

Date

Problem 7-5A

Reyes Co.

(a), (d) & (g)

Cash — No. 101

Date	Explanation	Ref.	Debit	Credit	Balance

Accounts Receivable — No. 112

Date	Explanation	Ref.	Debit	Credit	Balance

Merchandise Inventory — No. 120

Date	Explanation	Ref.	Debit	Credit	Balance

Store Supplies — No. 127

Date	Explanation	Ref.	Debit	Credit	Balance

Prepaid Rent — No. 131

Date	Explanation	Ref.	Debit	Credit	Balance

Accounts Payable — No. 201

Date	Explanation	Ref.	Debit	Credit	Balance

Reyes, Capital — No. 301

Date	Explanation	Ref.	Debit	Credit	Balance

(a), (d) & (g) (Continued)

Reyes, Drawing — No. 306

Date	Explanation	Ref.	Debit	Credit	Balance

Sales — No. 401

Date	Explanation	Ref.	Debit	Credit	Balance

Sales Discounts — No. 414

Date	Explanation	Ref.	Debit	Credit	Balance

Cost of Goods Sold — No. 505

Date	Explanation	Ref.	Debit	Credit	Balance

Supplies Expense — No. 631

Date	Explanation	Ref.	Debit	Credit	Balance

Rent Expense — No. 729

Date	Explanation	Ref.	Debit	Credit	Balance

(b)

Sales Journal — S1

	Date	Account Debited	Ref.	Accounts Receivable Dr. Sales Cr.	COGS Dr. Merchandise Inventory Cr.	
1						1
2						2
3						3
4						4
5						5
6						6

Name ______ Problem 7-5A Continued

Section ______

Date ______ Reyes Co.

(a), (b), (c) (Continued)

Cash Receipts Journal

CR1

	Date	Account Credited	Ref.	Cash Dr.	Sales Discounts Dr.	Accounts Receivable Cr.	Sales Cr.	Other Accounts Cr.	COGS Dr. Merch. Inv. Cr.	
1										1
2										2
3										3
4										4
5										5
6										6
7										7
8										8
9										9
10										10
11										11
12										12
13										13
14										14
15										15

Name

Section

Date

Problem 7-5A Continued

Reyes Co.

(c)

Accounts Receivable Subsidiary Ledger

Ewing Co.

Date	Explanation	Ref.	Debit	Credit	Balance

H. Prince

Date	Explanation	Ref.	Debit	Credit	Balance

W. Pitts

Date	Explanation	Ref.	Debit	Credit	Balance

S. Beauty

Date	Explanation	Ref.	Debit	Credit	Balance

Accounts Payable Subsidiary Ledger

C. Tabor

Date	Explanation	Ref.	Debit	Credit	Balance

A. Ernst

Date	Explanation	Ref.	Debit	Credit	Balance

M. Sneezy

Date	Explanation	Ref.	Debit	Credit	Balance

G. Clemens

Date	Explanation	Ref.	Debit	Credit	Balance

(c) (Continued)

J. Happy

Date	Explanation	Ref.	Debit	Credit	Balance

(e)

Reyes Co.
Trial Balance
July 31, 2008

	Debit	Credit

Name

Section

Date

Reyes Co.

(f)

Accounts payable balance:	
Subsidiary accounts balance:	
Accounts receivable balance:	
Subsidiary accounts balance:	

(g)

General Journal G1

Date	Account Titles	Ref.	Debit	Credit
July 31				
31				

Name
Section
Date

(h)

Reyes Co.
Adjusted Trial Balance
July 31, 2008

		Debit	Credit	
1	Cash			1
2	Accounts Receivable			2
3	Merchandise Inventory			3
4	Store Supplies			4
5	Prepaid Rent			5
6	Accounts Payable			6
7	Reyes, Capital			7
8	Reyes, Drawing			8
9	Sales			9
10	Sales Discounts			10
11	Cost of Goods Sold			11
12	Supplies Expense			12
13	Rent Expense			13
14				14
15				15
16				16

Name

Section

Date

Problem 7-6A

Cortez Co.

(b) & (c)

Cash Receipts Journal

CR1

	Date	Account Credited	Ref.	Cash Dr.	Sales Discounts Dr.	Accounts Receivable Cr.	Sales Cr.	Other Accounts Cr.	COGS Dr. Merch Inv Cr.	
1										1
2										2
3										3
4										4
5										5
6										6

Cash Payments Journal

CP1

	Date	Account Debited	Ref.	Other Accounts Dr.	Accounts Payable Dr.	Merchandise Inventory Cr.	Cash Cr.	
1								1
2								2
3								3
4								4
5								5
6								6
7								7
8								8

(b) & (c) (Continued)

Sales Journal

S1

Date	Account Debited	Ref.	Accounts Receivable Dr. Sales Cr.	COGS Dr. Merchandise Inventory Cr.

Purchases Journal

P1

Date	Account Credited	Ref.	Merchandise Inventory Dr. Acc. Pay. Cr.

General Journal

G1

Date	Account Titles	Ref.	Debit	Credit
Jan 14				
20				
30				

Name

Section

Date

Prtoblem 7-6A Continued

Cortez Co.

(a) and (c)

General Ledger

Cash

No. 101

Date	Explanation	Ref.	Debit	Credit	Balance
Jan. 1	Balance	√			41500

Accounts Receivable

No. 112

Date	Explanation	Ref.	Debit	Credit	Balance
Jan. 1	Balance	√			15000

Notes Receivable

No. 115

Date	Explanation	Ref.	Debit	Credit	Balance
Jan. 1	Balance	√			45000

Merchandise Inventory

No. 120

Date	Explanation	Ref.	Debit	Credit	Balance
Jan. 1	Balance	√			23000

Equipment

No. 157

Date	Explanation	Ref.	Debit	Credit	Balance
Jan. 1	Balance	√			6450

Accumulated Depreciation - Equipment

No. 158

Date	Explanation	Ref.	Debit	Credit	Balance
Jan. 1	Balance	√			1500

(a) and (c) (Continued)

Notes Payable — No. 200

Date	Explanation	Ref.	Debit	Credit	Balance

Accounts Payable — No. 201

Date	Explanation	Ref.	Debit	Credit	Balance
Jan. 1	Balance	√			43000

B. Cortez, Capital — No. 301

Date	Explanation	Ref.	Debit	Credit	Balance
Jan. 1	Balance	√			86450

Sales — No. 401

Date	Explanation	Ref.	Debit	Credit	Balance

Sales Returns and Allowances — No. 412

Date	Explanation	Ref.	Debit	Credit	Balance

Sales Discounts — No. 414

Date	Explanation	Ref.	Debit	Credit	Balance

Cost of Goods Sold — No. 505

Date	Explanation	Ref.	Debit	Credit	Balance

(a) and (c) (Continued)

Sales Salaries Expense No. 726

Date	Explanation	Ref.	Debit	Credit	Balance

Office Salaries Expense No. 727

Date	Explanation	Ref.	Debit	Credit	Balance

Rent Expense No. 729

Date	Explanation	Ref.	Debit	Credit	Balance

Accounts Receivable Subsidiary Ledger

J. Anders

Date	Explanation	Ref.	Debit	Credit	Balance
Jan. 1	Balance	√			2500

F. Cone

Date	Explanation	Ref.	Debit	Credit	Balance
Jan. 1	Balance	√			7500

T. Dudley

Date	Explanation	Ref.	Debit	Credit	Balance
Jan. 1	Balance	√			5000

M. Rensing

Date	Explanation	Ref.	Debit	Credit	Balance

(a) and (c) (Continued)

Accounts Payable Subsidiary Ledger

G. Marley

Date	Explanation	Ref.	Debit	Credit	Balance

J. Feeney

Date	Explanation	Ref.	Debit	Credit	Balance
Jan. 1	Balance	√			10000

D. Goodman

Date	Explanation	Ref.	Debit	Credit	Balance
Jan. 1	Balance	√			18000

K. Inwood

Date	Explanation	Ref.	Debit	Credit	Balance
Jan. 1	Balance	√			15000

E. Vietti

Date	Explanation	Ref.	Debit	Credit	Balance

Name
Section
Date

Problem 7-6A Concluded

Cortez Co.

(d)

Cortez Co.
Trial Balance
January 31, 2009

	Debit	Credit
Cash		
Accounts Receivable		
Notes Receivable		
Merchandise Inventory		
Equipment		
Accumulated Depreciation - Equipment		
Notes Payable		
Accounts Payable		
B. Cortez, Capital		
Sales		
Sales Returns and Allowances		
Sales Discounts		
Cost of Goods Sold		
Sales Salaries Expense		
Office Salaries Expense		
Rent Expense		

(e)

Accounts receivable subsidiary ledger:		
Account receivable control:		
Accounts payable subsidiary ledger:		
Accounts payable control:		

Name

Section

Date

Problem 7-1B

Darby Company

(a)

Cash Receipts Journal

CR1

Date	Account Credited	Ref.	Cash Dr.	Sales Discounts Dr.	Accounts Receivable Cr.	Sales Cr.	Other Accounts Cr.	COGS Dr. Merch Inv Cr.

(b)

General Ledger

Accounts Receivable — No. 112

Date	Explanation	Ref	Debit	Credit	Balance
June 1	Balance	√			7300

Accounts Receivable Subsidiary Ledger

Deering & Son

Date	Explanation	Ref	Debit	Credit	Balance
June 1	Balance	√			2500

Farley & Co.

Date	Explanation	Ref	Debit	Credit	Balance
June 1	Balance	√			1900

Grinnell Bros.

Date	Explanation	Ref	Debit	Credit	Balance
June 1	Balance	√			1600

Lenninger Co.

Date	Explanation	Ref	Debit	Credit	Balance
June 1	Balance	√			1300

(c)

1		1
2		2
3		3

Name

Section

Date

Problem 7-2B

Gonya Company

(a)

Cash Payments Journal

CP1

	Date	Ck. No.	Account Debited	Ref.	Other Accounts Dr.	Accounts Payable Dr.	Merchandise Inventory Cr.	Cash Cr.	
1									1
2									2
3									3
4									4
5									5
6									6
7									7
8									8
9									9
10									10
11									11
12									12
13									13
14									14
15									15
16									16
17									17
18									18
19									19
20									20

(b)

General Ledger

Accounts Payable — No. 201

Date	Explanation	Ref	Debit	Credit	Balance
Nov. 1	Balance	√			9350

Accounts Payable Subsidiary Ledger

A. Hess & Co.

Date	Explanation	Ref	Debit	Credit	Balance
Nov. 1	Balance	√			4500

C. Kimberlin

Date	Explanation	Ref	Debit	Credit	Balance
Nov. 1	Balance	√			2350

G. Ruttan

Date	Explanation	Ref	Debit	Credit	Balance
Nov. 1	Balance	√			1000

Wex Bros.

Date	Explanation	Ref	Debit	Credit	Balance
Nov. 1	Balance	√			1500

(c)

Accounts payable balance:	
Subsidiary account balances:	

Name | Problem 7-3B
Section
Date | Emley Company

(a)

Purchases Journal

P1

	Date	Account Credited (Debited)	Ref.	Other Accounts Dr.	Merchandise Inventory Dr.	Accounts Payable Cr.	
1							1
2							2
3							3
4							4
5							5
6							6
7							7
8							8
9							9
10							10
11							11
12							12
13							13
14							14
15							15
16							16
17							17
18							18

Sales Journal

S1

	Date	Account Debited	Ref.	Accounts Receiv. Dr. Sales Cr.	COGS Dr. Merchandise Inventory Cr.	
1						1
2						2
3						3
4						4
5						5
6						6
7						7
8						8
9						9
10						10

(a) (Continued)

General Journal G1

	Date	Account Titles	Ref.	Debit	Credit	
1						1
2						2
3						3
4						4
5						5
6						6
7						7
8						8
9						9
10						10
11						11
12						12

(b)

General Ledger

Accounts Receivable No. 112

Date	Explanation	Ref.	Debit	Credit	Balance

Merchandise Inventory No. 120

Date	Explanation	Ref.	Debit	Credit	Balance

Supplies No. 126

Date	Explanation	Ref.	Debit	Credit	Balance

Equipment No. 157

Date	Explanation	Ref.	Debit	Credit	Balance

Name
Section
Date

Problem 7-3B Continued

Emley Company

(b)(Continued)

Accounts Payable — No. 201

Date	Explanation	Ref.	Debit	Credit	Balance

Sales — No. 401

Date	Explanation	Ref.	Debit	Credit	Balance

Sales Returns and Allowances — No. 412

Date	Explanation	Ref.	Debit	Credit	Balance

Cost of Goods Sold — No. 505

Date	Explanation	Ref.	Debit	Credit	Balance

Advertising Expense — No. 610

Date	Explanation	Ref.	Debit	Credit	Balance

(b)(Continued)

Accounts Receivable Subsidiary Ledger

Ellie Company

Date	Explanation	Ref.	Debit	Credit	Balance

DeShazer Bros.

Date	Explanation	Ref.	Debit	Credit	Balance

Liu Company

Date	Explanation	Ref.	Debit	Credit	Balance

(b)(Continued) *Accounts Payable Subsidiary Ledger*

Ruden Freight

Date	Explanation	Ref.	Debit	Credit	Balance

Younger Company

Date	Explanation	Ref.	Debit	Credit	Balance

Rodriquez Supply

Date	Explanation	Ref.	Debit	Credit	Balance

Utley Company

Date	Explanation	Ref.	Debit	Credit	Balance

Zeider Company

Date	Explanation	Ref.	Debit	Credit	Balance

Amster Advertising

Date	Explanation	Ref.	Debit	Credit	Balance

(c)

Accounts receivable balance:

Subsidiary account balances:

Accounts payable balance:

Subsidiary account balances:

Name

Section

Date

Problem 7-4B

Litke Company

(a), (b), & (c)

Sales Journal

S1

	Date	Account Debited	Invoice No.	Ref.	Accounts Receivable Dr. Sales Cr.	COGS Dr. Merchandise Inventory Cr.	
1							1
2							2
3							3
4							4
5							5
6							6
7							7

Purchases Journal

P1

	Date	Account Credited	Ref.	Merchandise Inventory (Dr.) Acc. Pay (Cr.)	
1					1
2					2
3					3
4					4
5					5
6					6
7					7
8					8

General Journal

G1

	Date	Account Titles	Ref.	Debit	Credit	
1	Oct 13					1
2						2
3						3
4	25					4
5						5
6						6

Name

Section

Date

Problem 7-4B Continued

Litke Company

(a), (b), (c) (Continued)

Cash Receipts Journal

CR1

	Date	Account Credited	Ref.	Cash Dr.	Sales Discounts Dr.	Accounts Receivable Cr.	Sales Cr.	Other Accounts Cr.	COGS Dr. Merch Inv Cr.	
1										1
2										2
3										3
4										4
5										5
6										6
7										7
8										8
9										9
10										10

Name

Section

Date

Problem 7-4B Concluded

Litke Company

(a), (b), (c) (Continued)

Cash Payments Journal

CP1

	Date	Account Debited	Ref.	Other Accounts Dr.	Accounts Payable Dr.	Merchandise Inventory Cr.	Cash Cr.	
1								1
2								2
3								3
4								4
5								5
6								6
7								7
8								8
9								9
10								10
11								11

Name ______ Problem 7-5B

Section ______

Date ______ Wyrick Co.

(b)

Purchases Journal

P1

	Date	Account Credited	Ref.	Merchandise Inventory (Dr) Acc Pay (Cr)	
1					1
2					2
3					3
4					4
5					5
6					6
7					7

Cash Payments Journal

CP1

	Date	Account Debited	Ref.	Other Accounts Dr.	Accounts Payable Dr.	Merchandise Inventory Cr.	Cash Cr.	
1								1
2								2
3								3
4								4
5								5
6								6
7								7
8								8
9								9
10								10

Name

Section

Date

Problem 7-5B Continued

Wyrick Co.

(a), (d), & (g)

General Ledger

Cash — No. 101

Date	Explanation	Ref.	Debit	Credit	Balance

Accounts Receivable — No. 112

Date	Explanation	Ref.	Debit	Credit	Balance

Merchandise Inventory — No. 120

Date	Explanation	Ref.	Debit	Credit	Balance

Supplies — No. 126

Date	Explanation	Ref.	Debit	Credit	Balance

Equipment — No. 157

Date	Explanation	Ref.	Debit	Credit	Balance

Accumulated Depreciation - Equipment — No. 158

Date	Explanation	Ref.	Debit	Credit	Balance

(a), (d) and (g) (Continued)

Accounts Payable — No. 201

Date	Explanation	Ref.	Debit	Credit	Balance

A. Wyrick, Capital — No. 301

Date	Explanation	Ref.	Debit	Credit	Balance

A. Wyrick, Drawing — No. 306

Date	Explanation	Ref.	Debit	Credit	Balance

Sales — No. 401

Date	Explanation	Ref.	Debit	Credit	Balance

Sales Discounts — No. 414

Date	Explanation	Ref.	Debit	Credit	Balance

Cost of Goods Sold — No. 505

Date	Explanation	Ref.	Debit	Credit	Balance

Supplies Expense — No. 631

Date	Explanation	Ref.	Debit	Credit	Balance

Depreciation Expense — No. 711

Date	Explanation	Ref.	Debit	Credit	Balance

Name

Section

Date

Problem 7-5B Continued

Wyrick Co.

(c)

Accounts Receivable Subsidiary Ledger

S. Arndt

Date	Explanation	Ref.	Debit	Credit	Balance

F. Catt

Date	Explanation	Ref.	Debit	Credit	Balance

C. Boyd

Date	Explanation	Ref.	Debit	Credit	Balance

M. Didde

Date	Explanation	Ref.	Debit	Credit	Balance

Accounts Payable Subsidiary Ledger

G. Reedy

Date	Explanation	Ref.	Debit	Credit	Balance

J. Vopat

Date	Explanation	Ref.	Debit	Credit	Balance

P. Kneiser

Date	Explanation	Ref.	Debit	Credit	Balance

(c) (Continued)

J. Nunez

Date	Explanation	Ref.	Debit	Credit	Balance

(e)

Wyrick Co.
Trial Balance
February 28, 2008

	Debit	Credit
Cash		
Accounts Receivable		
Merchandise Inventory		
Supplies		
Equipment		
Accounts Payable		
A. Wyrick, Capital		
A. Wyrick, Drawing		
Sales		
Sales Discounts		
Cost of Goods Sold		

(f)

Accounts receivable control account:

Accounts receivable subsidiary accounts:

Accounts payable control account:

Accounts payable subsidiary accounts:

Name

Section

Date

Problem 7-5B Concluded

Wyrick Co.

(g)

General Journal

G1

Date	Account Titles	Ref.	Debit	Credit
Feb 28				
28				

(h)

Wyrick Co.

Adjusted Trial Balance

February 28, 2008

	Debit	Credit
Cash		
Accounts Receivable		
Merchandise Inventory		
Supplies		
Equipment		
Accumulated Depreciation - Equipment		
Accounts Payable		
A. Wyrick, Capital		
A. Wyrick, Drawing		
Sales		
Sales Discounts		
Cost of Goods Sold		
Supplies Expense		
Depreciation Expense		

Name

Section

Date

Packard Company

(a)

Sales Journal S1

	Date	Account Debited	Invoice No.	Ref.	Accounts Receiv. Dr. Sales Cr.	
1						1
2						2
3						3
4						4
5						5
6						6
7						7
8						8
9						9
10						10
11						11
12						12

Purchases Journal P1

	Date	Account Credited	Terms	Ref.	Purchases Dr. Acc. Pay Cr.	
1						1
2						2
3						3
4						4
5						5
6						6
7						7
8						8
9						9
10						10
11						11
12						12

Name

Section

Date

Packard Company

(a) (Continued)

Cash Receipts Journal

CR1

	Date	Explanation	Account Credited	Ref.	Cash Dr.	Accounts Receivable Cr.	Sales Cr.	Other Accounts Cr.	
1									1
2									2
3									3
4									4
5									5
6									6
7									7
8									8
9									9
10									10
11									11
12									12
13									13
14									14
15									15

Name

Section

Date

Packard Company

(a) (Continued)

Cash Payments Journal

CR1

	Date	Explanation	Cash Cr.	Accounts Payable Dr.	Office Supplies Dr.	Accounts Debited	Ref.	Other Accounts Dr.	
1									1
2									2
3									3
4									4
5									5
6									6
7									7
8									8
9									9
10									10
11									11
12									12
13									13
14									14
15									15

Name

Section

Date

(a) and (e)

General Journal

G1

Date	Account Titles	Ref	Debit	Credit

Name

Section

Date

Comprehensive Problem: Chapters 3 to 7

Packard Company

(a) and (e)

General Journal G1

Date	Account Titles	Ref	Debit	Credit

(b) and (e)

General Ledger

Cash — No. 101

Date	Explanation	Ref.	Debit	Credit	Balance
Jan. 1	Balance	√			33750

Accounts Receivable — No. 112

Date	Explanation	Ref.	Debit	Credit	Balance
Jan. 1	Balance	√			13000

Notes Receivable — No. 115

Date	Explanation	Ref.	Debit	Credit	Balance
Jan. 1	Balance	√			39000

Merchandise Inventory — No. 120

Date	Explanation	Ref.	Debit	Credit	Balance
Jan. 1	Balance	√			20000

Office Supplies — No. 125

Date	Explanation	Ref.	Debit	Credit	Balance
Jan. 1	Balance	√			1000

Prepaid Insurance — No. 130

Date	Explanation	Ref.	Debit	Credit	Balance
Jan. 1	Balance	√			2000

(b) and (e) (Continued)

Equipment No. 157

Date	Explanation	Ref.	Debit	Credit	Balance
Jan. 1	Balance	√			6450

Accumulated Depreciation - Equipment No. 158

Date	Explanation	Ref.	Debit	Credit	Balance
Jan. 1	Balance	√			1500

Notes Payable No. 200

Date	Explanation	Ref.	Debit	Credit	Balance
	Balance				

Accounts Payable No. 201

Date	Explanation	Ref.	Debit	Credit	Balance
Jan. 1	Balance	√			35000

Interest Payable No. 230

Date	Explanation	Ref.	Debit	Credit	Balance

I. Packard, Capital No. 301

Date	Explanation	Ref.	Debit	Credit	Balance
Jan. 1	Balance	√			78700

I. Packard, Drawing No. 306

Date	Explanation	Ref.	Debit	Credit	Balance

(b) and (e) (Continued)

Income Summary — No. 350

Date	Explanation	Ref.	Debit	Credit	Balance

Sales — No. 401

Date	Explanation	Ref.	Debit	Credit	Balance

Sales Returns and Allowances — No. 412

Date	Explanation	Ref.	Debit	Credit	Balance

Purchases — No. 510

Date	Explanation	Ref.	Debit	Credit	Balance

Purchase Returns and Allowances — No. 512

Date	Explanation	Ref.	Debit	Credit	Balance

Freight-in — No. 516

Date	Explanation	Ref.	Debit	Credit	Balance

Sales Salaries Expense — No. 627

Date	Explanation	Ref.	Debit	Credit	Balance

(b) and (e) (Continued)

Depreciation Expense — No. 711

Date	Explanation	Ref.	Debit	Credit	Balance

Interest Expense — No. 718

Date	Explanation	Ref.	Debit	Credit	Balance

Insurance Expense — No. 722

Date	Explanation	Ref.	Debit	Credit	Balance

Office Salaries Expense — No. 727

Date	Explanation	Ref.	Debit	Credit	Balance

Office Supplies Expense — No. 728

Date	Explanation	Ref.	Debit	Credit	Balance

Rent Expense — No. 729

Date	Explanation	Ref.	Debit	Credit	Balance

(b) and (e) (Continued)

Accounts Receivable Subsidiary Ledger

R. Draves

Date	Explanation	Ref.	Debit	Credit	Balance
Jan. 1	Balance	√			1500

J. Fine

Date	Explanation	Ref.	Debit	Credit	Balance

B. Hachinski

Date	Explanation	Ref.	Debit	Credit	Balance
Jan. 1	Balance	√			7500

S. Ingles

Date	Explanation	Ref.	Debit	Credit	Balance
Jan. 1	Balance	√			4000

B. Remy

Date	Explanation	Ref.	Debit	Credit	Balance

(b) and (e) (Continued)

Accounts Payable Subsidiary Ledger

D. Laux

Date	Explanation	Ref.	Debit	Credit	Balance

S. Kosko

Date	Explanation	Ref.	Debit	Credit	Balance
Jan. 1	Balance	√			9000

R. Mikush

Date	Explanation	Ref.	Debit	Credit	Balance
Jan. 1	Balance	√			15000

D. Moreno

Date	Explanation	Ref.	Debit	Credit	Balance
Jan. 1	Balance	√			11000

S. Yost

Date	Explanation	Ref.	Debit	Credit	Balance

Comprehensive Problem: Chapters 3 to 7

Packard Company

See Appendix

(d)

Packard Company
Income Statement
For the Month Ended January 31, 2008

(d) (Continued)

Packard Company
Statement of Owner's Equity
For the Month Ended January 31, 2008

Packard Company
Balance Sheet
January 31, 2008

Assets

Liabilities and Owner's Equity

(f)

Packard Company
Post-Closing Trial Balance
January 31, 2008

	Debit	Credit
Cash		
Notes Receivable		
Accounts Receivable		
Merchandise Inventory		
Office Supplies		
Prepaid Insurance		
Equipment		
Accumulated Depreciation - Equipment		
Notes Payable		
Accounts Payable		
Interest Payable		
I. Packard, Capital		

Accounts Receivable balance:		
Subsidiary account balances:		
Accounts Payable balance:		
Subsidiary account balances:		

Name | Chapter 7 Financial Reporting Problem

Section

Date | Bluma Co.

Sales Journal

S1

Date	Account Debited	Invoice No.	Ref.	Accounts Receiv. Dr. Sales Cr.	COGS Dr. Merchandise Inventory Cr.

Purchases Journal

P1

Date	Account Credited	Terms	Ref.	Merchandise Inventory (Dr.) Acc. Pay (Cr.)

Name

Section

Date

Bluma Co.

(a) (Continued)

Cash Receipts Journal

CR1

	Date	Account Credited	Ref.	Cash Dr.	Sales Discounts Dr.	Accounts Receivable Cr.	Sales Cr.	Other Accounts Cr.	COGS Dr. Inventory Cr.	
1										1
2										2
3										3
4										4
5										5
6										6
7										7
8										8
9										9
10										10
11										11
12										12
13										13
14										14
15										15

Name

Section

Date

Bluma Co.

(a) (Continued)

Cash Payments Journal

CP1

	Date	Account Debited	Ref.	Other Accounts Dr.	Accounts Payable Dr.	Office Supplies Dr.	Merchandise Inventory Cr.	Cash Cr.	
1									1
2									2
3									3
4									4
5									5
6									6
7									7
8									8
9									9
10									10
11									11
12									12
13									13
14									14
15									15

(a) and (e)

General Journal G1

Date	Account Titles	Ref	Debit	Credit

(a) and (e) (Continued)

General Journal G1

Date	Account Titles	Ref	Debit	Credit

(b) and (e)

General Ledger

Cash — No. 101

Date	Explanation	Ref.	Debit	Credit	Balance
Jan. 1	Balance	√			35750

Accounts Receivable — No. 112

Date	Explanation	Ref.	Debit	Credit	Balance
Jan. 1	Balance	√			13000

Notes Receivable — No. 115

Date	Explanation	Ref.	Debit	Credit	Balance
Jan. 1	Balance	√			39000

Merchandise Inventory — No. 120

Date	Explanation	Ref.	Debit	Credit	Balance
Jan. 1	Balance	√			18000

Office Supplies — No. 125

Date	Explanation	Ref.	Debit	Credit	Balance
Jan. 1	Balance	√			1000

Prepaid Insurance — No. 130

Date	Explanation	Ref.	Debit	Credit	Balance
Jan. 1	Balance	√			2000

(b) and (e) (Continued)

Equipment No. 157

Date	Explanation	Ref.	Debit	Credit	Balance
Jan. 1	Balance	√			6450

Accumulated Depreciation - Equipment No. 158

Date	Explanation	Ref.	Debit	Credit	Balance
Jan. 1	Balance	√			1500

Notes Payable No. 200

Date	Explanation	Ref.	Debit	Credit	Balance

Accounts Payable No. 201

Date	Explanation	Ref.	Debit	Credit	Balance
Jan. 1	Balance	√			35000

Interest Payable No. 230

Date	Explanation	Ref.	Debit	Credit	Balance

M.Bluma, Capital No. 301

Date	Explanation	Ref.	Debit	Credit	Balance
Jan. 1	Balance	√			78700

M. Bluma, Drawing No. 306

Date	Explanation	Ref.	Debit	Credit	Balance

(b) and (e) (Continued)

Income Summary — No. 350

Date	Explanation	Ref.	Debit	Credit	Balance

Sales — No. 401

Date	Explanation	Ref.	Debit	Credit	Balance

Sales Returns and Allowances — No. 412

Date	Explanation	Ref.	Debit	Credit	Balance

Sales Discounts — No. 414

Date	Explanation	Ref.	Debit	Credit	Balance

Cost of Goods Sold — No. 505

Date	Explanation	Ref.	Debit	Credit	Balance

Sales Salaries Expense — No. 627

Date	Explanation	Ref.	Debit	Credit	Balance

Depreciation Expense — No. 711

Date	Explanation	Ref.	Debit	Credit	Balance

(b) and (e) (Continued)

Interest Expense No. 718

Date	Explanation	Ref.	Debit	Credit	Balance

Insurance Expense No. 722

Date	Explanation	Ref.	Debit	Credit	Balance

Office Salaries Expense No. 727

Date	Explanation	Ref.	Debit	Credit	Balance

Office Supplies Expense No. 728

Date	Explanation	Ref.	Debit	Credit	Balance

Rent Expense No. 729

Date	Explanation	Ref.	Debit	Credit	Balance

(b) and (e) (Continued)

Accounts Receivable Subsidiary Ledger

R. Dvorak

Date	Explanation	Ref.	Debit	Credit	Balance
Jan. 1	Balance	√			1500

J. Forbes

Date	Explanation	Ref.	Debit	Credit	Balance

B. Garcia

Date	Explanation	Ref.	Debit	Credit	Balance
Jan. 1	Balance	√			7500

S. LaDew

Date	Explanation	Ref.	Debit	Credit	Balance
Jan. 1	Balance	√			4000

B. Richey

Date	Explanation	Ref.	Debit	Credit	Balance

(b) and (e) (Continued)

Accounts Payable Subsidiary Ledger

D. Lynch

Date	Explanation	Ref.	Debit	Credit	Balance

S. Hoyt

Date	Explanation	Ref.	Debit	Credit	Balance
Jan. 1	Balance	√			9000

R. Moses

Date	Explanation	Ref.	Debit	Credit	Balance
Jan. 1	Balance	√			15000

D. Omara

Date	Explanation	Ref.	Debit	Credit	Balance
Jan. 1	Balance	√			11000

S. Vogel

Date	Explanation	Ref.	Debit	Credit	Balance

Chapter 7 Financial Reporting Problem

Bluma Co.

See Appendix

(d)

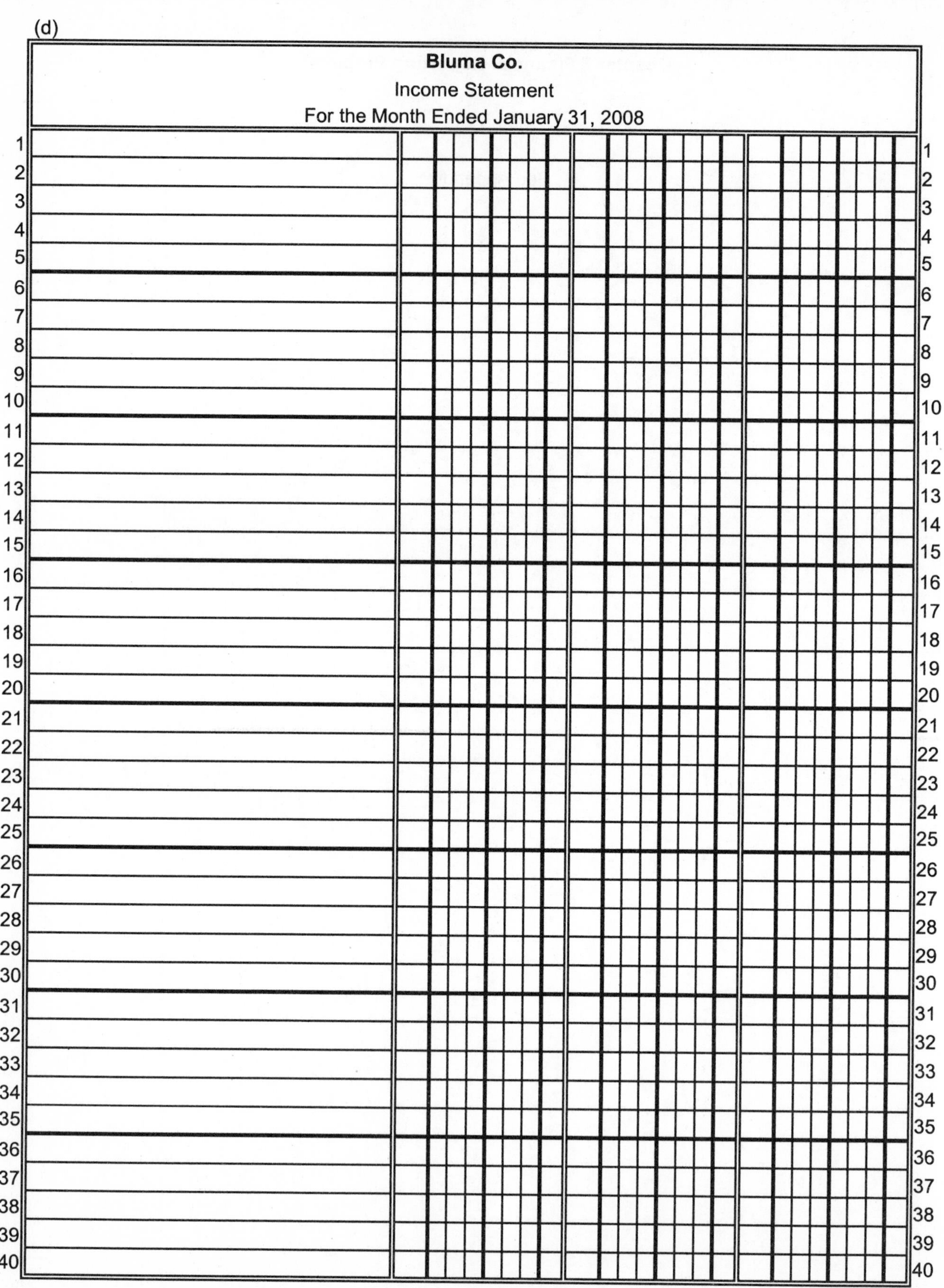
Bluma Co.
Income Statement
For the Month Ended January 31, 2008

(d) (Continued)

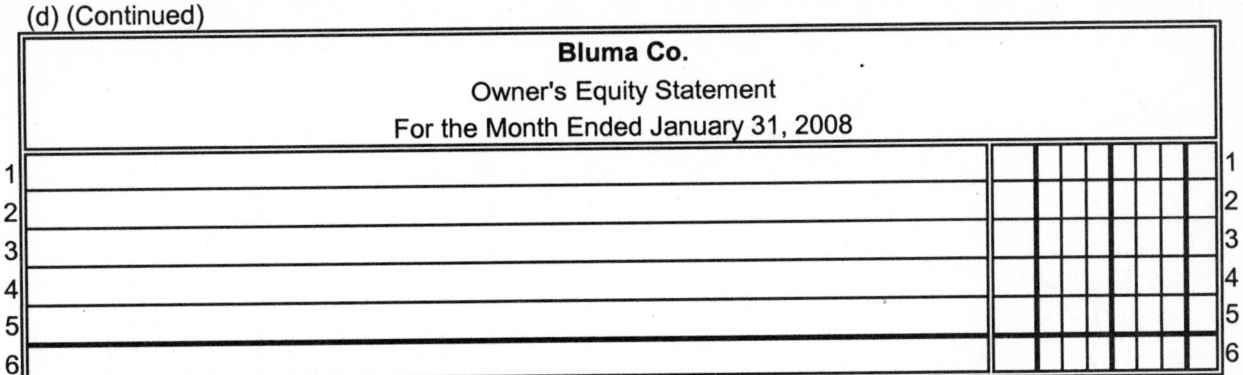

Bluma Co.
Owner's Equity Statement
For the Month Ended January 31, 2008

Bluma Co.
Balance Sheet
January 31, 2008

Assets

Liabilities and Owner's Equity

(f)

Bluma Co.
Post-Closing Trial Balance
January 31, 2008

	Debit	Credit
Cash		
Notes Receivable		
Accounts Receivable		
Merchandise Inventory		
Office Supplies		
Prepaid Insurance		
Equipment		
Accumulated Depreciation - Equipment		
Notes Payable		
Accounts Payable		
Interest Payable		
M. Bluma, Capital		

Accounts Receivable balance:		
Subsidiary account balances:		
Accounts Payable balance:		
Subsidiary account balances:		

Name

Section

Date

BE8-6

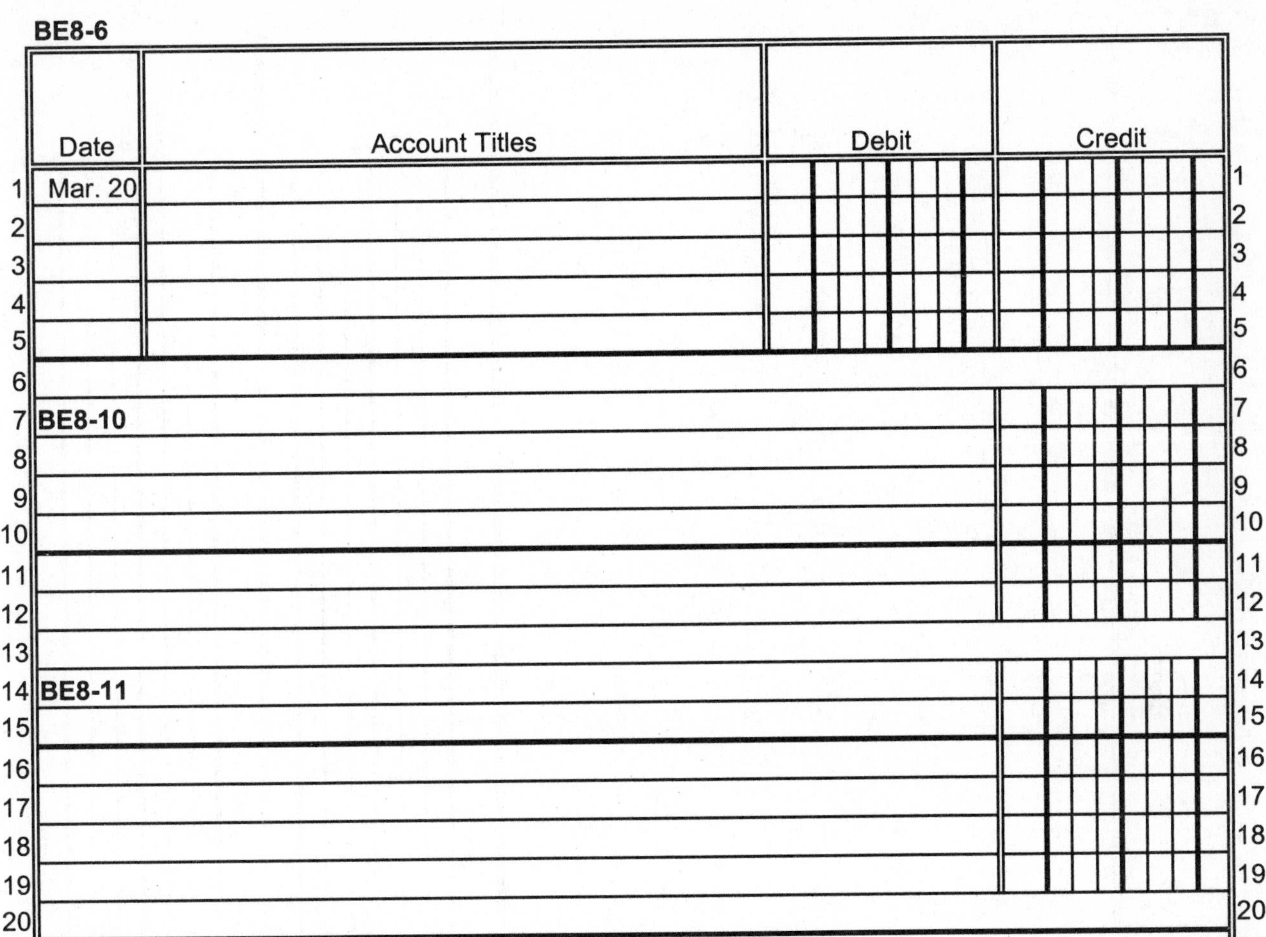

Date	Account Titles	Debit	Credit
Mar. 20			

BE8-10

BE8-11

Name

Section

Date

E8-7

Date	Account Titles	Debit	Credit
May 1			
June 1			
July 1			
July 10			

Name

Section

Name

E8-8

Date	Account Titles	Debit	Credit
Mar. 1			
15			
20			

E8-9 (a)

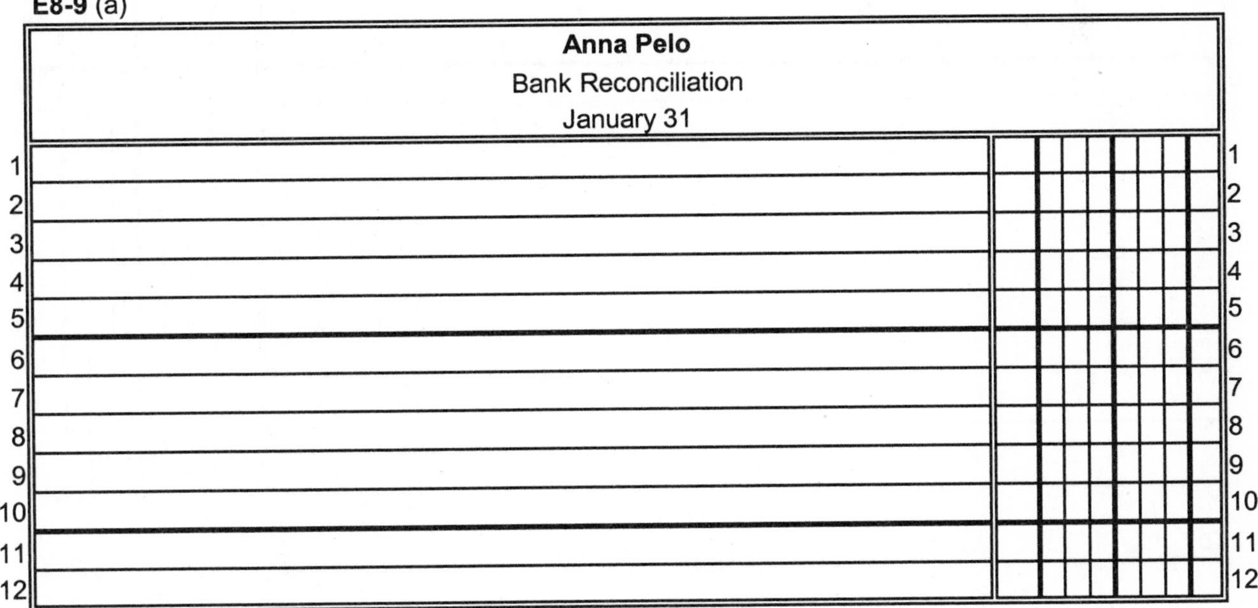

Anna Pelo

Bank Reconciliation

January 31

(b)

Date	Account Titles	Debit	Credit

Name

Section

Name

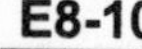

E8-10

		No.	Amount	
1				1
2				2
3				3
4				4
5				5

E8-11 (a)

Family Video Company
Bank Reconciliation
July 31

1			1
2			2
3			3
4			4
5			5
6			6
7			7
8			8
9			9
10			10
11			11
12			12
13			13
14			14
15			15
16			16

(b)

	Date	Account Titles	Debit	Credit	
1	July 31				1
2					2
3					3
4					4
5					5
6	31				6
7					7
8					8
9					9
10					10

Name

Section

Date

Exercise 8-12

Robertson Company

(a)

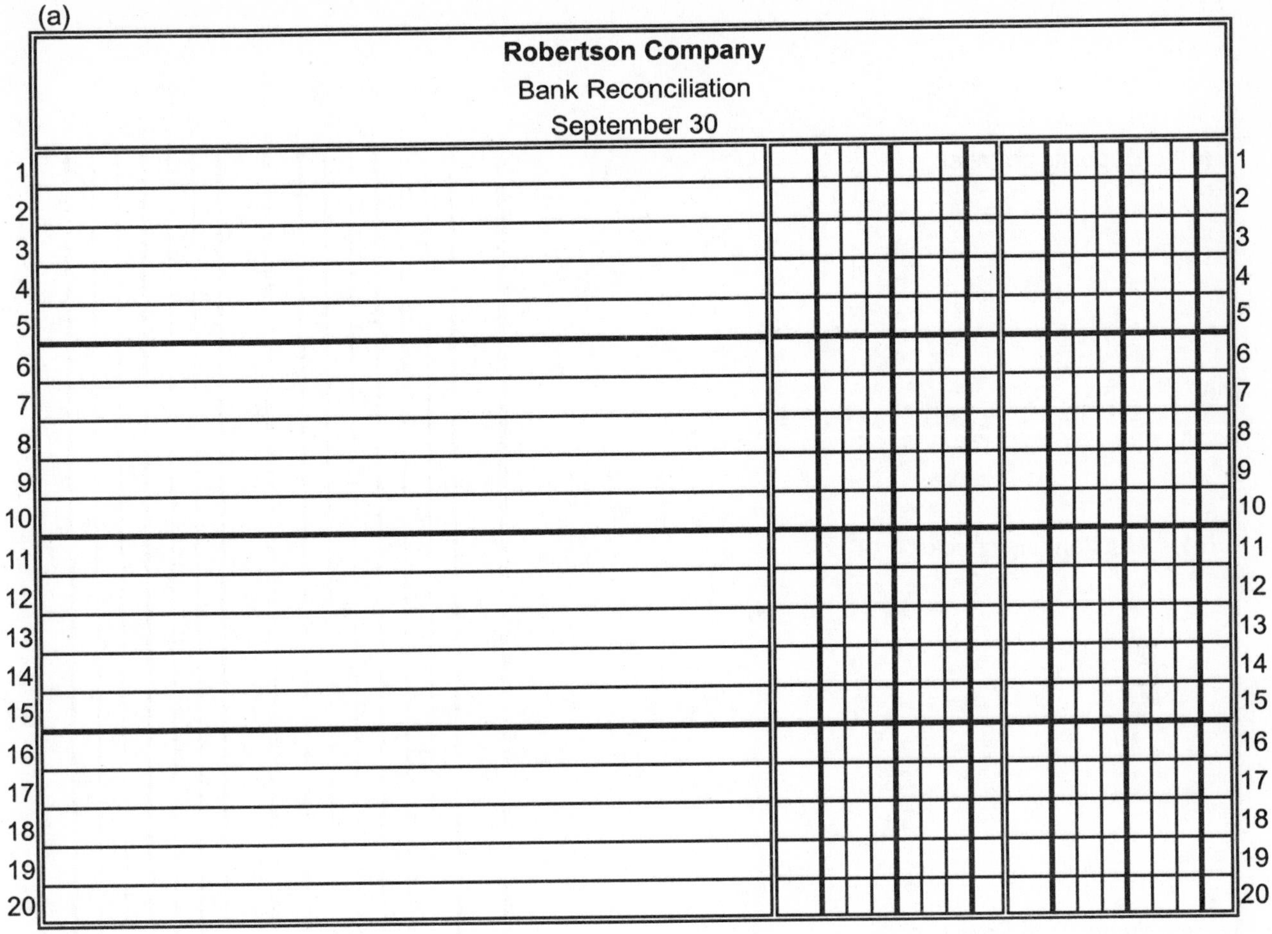

(b)

Date	Account Titles	Debit	Credit
Sept. 30			
30			
30			
30			

Name

Section

Date

Exercise 8-13

Givens Company

(a) Deposits in transit:

(b) Outstanding checks:

(c) Deposits in transit:

(d) Outstanding checks:

Name

Section

Date

Exercise 8-14

Lipkus Company

(a)

(b)

(c)

Name

Section

Date

Problem 8-2A

Winningham Company

(a)

General Journal

Date	Account Titles	Debit	Credit
July 1			
15			
31			
Aug. 15			
16			
31			

(b)

Petty Cash

Date	Explanation	Ref.	Debit	Credit	Balance

(c)

Name
Section
Date

Problem 8-3A

James Logan Company

(a)

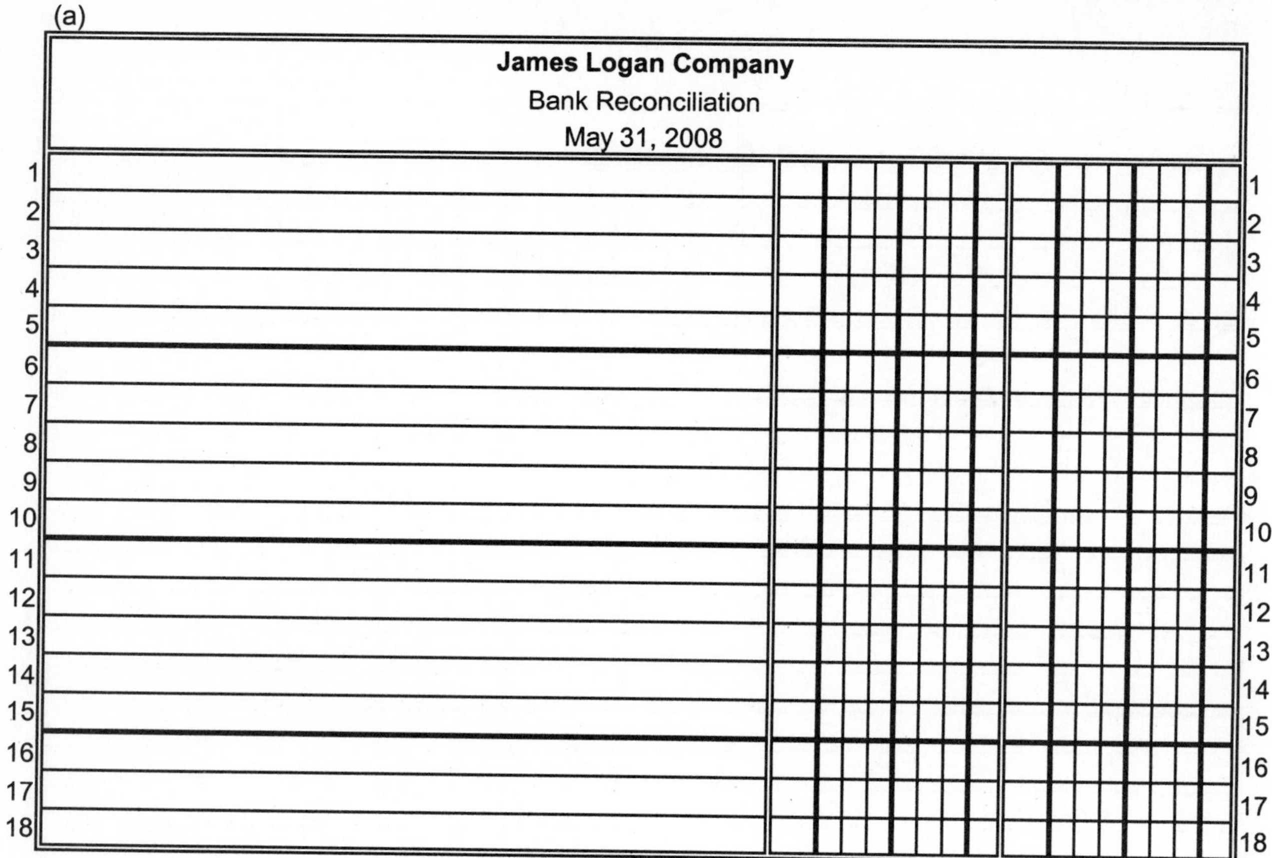

James Logan Company
Bank Reconciliation
May 31, 2008

(b)

General Journal

Date	Account Titles	Debit	Credit
May 31			
31			
31			
31			
31			

(a)

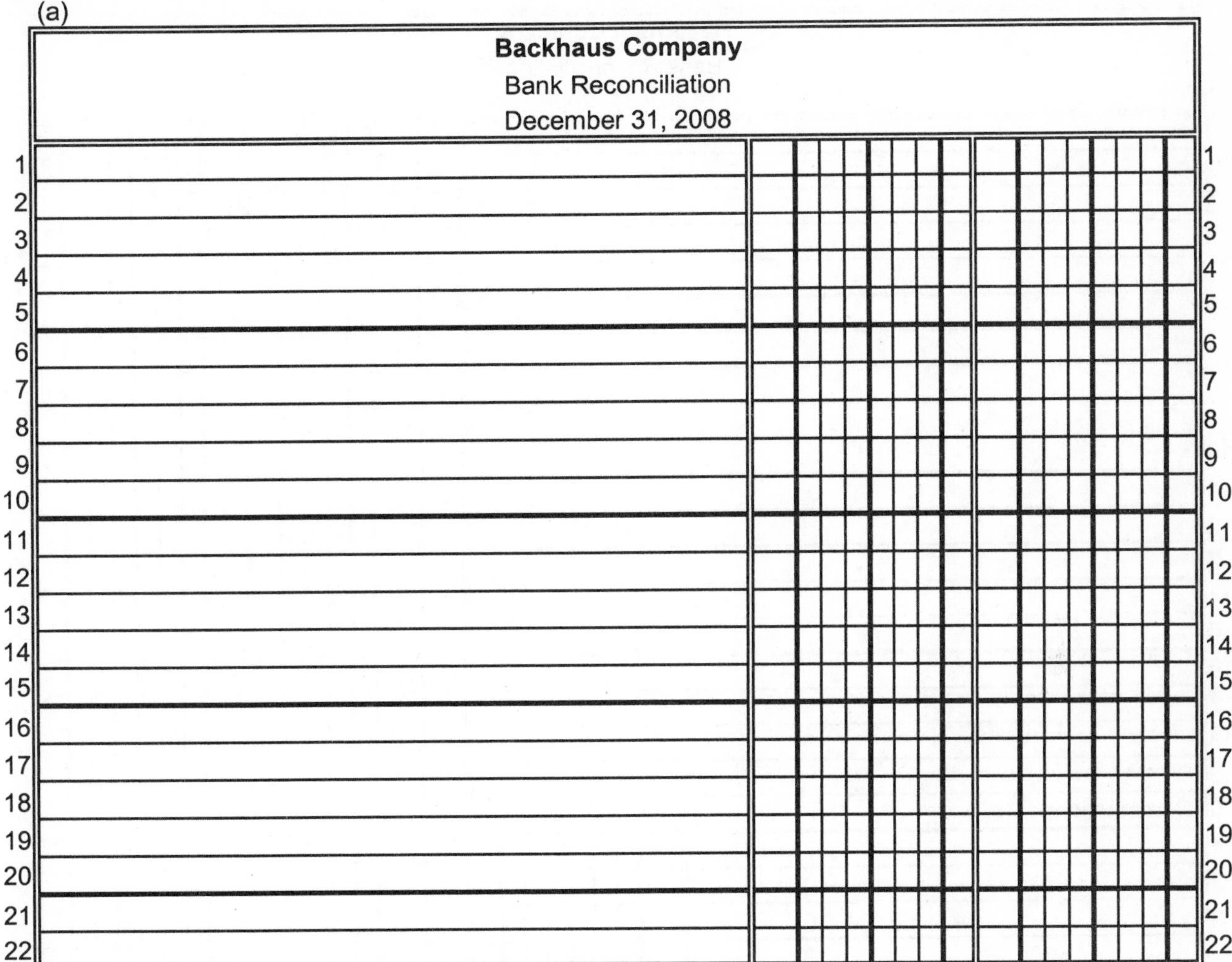

Backhaus Company
Bank Reconciliation
December 31, 2008

(b)

General Journal

Date	Account Titles	Debit	Credit
Dec. 31			
31			
31			
31			

Name
Section
Date

Problem 8-5A

Haverman Company

(a)

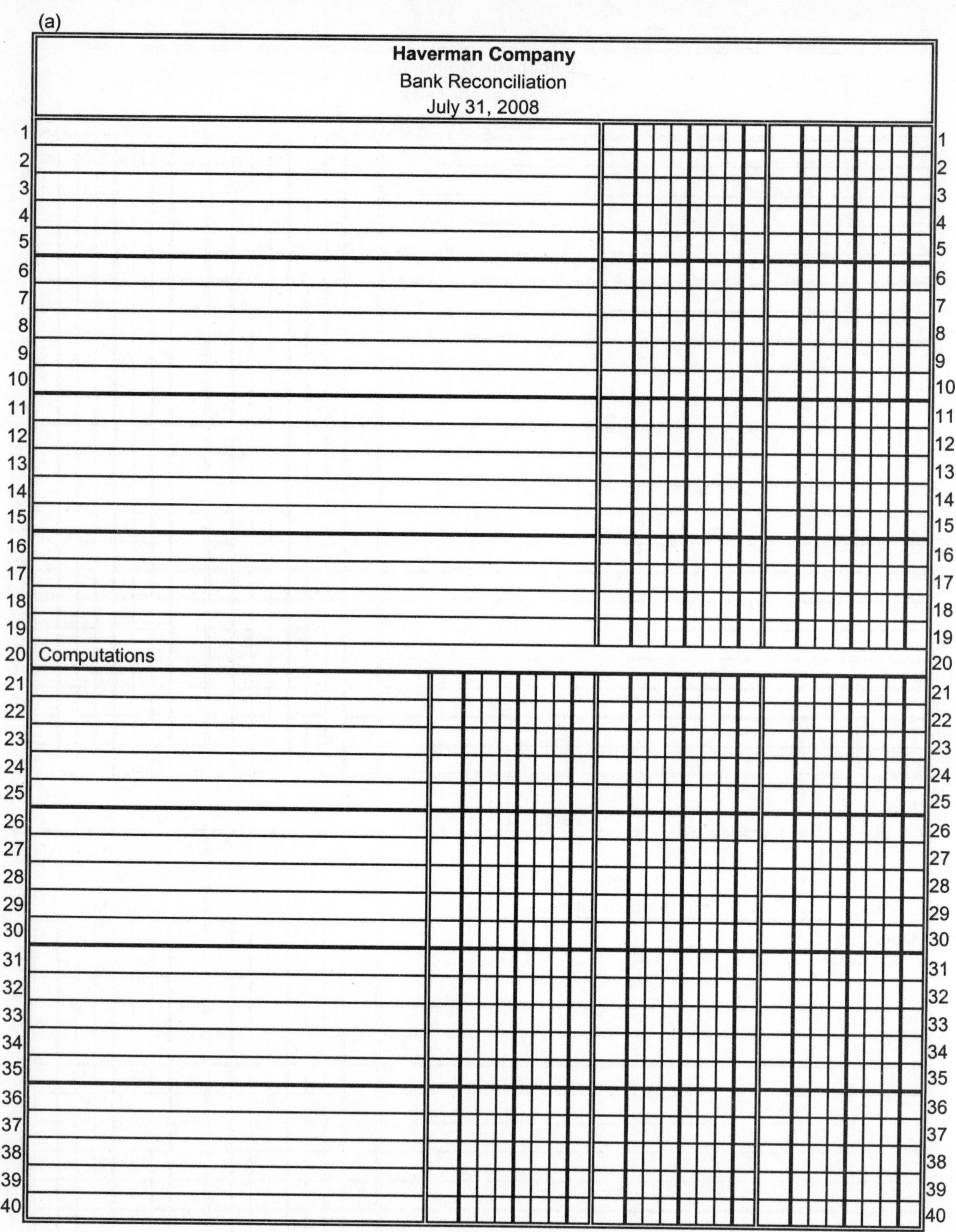

Haverman Company
Bank Reconciliation
July 31, 2008

Computations

Name

Section

Date

Haverman Company

(b)

General Journal

	Date	Account Titles	Debit	Credit	
1	July 31				1
2					2
3					3
4					4
5	31				5
6					6
7					7
8	31				8
9					9
10					10
11					11
12					12
13					13
14					14
15					15
16					16
17					17
18					18
19					19
20					20

Name

Section

Date

Problem 8-2B

Cushenberry Company

(a)

General Journal

Date	Account Titles	Debit	Credit
July 1			
15			
31			
Aug. 15			
16			
31			

Name

Section

Date

Cushenberry Company

(b)

Petty Cash

Date	Explanation	Ref.	Debit	Credit	Balance

(c)

Name

Section

Date

Problem 8-3B

Flint Hills Genetics Company

(a)

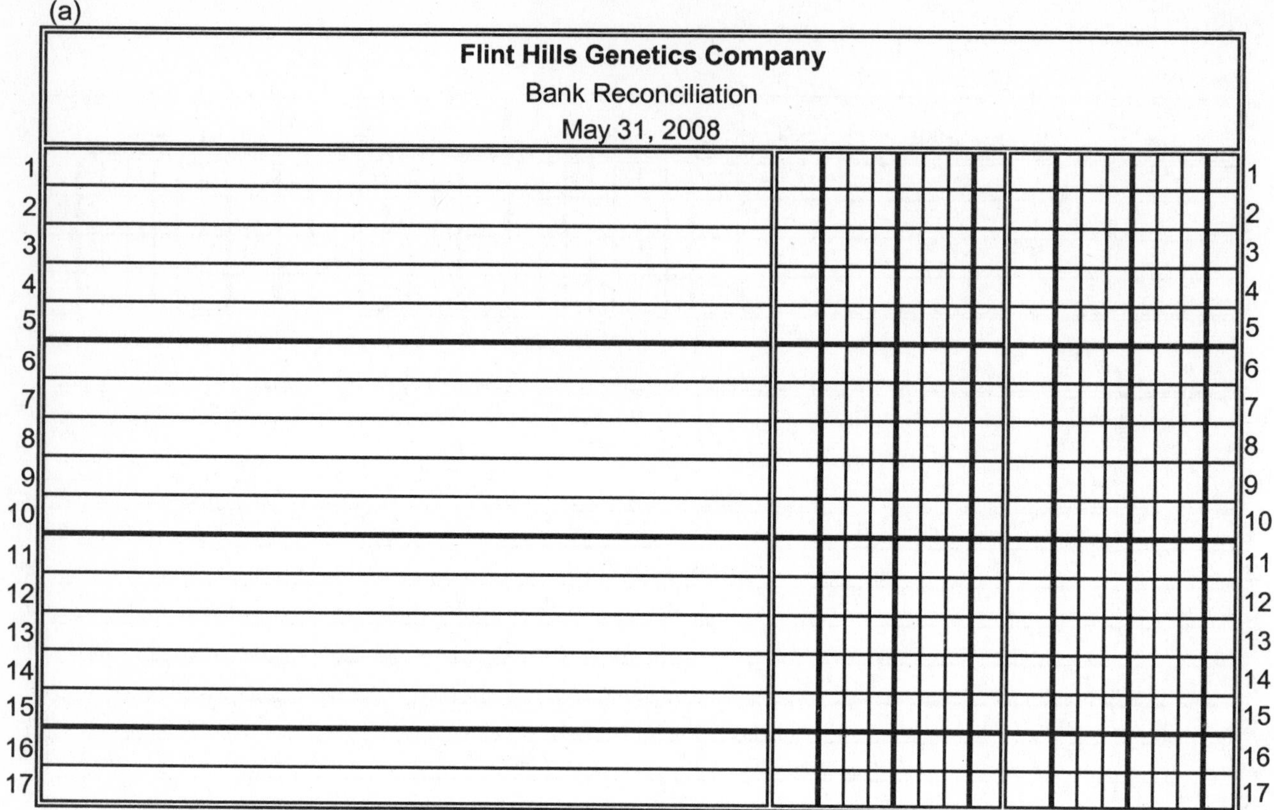

(b)

General Journal

Date	Account Titles	Debit	Credit
May 31			
31			
31			
31			
31			

Name | Problem 8-4B

Section

Date | Conlin Company

(a)

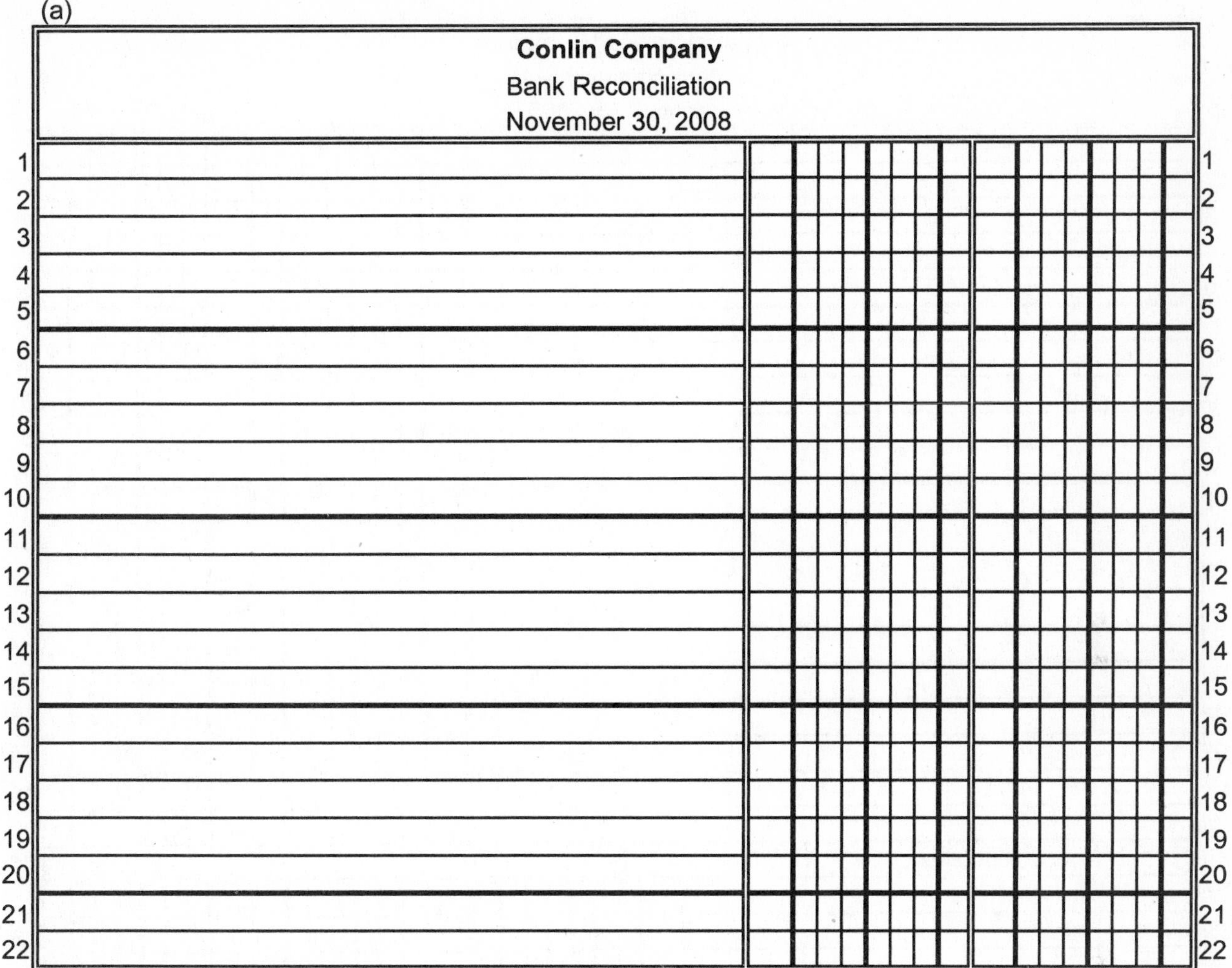

(b) General Journal

Date	Account Titles	Debit	Credit
Nov. 30			
30			
30			
30			

Name

Section

Date

Problem 8-5B

Baumgardner Company

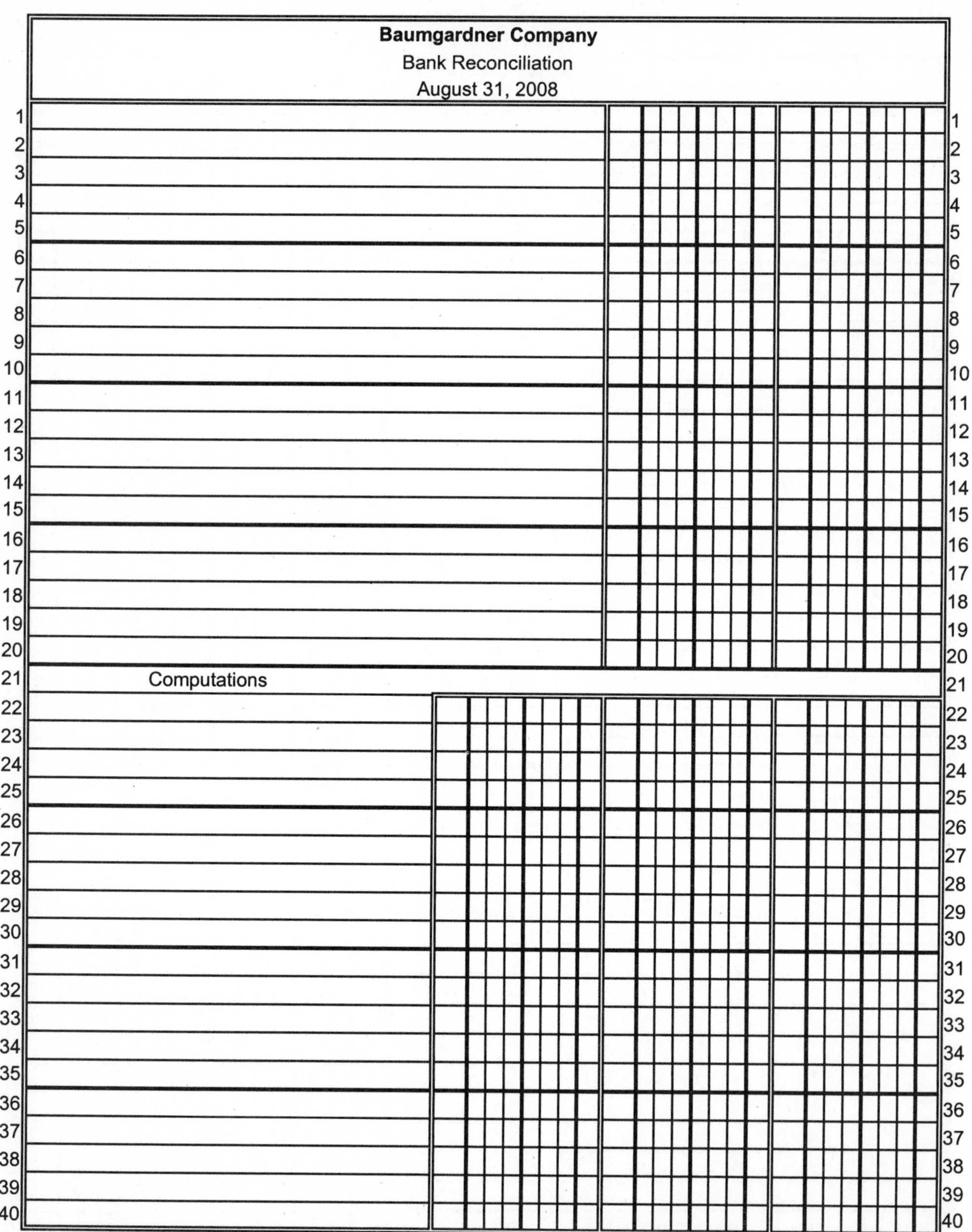

Baumgardner Company

Bank Reconciliation

August 31, 2008

Computations

(b)

General Journal

Date	Account Titles	Debit	Credit
Aug. 31			
31			
31			
31			

Name Problem 8-6B

Section

Date Richardson Company

(a)

Richardson Company

Bank Reconciliation

October 31, 2008

(b)

(c)

Name

Section

Date

PepsiCo, Inc. versus Coca-Cola Company

(a) (In millions)	PepsiCo	Coca-Cola
(1) Cash and cash equivalents at year-end 2002		
(2) Increase/decrease in cash and cash equivalents from 2004 to 2005		
(3) Cash provided by operating activities during year ended Dec. 31, 2005		

(b)

Name
Section
Date

BE9-1

(a)

(b)

(c)

BE9-2	Account Titles	Debit	Credit
(a)			
(b)			
(c)			

BE9-3	Account Titles	Debit	Credit
(a)			

(b) Current assets:

BE9-4	Account Titles	Debit	Credit
(a)			

(b)	(1) Before Write-Off	(2) After Write-Off

BE9-5	Account Titles	Debit	Credit
BE9-6			
BE9-7			
(a)			
(b)			

BE9-8	Account Titles	Debit	Credit
(a)			
(b)			

BE9-9		Interest	Maturity Date
(a)			
(b)			
(c)			

BE9-10	Date of Note	Maturity Date	Annual Interest Rate	Total Interest
(a)	April 1		9%	
(b)	July 2			$ 600
(c)	March 7		10%	

Name

Section

Date

BE9-11	Account Titles	Debit	Credit
Date			
Jan. 10			
Feb. 9			

BE9-12

Accounts receivable turnover ratio:

Average collection period for accounts receivable:

Name

Section

Date

E9-1

Date	Account Titles	Debit	Credit
March 1			
3			
9			
15			
31			
E9-2			
(a)			
Jan. 6			
16			
(b)			
Jan. 10			
Feb. 12			
Mar. 10			

Name

Section

Date

E9-3

Date	Account Titles	Debit	Credit
(a)			
Dec. 31			
(b) (1)			
Dec. 31			
(2)			
Dec. 31			
(c) (1)			
Dec. 31			
(2)			
Dec. 31			

E9-4

(a)

Accounts Receivable	Amount	%	Estimated Uncollectible
1 - 30 days			
30 - 60 days			
60 - 90 days			
Over 90 days			

(b)

Date	Account Titles	Debit	Credit
Mar. 31			

Name

Section

Date

E9-5

Date	Account Titles	Debit	Credit

E9-6

Date	Account Titles	Debit	Credit
2005			
Dec. 31			
2006			
5/11/04			
2006			
Jun. 12			

Name

Section

Date

E9-7

Date	Account Titles	Debit	Credit
(a)			
Mar. 3			
(b)			
May 10			
E9-8			
(a)			
Apr. 2			
May 3			
Jun. 1			
(b)			
July 4			

Name

Section

Date

E9-9

Date	Account Titles	Debit	Credit
(a)			
Jan. 15			
20			
Feb 10			
15			

(b)

E9-10

Date	Account Titles	Debit	Credit
(a)	2008		
Nov. 1			
Dec. 11			
16			
31			
	Calculation of interest:		
(b)	2009		
Nov. 1			

Name

Section

Date

E9-11

Date	Account Titles	Debit	Credit
	2008		
May 1			
Dec. 31			
31			
	2009		
May 1			
E9-12			
4/1/08			
7/1/08			
12/31/08			
4/1/09			

Name

Section

Date

E9-13

Date	Account Titles	Debit	Credit
(a)			
May 2			
(b)			
Nov. 2			
(c)			
Nov. 2			

E9-14

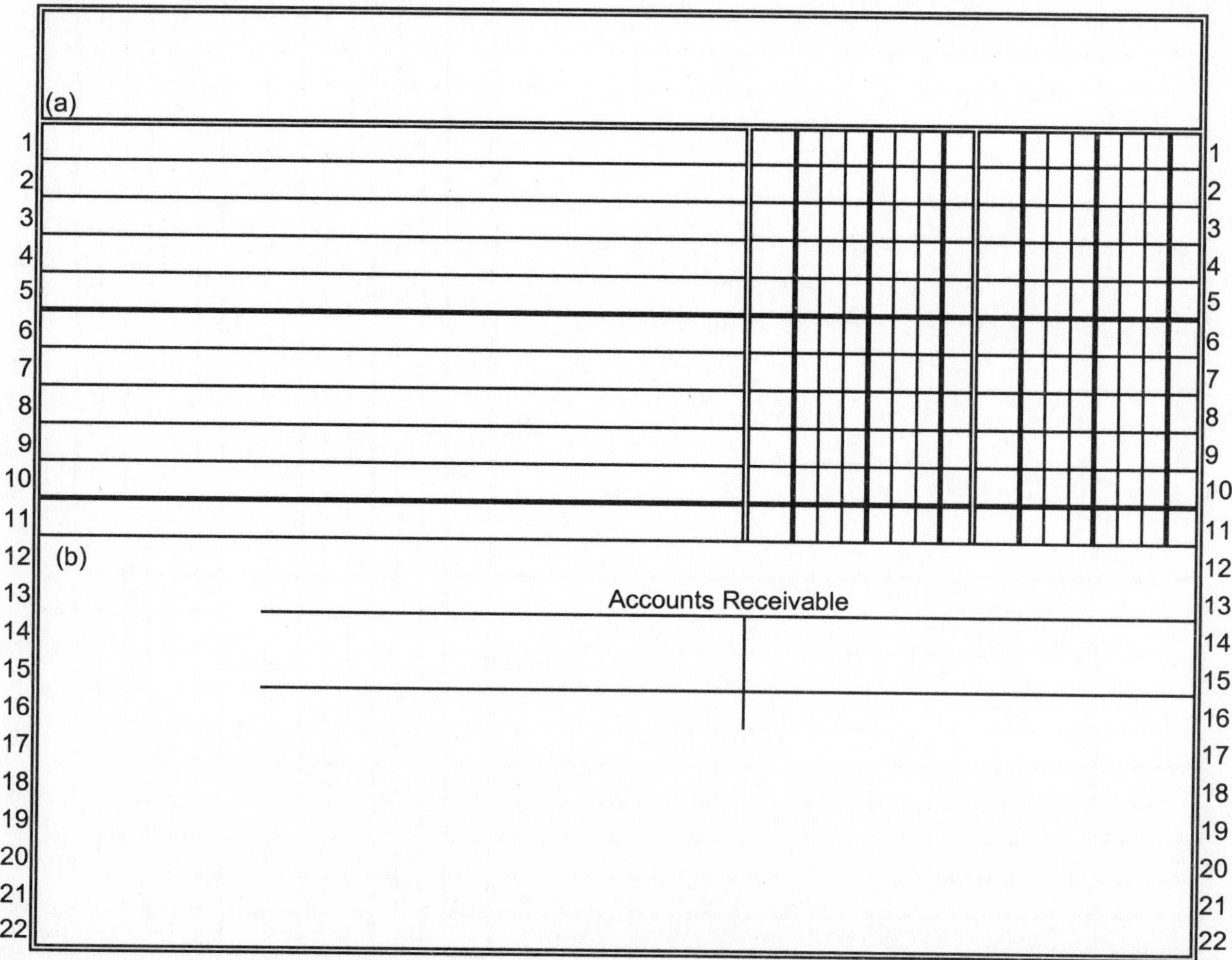

Name Exercise 9-15

Section

Date Bledel Company

(a)

(b)

(c)

Name

Section

Date

Problem 9-1A

Leis Co.

		Account Titles	Debit	Credit	
1	1.				1
2					2
3					3
4	2.				4
5					5
6					6
7	3.				7
8					8
9					9
10	4.				10
11					11
12					12
13	5.				13
14					14
15					15
16					16
17					17
18					18
19					19
20					20

(b)

Accounts Receivable

Bal. 960,000	

Allowance for Doubtful Accounts

	Bal. 80,000

(c)

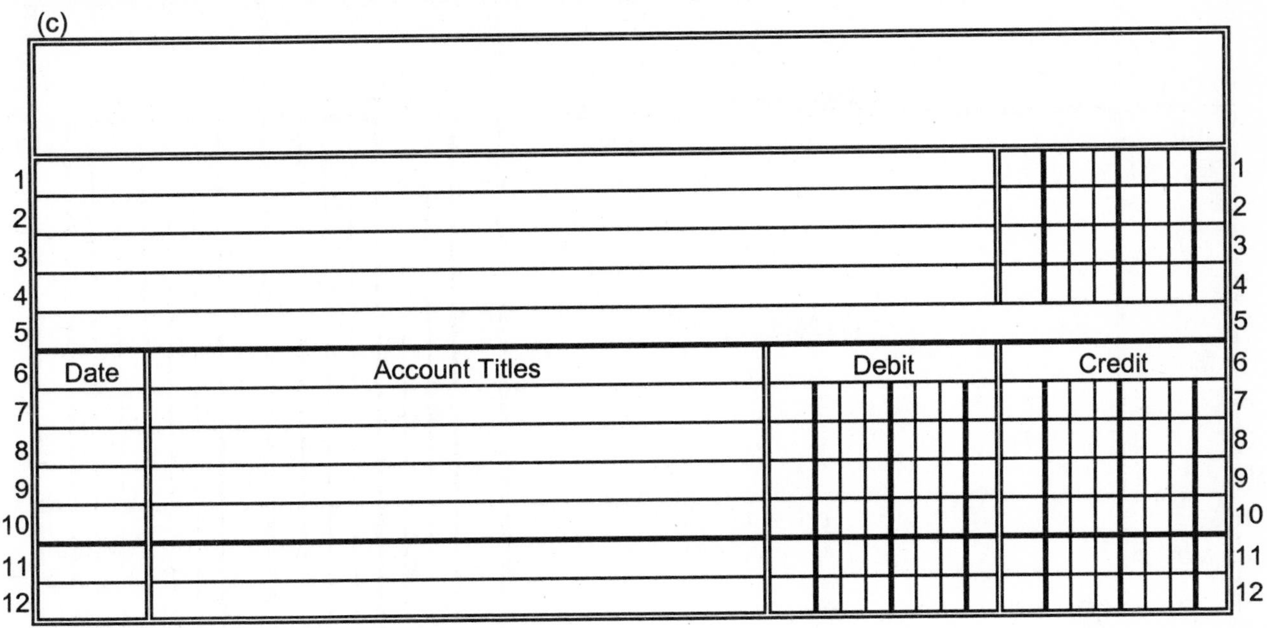

Date	Account Titles	Debit	Credit

(d)

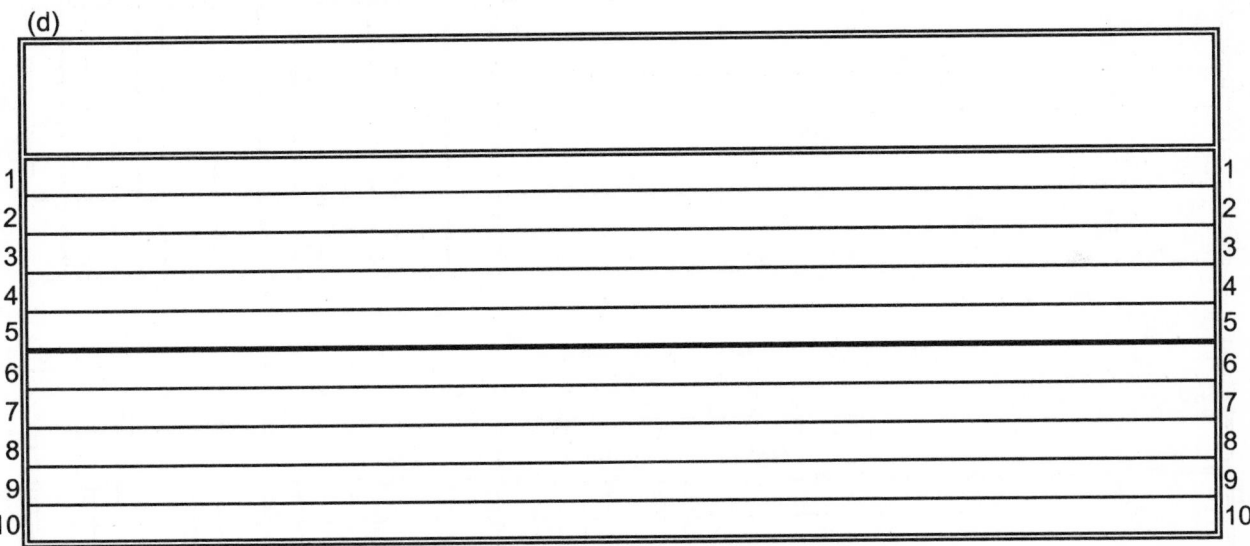

Name

Section

Date

Problem 9-3A

Zillmann Company

(a), (b), and (c)

General Journal

Date	Account Titles	Debit	Credit
(a)			
Dec. 31			
(b)	(1) 2006		
Mar. 31			
	(2)		
May 31			
31			
(c)	2006		
Dec. 31			

(a) & (b)

Bad Debt Expense

Date	Explanation	Ref.	Debit	Credit	Balance

Allowance for Doubtful Accounts

Date	Explanation	Ref.	Debit	Credit	Balance
2008					
Dec. 31	Balance	√			12000

Name

Section

Date

Problem 9-4A

Wall Inc.

(a)

		Total	Number of Days Outstanding					
			0 - 30	31 - 60	61 - 90	91 - 120	Over 120	
1	Accounts receivable	$ 375000	$ 220000	$ 90000	$ 40000	$ 10000	$ 15000	1
2								2
3	% uncollectible		1%	4%	5%	8%	10%	3
4								4
5	Estimated Bad Debts							5

Name
Section
Date

Problem 9-4A Concluded

Wall Inc.

Date	Account Titles	Debit	Credit
(b)			
(c)			
(d)			

(e)

Name Problem 9-5A

Section

Date Worcester Company

(a)

Date	Account Titles	Debit	Credit
(b) (1)			
Dec. 31			
(2)			
Dec. 31			
(c) (1)			
Dec. 31			
(2)			
Dec. 31			
(d)			
(e)			

(f)

Name Problem 9-6A

Section

Date Mendosa Company

(a) General Journal

Date	Account Titles	Debit	Credit
Oct. 7			
12			
15			
15			
24			
31			

Name

Section

Date

Problem 9-6A Concluded

Mendosa Company

(b)

Notes Receivable

Date	Explanation	Ref.	Debit	Credit	Balance
Oct 1	Balance	√			33000

Accounts Receivable

Date	Explanation	Ref.	Debit	Credit	Balance

Interest Receivable

Date	Explanation	Ref.	Debit	Credit	Balance
Oct 1	Balance	√			170

(c)

Assets		
Current Assets		

Name | Problem 9-7A

Section

Date | Kloppenberg Company

General Journal

Date	Account Titles	Debit	Credit
Jan. 5			
20			
Feb. 18			
Apr. 20			
30			
May 25			
Aug. 18			
25			
Sept. 1			

Name | Problem 9-1B

Section

Date | Pickeril Imports

		Account Titles	Debit	Credit	
1	1.				1
2					2
3					3
4	2.				4
5					5
6					6
7	3.				7
8					8
9					9
10	4.				10
11					11
12					12
13	5.				13
14					14
15					15
16					16
17					17
18					18
19					19
20					20

(b)

Accounts Receivable

Debit		Credit
Bal.	1,000,000	

Allowance for Doubtful Accounts

Debit	Credit	
	Bal.	60,000

Name
Section
Date

Problem 9-1B Concluded

Pickeril Imports

(c)

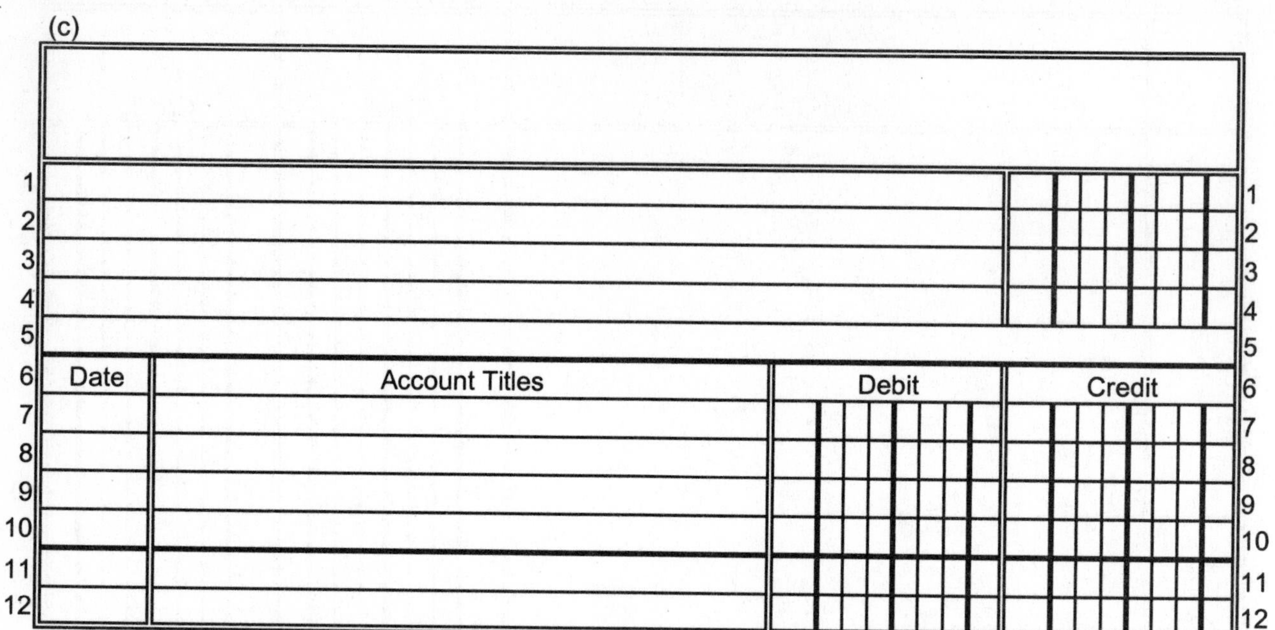

(d)

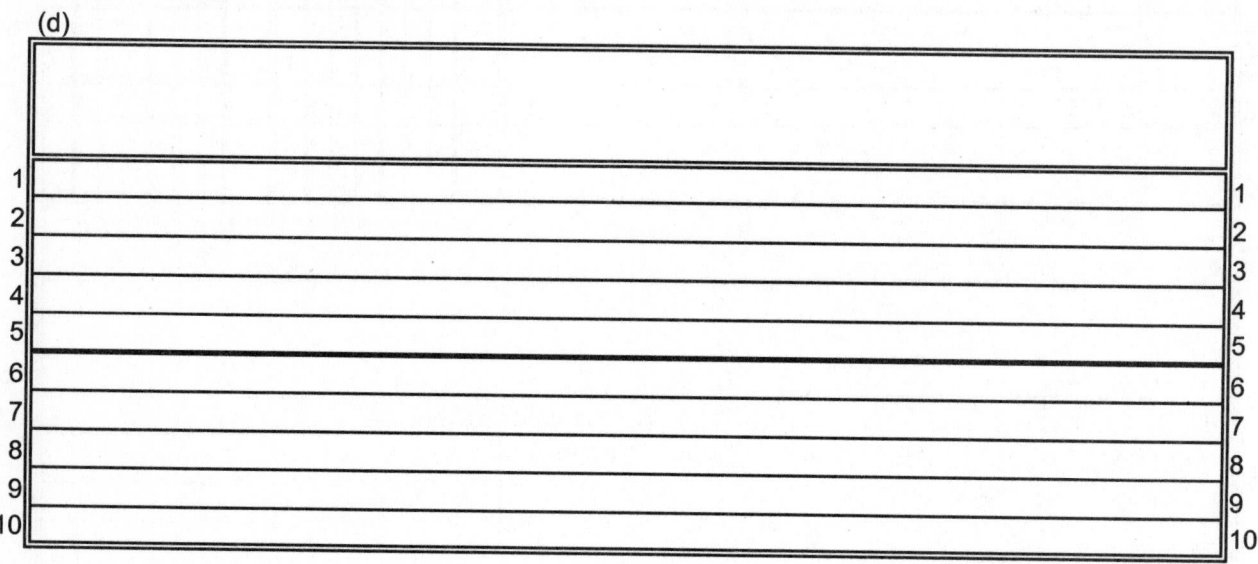

Name | Problem 9-3B
Section
Date | Lawrenz Company

(a), (b), and (c)

General Journal

	Date	Account Titles	Debit	Credit	
1	(a)				1
2	Dec. 31				2
3					3
4					4
5					5
6	(b)	(1) 2009			6
7	Mar. 1				7
8					8
9					9
10					10
11		(2)			11
12	May 1				12
13					13
14					14
15	1				15
16					16
17					17
18					18
19	(c)	2009			19
20	Dec. 31				20
21					21
22					22

(a) & (b)

Bad Debt Expense

	Date	Explanation	Ref.	Debit	Credit	Balance	
1							1
2							2
3							3

Allowance for Doubtful Accounts

	Date	Explanation	Ref.	Debit	Credit	Balance	
1	2008						1
2	Dec. 31	Balance	√			10000	2
3							3
4							4
5							5
6							6
7							7

Name

Section

Date

Problem 9-4B

Aging Accounts Receivable

(a)

		Total	Number of Days Outstanding					
			0 - 30	31 - 60	61 - 90	91 - 120	Over 120	
1	Accounts receivable	$ 260000	$ 100000	$ 60000	$ 50000	$ 30000	$ 25000	1
2								2
3	% uncollectible		1%	5%	8%	10%	15%	3
4								4
5	Estimated Bad Debts							5

	Date	Account Titles	Debit	Credit	
1	(b)				1
2					2
3					3
4	(c)				4
5					5
6					6
7	(d)				7
8					8
9					9
10					10
11					11
12					12
13					13
14					14
15					15

(e)

1		1
2		2
3		3
4		4
5		5

Name | Problem 9-5B

Section

Date | Schnakenberg Company

General Journal

Date	Account Titles	Debit	Credit
(a) (1)			
Dec. 31			
(2)			
Dec. 31			
(b) (1)			
Dec. 31			
(2)			
Dec. 31			
(c)			
(d)			
(e)			
(1)			
(2)			

Name Problem 9-6B

Section

Date Schottenheimer Co.

(a) General Journal

Date	Account Titles	Debit	Credit
July 5			
14			
14			
15			
25			
31			

(b)

Notes Receivable

Date	Explanation	Ref.	Debit	Credit	Balance
July 1	Balance	√			46000

Accounts Receivable

Date	Explanation	Ref.	Debit	Credit	Balance

Interest Receivable

Date	Explanation	Ref.	Debit	Credit	Balance
July 1	Balance	√			300

(c)

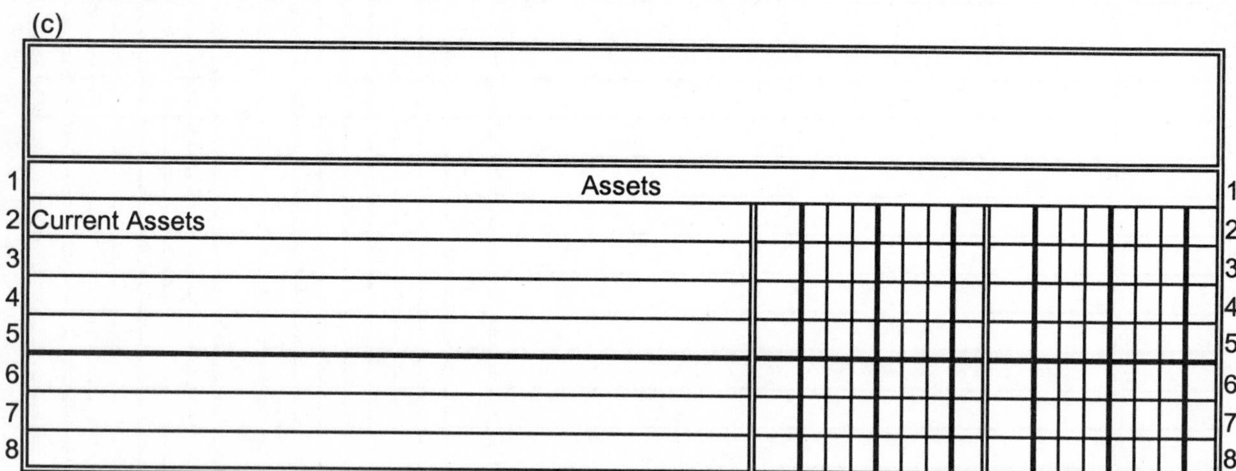

Assets		
Current Assets		

Name Problem 9-7B

Section

Date Frybendall Company

General Journal

Date	Account Titles	Debit	Credit
Jan. 5			
Feb. 2			
12			
26			
Apr. 5			
12			
June 2			
July 5			
15			
Oct. 15			

(a)

SEK Company
Accounts Receivable Aging Schedule
May 31, 2008

	Proportion of Total %	Amount in Category	Probability of Non-Collection %	Estimated Uncollectible Amount
Not yet due				
Less than 30 days past due				
30 to 60 days past due				
61 to 120 days past due				
121 to 180 days past due				
Over 180 days past due				
Totals				

(b)

CAF Company
Analysis of Allowance for Doubtful Accounts
May 31, 2008

Account Titles	Debit	Credit

Name

Section

Date

Campus Fashions

(a)	2008	2007	2006
Net credit sales			
Credit and collection expenses			
Collection agency fees			
Salary of accounts receivable clerk			
Uncollectible accounts			
Billing and mailing costs			
Credit investigation fees			
Total			
Total expenses as a percentage of net credit sales			
(b) Average accounts receivable			
Investment earnings			
Total credit and collection expenses per above			
Add: Investment earnings			
Net credit and collection expenses			
Net expenses as a percentage of net credit sales			

(c)

Name

Section

Date

BE10-1

BE10-2

BE10-3

BE10-4

BE10-5

	Year	Book Value	X	Rate	=	Depreciation
	1					
	2					

BE10-6

Depreciation cost per unit:

	Year	
	1	
	2	

Name

Section

Date

BE10-7

BE10-8 Account Titles	Debit	Credit
1.		
2.		

BE10-9 Account Titles	Debit	Credit
(a)		
(b)		

Calculations:

Name

Section

Date

BE10-10

Account Titles	Debit	Credit
(a)		
(b)		

Calculations:

BE10-11

(a) Depletion cost per unit =

Depletion expense =

Account Titles	Debit	Credit
(b)		

BE10-12 Account Titles	Debit	Credit
(a)		

(b)

Name

Section

Date

BE10-13

Spain Company

Balance Sheet (Partial)

December 31, 2008

BE10-14

***BE10-1!** Account Titles	Debit	Credit

Calculations:

Name

Section

Date

*BE10-16 Account Titles	Debit	Credit

Calculations:

Name

Section

Date

E10-3

(a) Cost of land:

(b)

E10-4

1.

2.

3.

4.

5.

6.

7.

8.

9.

10.

Name

Section

Date

E10-5

(a)

(b) Year	Computation: Units of Activity	X	Computation: Depreciation Cost/Unit	=	Annual Depreciation Expense	End of Year Accumulated Depreciation	Book Value
2008							
2009							
2010							
2011							

E10-6

(a) Straight-line method:

(b) Units-of-activity method:

(c) Declining-balance method:

Name

Section

Date

Exercise 10-7

Brainiac Company

(a)

(1) 2008:

2009:

(2) Calculation of depreciation cost per unit:

2008:

2009:

(3) 2008:

2009:

(b)

	Account Tiles	Debit	Credit
(1)			

(2) Balance sheet presentation:

Name

Section

Date

E10-8

Type of Asset	Building	Warehouse
(a)		

(b)

Date	Account Titles	Debit	Credit
Dec. 31			

E10-9

Date	Account Titles	Debit	Credit
Jan. 1			
June 30			
30			
Dec. 31			
31			

Name

Section

Date

Exercise 10-10

Beka Company

	Account Titles	Debit	Credit
(a)			
(b)			
(c)			
(d)			

Name
Section
Date

E10-11

Date	Account Titles	Debit	Credit
(a)			
Dec. 31			

Calculations

(b)

E10-12

Date	Account Titles	Debit	Credit
Dec. 31			

E10-13

Date	Account Titles	Debit	Credit
1/2/08			
4/1/08			
7/1/08			
9/1/08			
12/31/08			

Ending balances:

Patent	
Goodwill	
Franchise	
R&D expense	

E10-14

Asset turnover ratio

***E10-15**

Account Titles	Debit	Credit
(a)		

Calculations:

(b) Account Titles	Debit	Credit

Calculations:

Name | *Exercise 10-16
Section
Date | Coran's Delivery Company

Date	Account Titles	Debit	Credit
(a)			

Calculations:

(b)

Account Titles	Debit	Credit

Calculations:

Name

Section

Date

Problem 10-1A

Diaz Company

Item	Land	Building	Other Accounts	
			Amount	Account Titles
1.				
2.				
3.				
4.				
5.				
6.				
7.				
8.				
9.				
10.				

Name

Section

Date

Problem 10-2A

Juresic Transportation

	Year	Computation	Cumulative, 12/31
(a)		BUS 1	
	2006		
	2007		
	2008		
		BUS 2	
	2006		
	2007		
	2008		
		BUS 3	
	2007		
	2008		

	Year	Depreciation Computation	Expense
(b)		BUS 2	
	(1) 2006		
	(2) 2007		

Name

Section

Date

Problem 10-3A

Pele Company

Total cost of machinery:

(a) (1)

Account Titles	Debit	Credit

(2) Annual depreciation:

Account Titles	Debit	Credit

(b) (1)

(2)

Year	Book Value at Beginning of Year	DDB Rate	Annual Depreciation Expense	Accumulated Depreciation
2008				
2009				
2010				
2011				

Name
Section
Date

Pele Company

(b) (Continued) and (c)

(b) (3) Depreciation cost per unit:

Year	Computation	Depreciation Expense
2008		
2009		
2010		
2011		

(c)

Name

Section

Date

Problem 10-4A

Lehman Company

Year		Depreciation Expense	Accumulated Depreciation
2006			
2007			
2008			
2009			
2010			
2011			
2012			

Supporting calculations:

Name Problem 10-5A

Section

Date Jimenez Company

(a) General Journal

Date	Account Titles	Debit	Credit
Apr. 1			
May 1			
1			

Calculations:

Date	Account Titles	Debit	Credit
June 1			
July 1			
Dec. 31			
31			

Calculations:

Name

Section

Date

Problem 10-5A Continued

Jiminez Company

(b)

General Journal

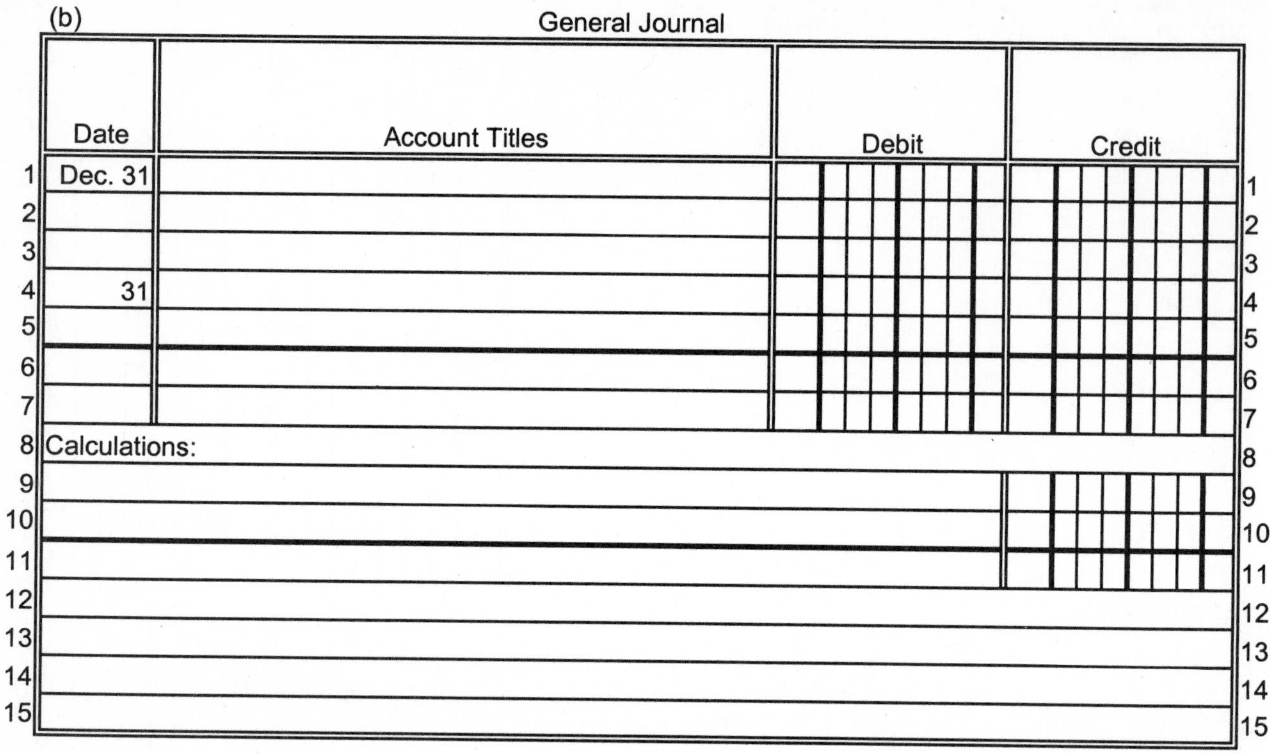

Date	Account Titles	Debit	Credit
Dec. 31			
31			

Calculations:

(c)

Jimenez Company

Partial Balance Sheet

December 31, 2009

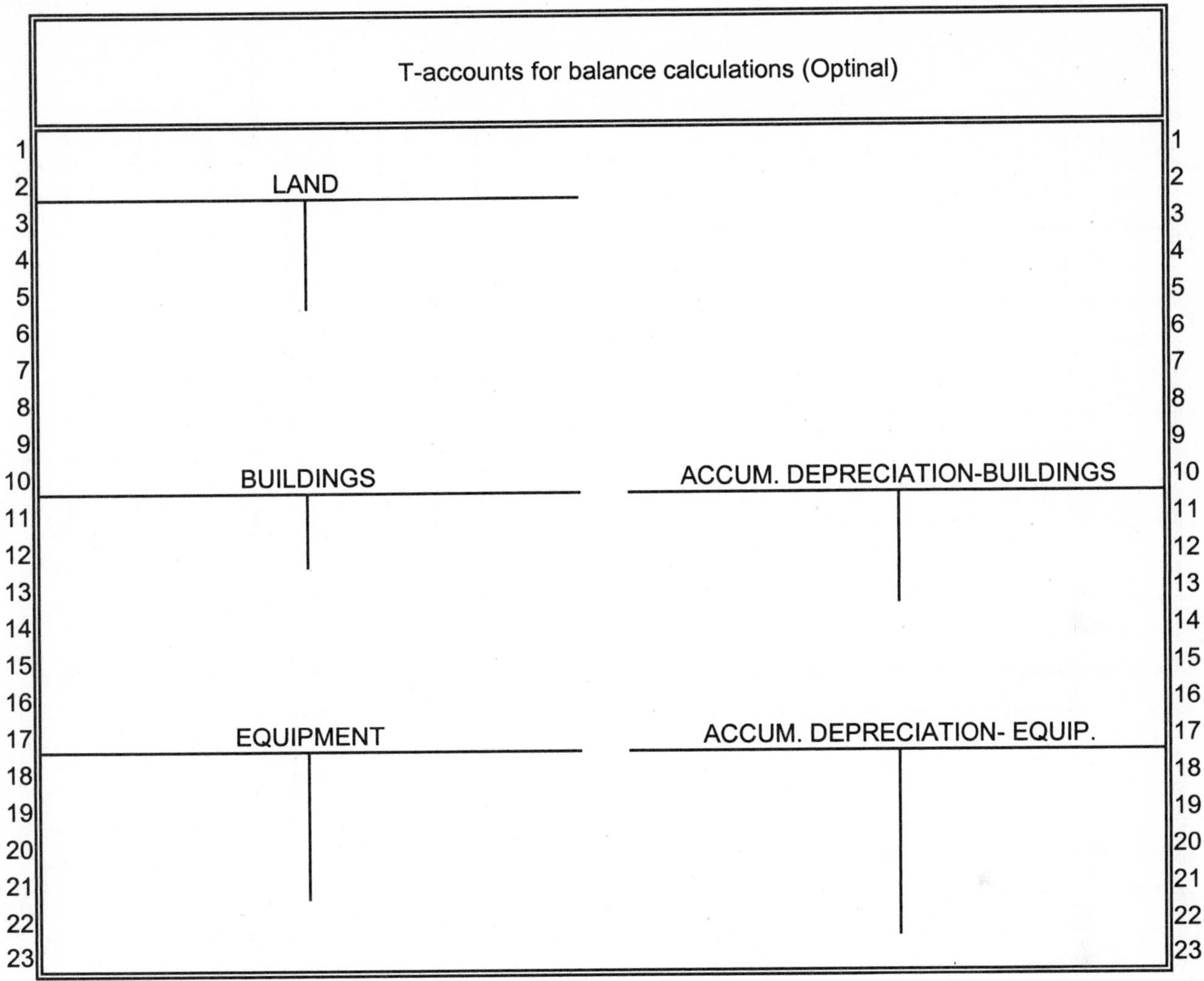
T-accounts for balance calculations (Optinal)
LAND
BUILDINGS
ACCUM. DEPRECIATION-BUILDINGS
EQUIPMENT
ACCUM. DEPRECIATION- EQUIP.

Name

Section

Date

Problem 10-6A

Puckett Co.

	Account Titles	Debit	Credit
(a)			
(b)			
(c)			

Name Problem 10-7A

Section

Date Redeker Company

General Journal

Date	Account Titles	Debit	Credit
(a)			
Jan. 2			
Jan. -			
June			
Sept. 1			
Oct. 1			
(b)			
Dec. 31			
31			

(c) Intangible Assets:

Name

Section

Date

Problem 10-8A

Thorne Company

General Journal

	Account Titles	Debit	Credit
1.			
2.			

Name

Section

Date

Problem 10-1B

Selmon Company

Item	Land	Building	Other Accounts	
			Amount	Account Titles
1.				
2.				
3.				
4.				
5.				
6.				
7.				
8.				
9.				
10.				

Name

Section

Date

Problem 10-2B

Escobar Company

	Year	Computation	Cumulative, 12/31
(a)		MACHINE 1	
	2005		
	2006		
	2007		
	2008		
		MACHINE 2	
	2006		
	2007		
	2008		
		MACHINE 3	
	2008		

	Year	Depreciation Computation	Expense
(b)		MACHINE 2	
	(1) 2006		
	(2) 2007		

Name | Problem 10-3B

Section

Date | Guthrie Company

Total cost of machinery:

(a) (1)

Account Titles	Debit	Credit

(2) Annual depreciation:

Account Titles	Debit	Credit

(b) (1)

(2)

Year	Book Value at Beginning of Year	DDB Rate	Annual Depreciation Expense	Accumulated Depreciation
2008				
2009				
2010				
2011				

(b) (Continued) and (c)

(b) (3) Depreciation cost per unit:

	Year	Computation	Depreciation Expense
	2008		
	2009		
	2010		
	2011		

(c)

Name | Problem 10-4B
Section
Date | Hadaway Company

Year		Depreciation Expense	Accumulated Depreciation
2006			
2007			
2008			
2009			
2010			
2011			
2012			

Supporting calculations:

Name | Problem 10-5B
Section
Date | Yockey Company

(a) General Journal

Date	Account Titles	Debit	Credit
Apr. 1			
May 1			
1			

Calculations:

Date	Account Titles	Debit	Credit
June 1			
July 1			
Dec. 31			
31			

Calculations:

(b) General Journal

Date	Account Titles	Debit	Credit
Dec. 31			
31			

Calculations:

(c)

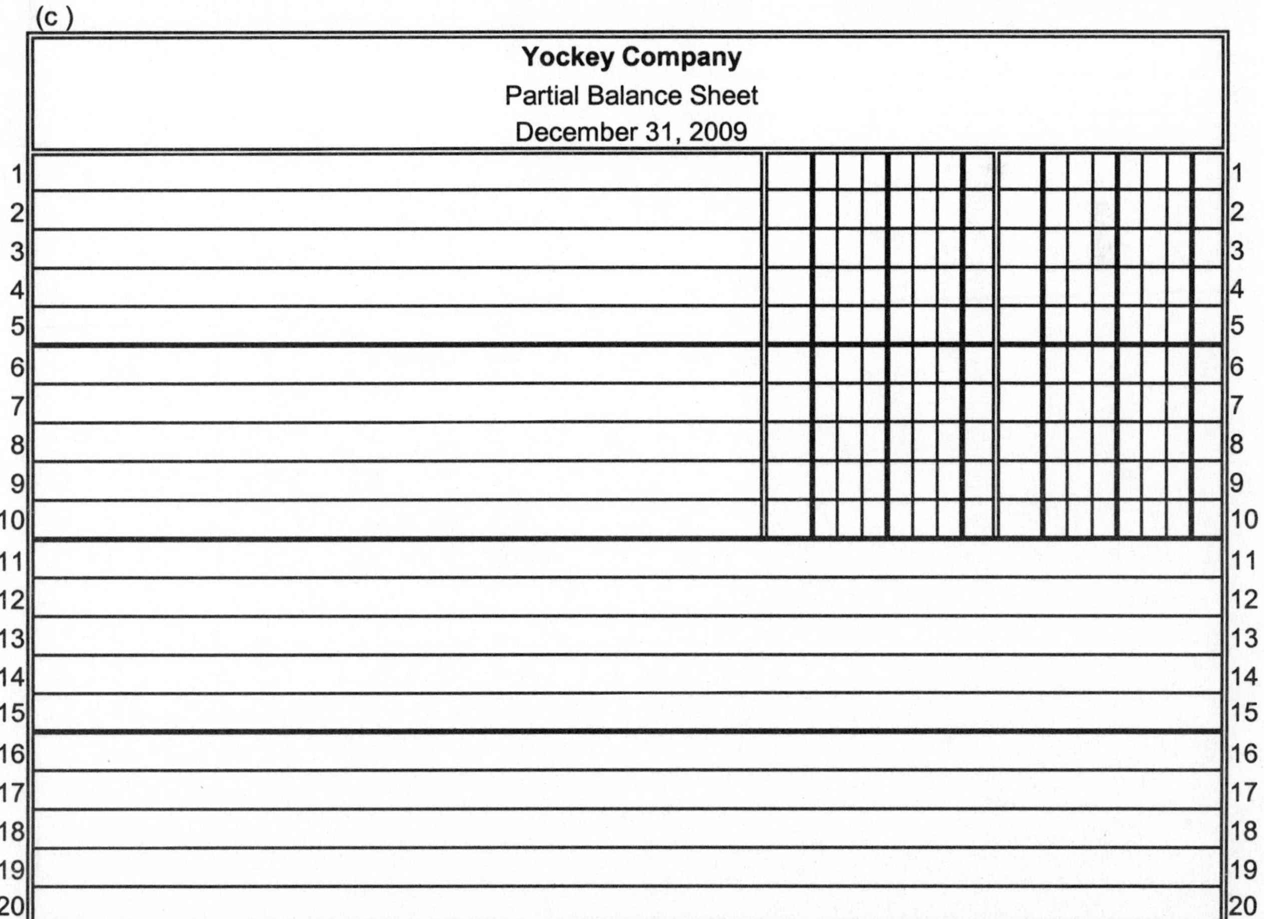

Yockey Company
Partial Balance Sheet
December 31, 2009

Name | Problem 10-5B Concluded
Section
Date | Yockey Company

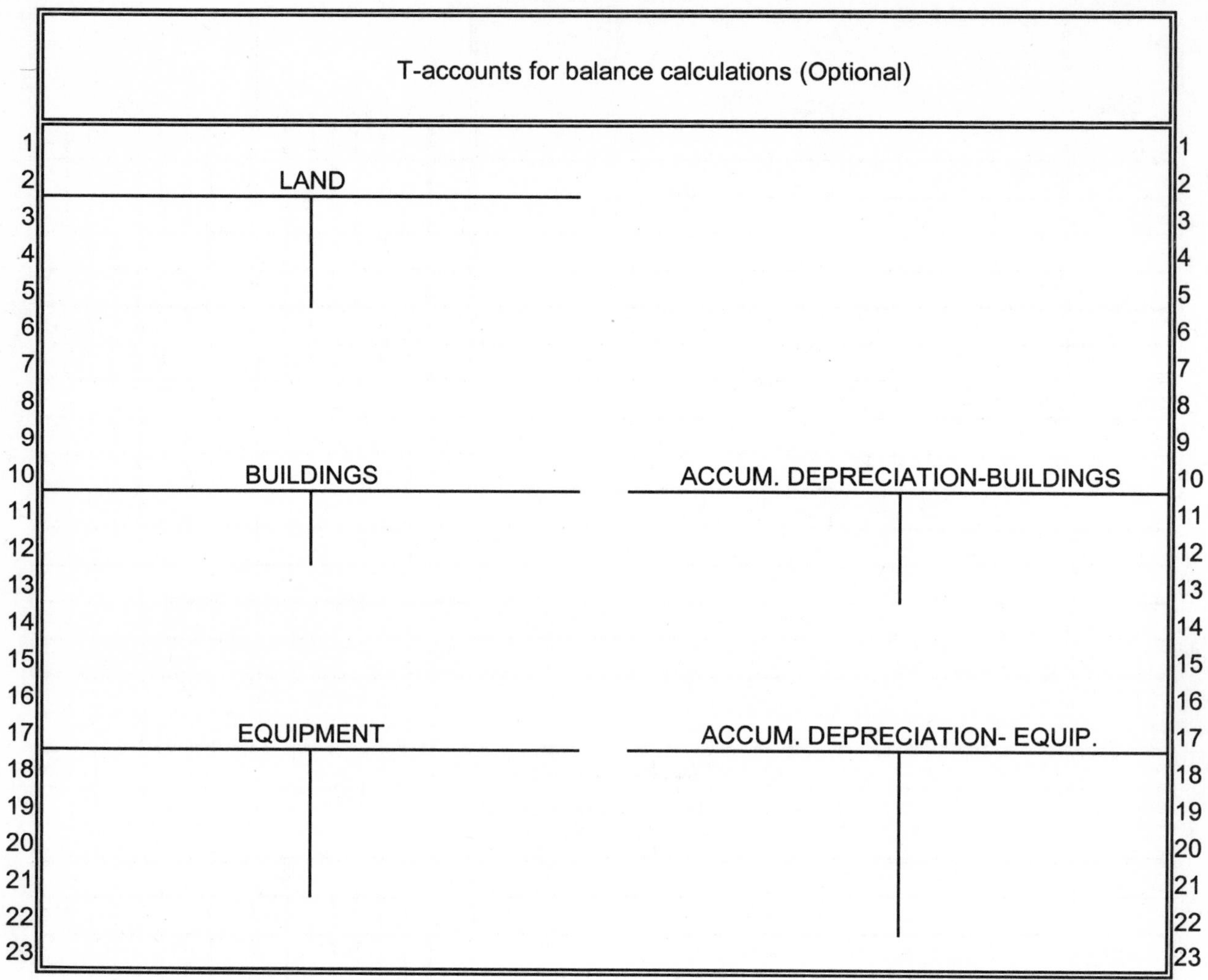

Name

Section

Date

Problem 10-6B

Riggs Co.

Account Titles	Debit	Credit
(a)		
(b)		
(c)		

Name | Problem 10-7B

Section

Date | Justen Company

General Journal

Date	Account Titles	Debit	Credit
(a)			
Jan. 2			
Jan -			
June			
Sept. 1			
Oct. 1			
(b)			
Dec. 31			
31			

(c) Intangible Assets:

(d)

Name Problem 10-8B

Section

Date Duby Company

General Journal

	Account Titles	Debit	Credit
1.			
2.			

(a)

	Account Titles	Debit	Credit
1.			
2.			
3.			
4.			
5.			
6.			
7.			
8.			
9.			
10.			

(a) (Continued)

	Account Titles	Debit	Credit
11.			
12.			
13.			

(b)

Winterschid Company
Trial Balance
December 31, 2008

	Debits	Credits
Cash		
Accounts Receivable		
Notes Receivable		
Interest Receivable		
Merchandise Inventory		
Prepaid Insurance		
Land		
Building		
Equipment		
Patent		
Allowance for Doubtful Accounts		
Accumulated Depreciation - Building		
Accumulated Depreciation - Equipment		
Accounts Payable		
Salaries Payable		
Unearned Rent		
Notes Payable (short-term)		
Interest Payable		
Notes Payable (long-term)		
Winterschid, Capital		
Winterschid, Drawing		
Sales		
Interest Revenue		
Rent Revenue		
Gain on Disposal		
Bad Debts Expense		
Cost of Goods Sold		
Depreciation Expense - Building		
Depreciation Expense - Equipment		
Insurance Expense		
Interest Expense		
Other Operating Expense		
Amortization Expense - Patents		
Salaries Expense		
Totals		

Name

Section

Date

(c)

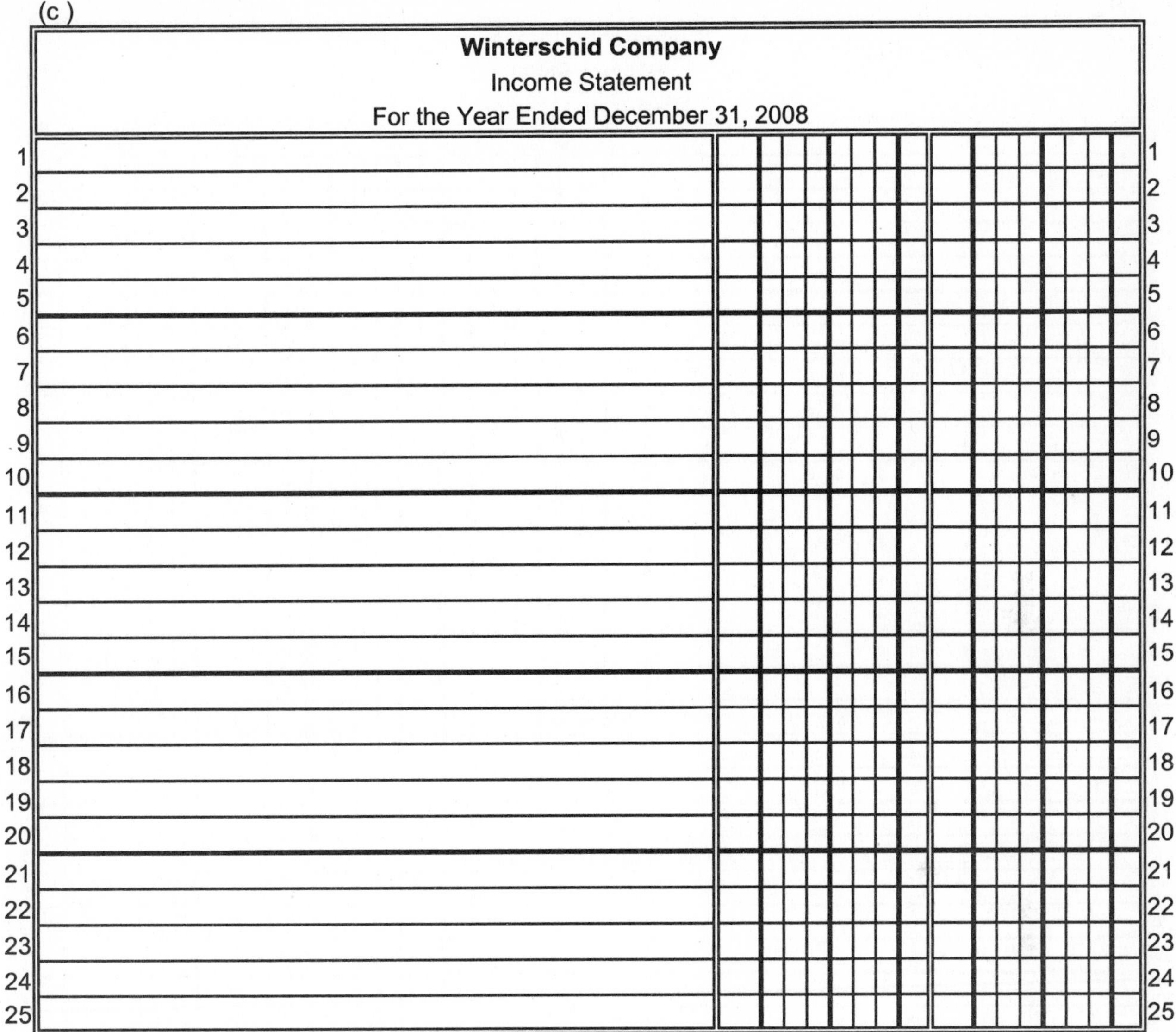

Winterschid Company
Income Statement
For the Year Ended December 31, 2008

Winterschid Company

Owner's Equity Statement

For the Year Ended December 31, 2008

(d)

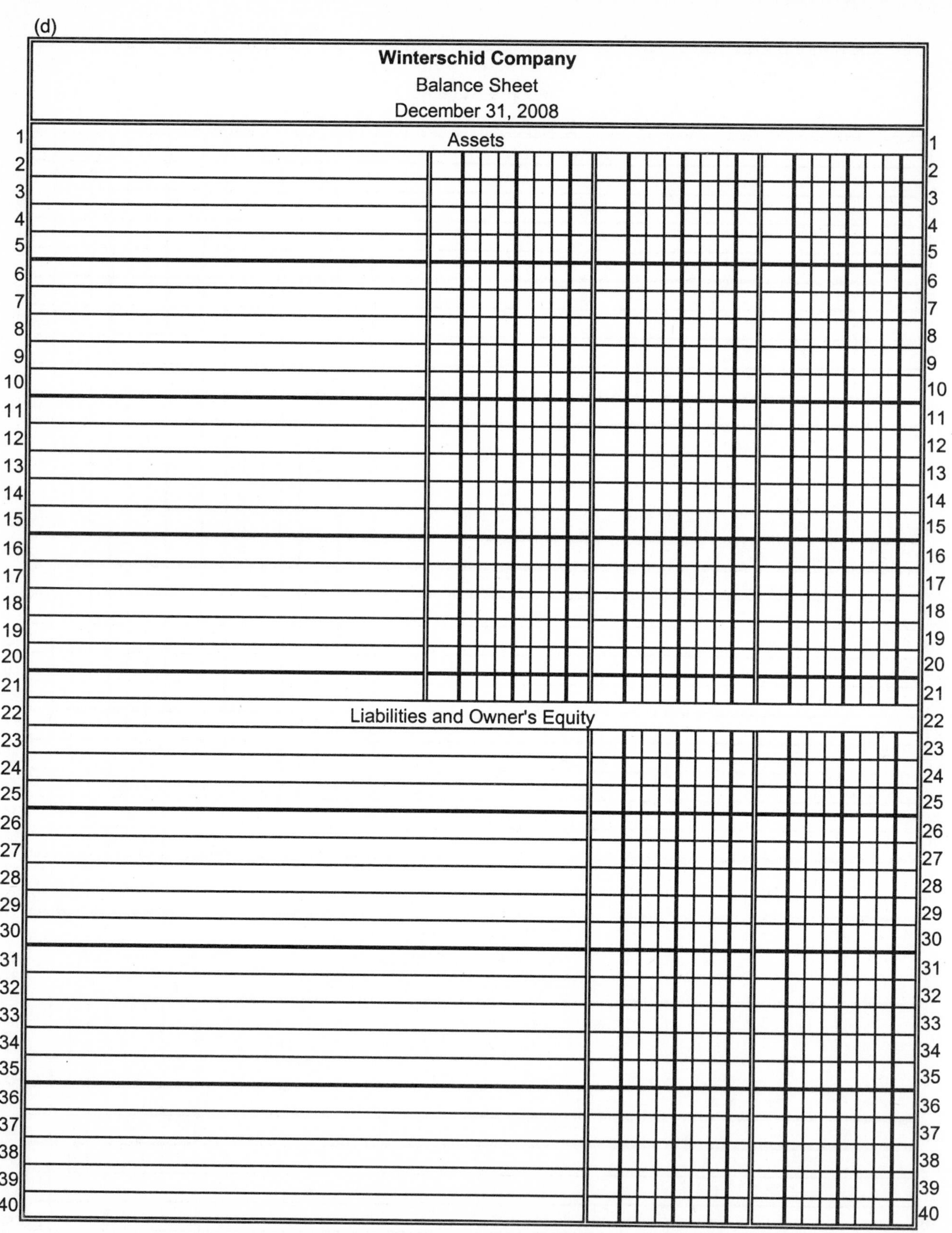

Winterschid Company
Balance Sheet
December 31, 2008

Assets

Liabilities and Owner's Equity

(a) Reimer Company- Straight-line method

Lingo Company- Double-declining-balance method

Year	Asset	Computation	Annual Depreciation	Accumulated Depreciation
2006	Building			
	Equipment			
2007	Building			
	Equipment			
2008	Building			
	Equipment			

(b) Year	Reimer Company Net Income	Lingo Co. Net Inc. as Adjusted	Computations for Lingo Company
2006			
2007			
2008			
Total			

(c)

Name

Section

Date

Chapter 10 Ethics Case

Buster Container Company

(a)

(b)

(c)

Old Estimates

Revised Estimates

Name

Section

Date

BE11-1

(a)

(b)

(c)

(d)

BE11-2

Date	Account Titles	Debit	Credit
July 1			
Dec 31			

BE11-3

Date	Account Titles	Debit	Credit
Mar. 16			

Name
Section
Date

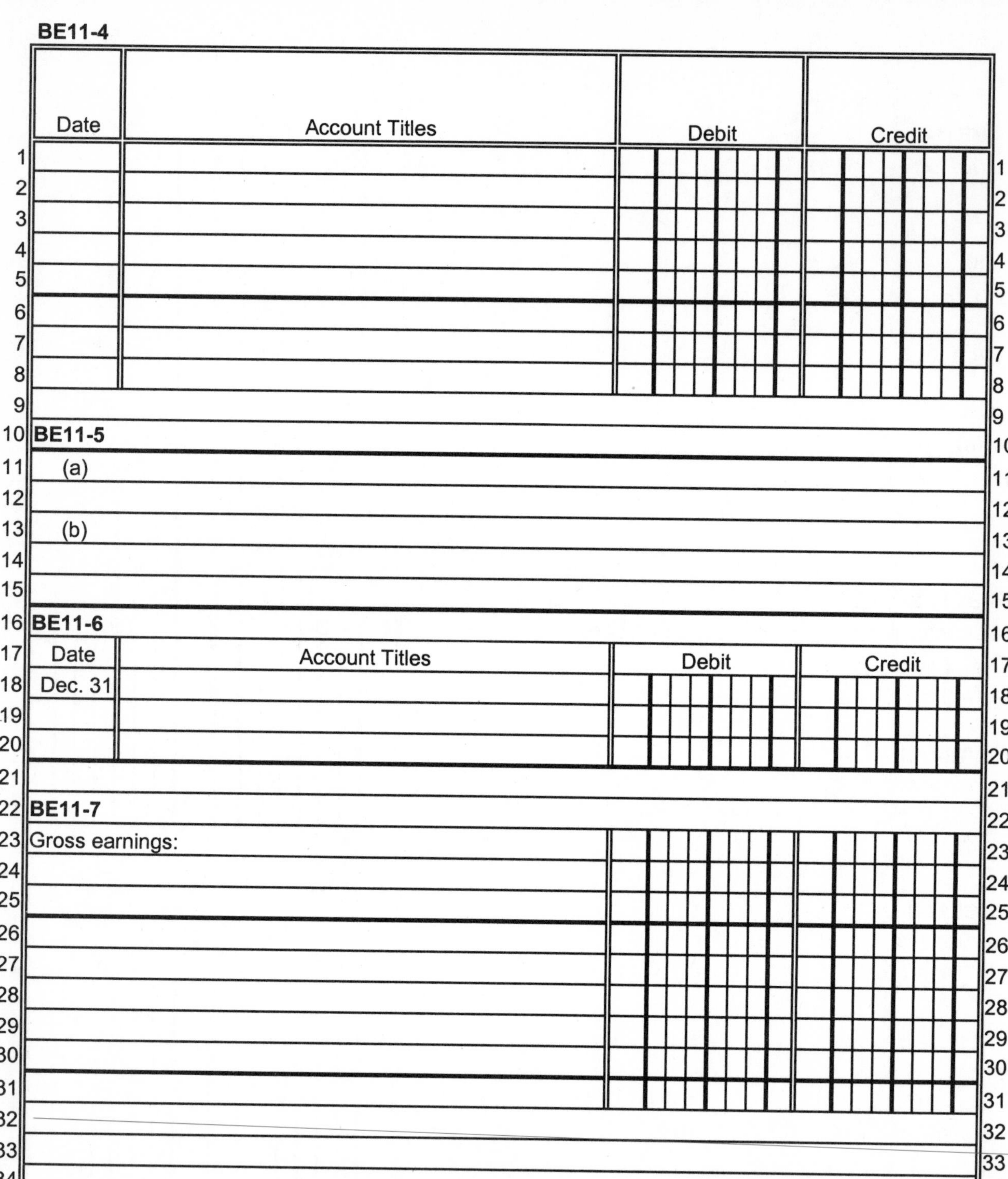

BE11-4

Date	Account Titles	Debit	Credit

BE11-5

(a)

(b)

BE11-6

Date	Account Titles	Debit	Credit
Dec. 31			

BE11-7

Gross earnings:

Name

Section

Date

BE11-8

Date	Account Titles	Debit	Credit
Jan. 15			
15			

BE11-9

Date	Account Titles	Debit	Credit
Jan. 31			

BE11-10

(a)

(b)

(c)

(d)

***BE11-11**

Date	Account Titles	Debit	Credit
Jan. 31			

Name

Section

Date

Exercise 11-1

Rob Judson Company

Date	Account Titles	Debit	Credit
	July 1, 2008		
	November 1, 2008		
	December 31, 2008		
	February 1, 2009		
	April 1, 2009		

Name

Section

Date

E11-2

Date	Account Titles	Debit	Credit
(a)			
June 1			
(b)			
June 30			
(c)			
Dec. 1			

(d)

E11-3

Date	Account Titles	Debit	Credit
	Warkentinne Company		
Apr. 10			
	Rivera Company		
15			

Name

Section

Date

E11-4

Date	Account Titles	Debit	Credit
(a)			
Nov. 30			
(b)			
Dec. 31			
(c)			
Mar. 31			

E11-5

(a) Estimated warrranties outstanding:

Month	Estimate	Units Defective	Outstanding
November			
December			
Total			

Date	Account Titles	Debit	Credit
(b)			
(c)			

Name

Section

Date

E11-6

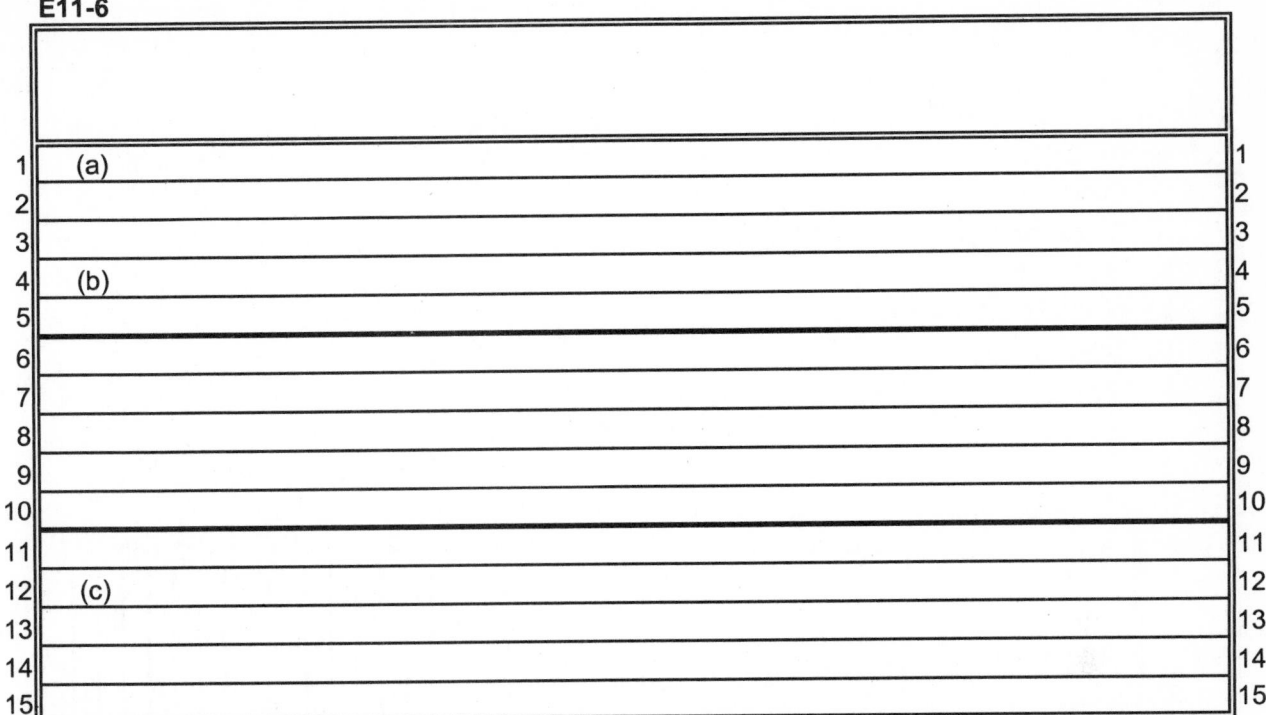

E11-7 (a)

Jewett Online Company

Partial Balance Sheet

(b)

Name

Section

Date

E11-10

(a)

(1) Reular

Overtime

Gross earnings

(2) FICA taxes

(3) Federal income taxes

(4) State income taxes

(5) Net pay

(b)

Date	Account Titles	Debit	Credit

E11-11

C. Ogle

D. Delgado

L. Jeter

T. Spivey

Name | Exercise 11-12

Section

Date | Alvamar Company

(a)

Alvamar Company
Payroll Register
For the Week Ending January 31

Employee	Total Hours	Earnings: Regular	Earnings: Overtime	Earnings: Gross Pay
M. Hashmi				
E. Benson				
K. Kern				
Totals				

(a) Continued

Alvamar Company
Payroll Register (continued)
For the Week Ending January 31

	Deductions: FICA Taxes	Deductions: Federal Income Taxes	Deductions: Health Insurance	Deductions: Total	Net Pay
Hashmi					
Benson					
Kern					
Totals					

(b)

Date	Account Titles	Debit	Credit
Jan 31			
31			

Name

Section

Date

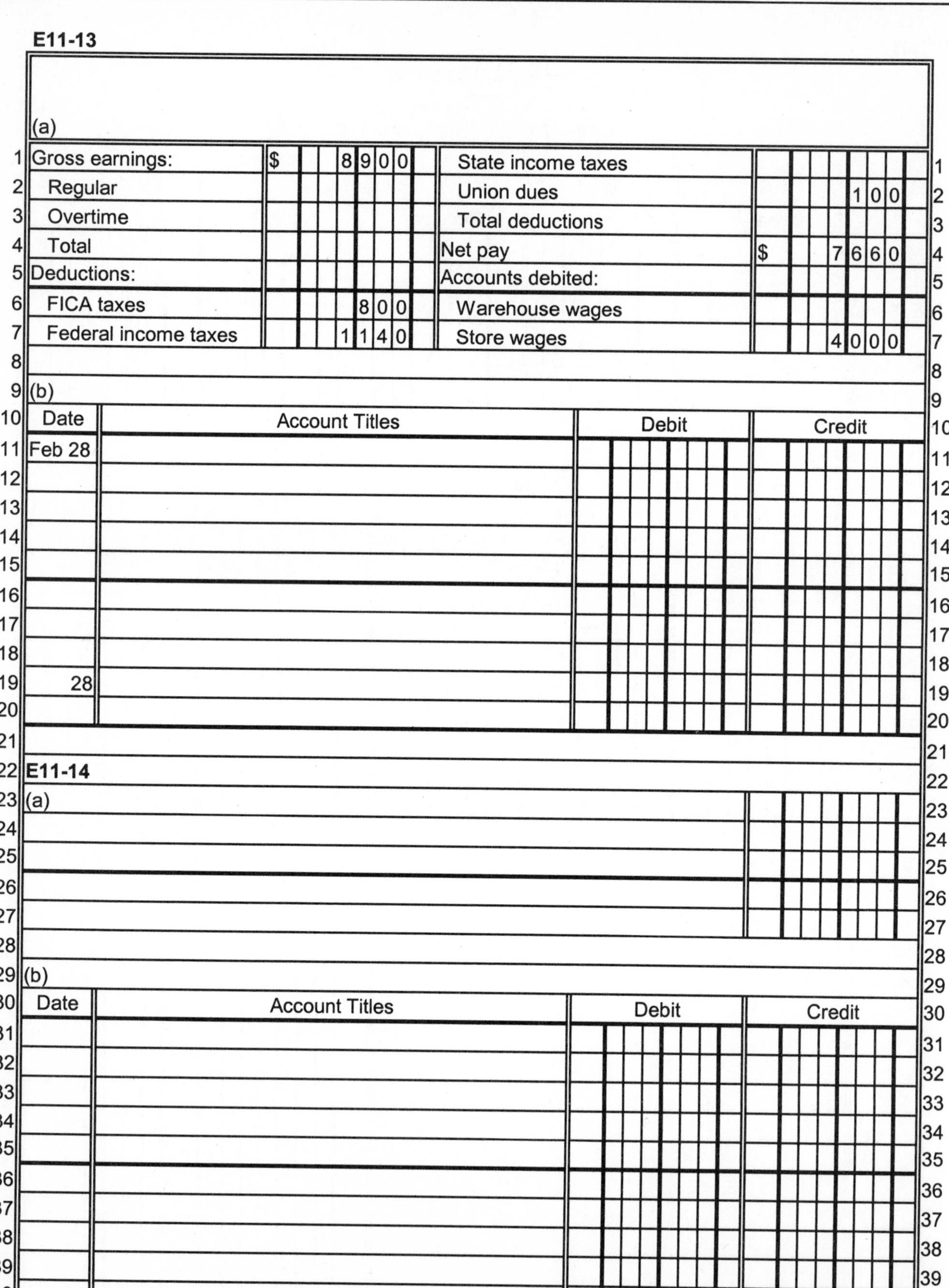

E11-13

(a)

Gross earnings:	$ 8900	State income taxes	
Regular		Union dues	100
Overtime		Total deductions	
Total		Net pay	$ 7660
Deductions:		Accounts debited:	
FICA taxes	800	Warehouse wages	
Federal income taxes	1140	Store wages	4000

(b)

Date	Account Titles	Debit	Credit
Feb 28			
28			

E11-14

(a)

(b)

Date	Account Titles	Debit	Credit

Name

Section

Date

*Exercises 11-15 and 11-16

***E11-15**

Date	Account Titles	Debit	Credit
Mar. 31			
31			

***E11-16**

Date	Account Titles	Debit	Credit
1.			
2.			
3.			

Name

Section

Date

Problem 11-1A

Mane Company

Date	Account Titles	Debit	Credit
(a)			
Jan 5			
12			
14			
20			
21			
25			
(b) (1)			
Jan 31			
(2)			
31			

Name

Section

Date

(c)

Mane Company Balance Sheet (Partial) January 31, 2008		
Current liabilities:		

Name | Problem 11-2A
Section
Date | Winsky Company

(a)

Date	Account Titles	Debit	Credit
Jan 2			
Feb 1			
Mar 31			
Apr 1			
July 1			
Sept 30			
Oct 1			
Dec 1			
Dec 31			

(c)

Winsky Company
Balance Sheet (Partial)
December 31

Current liabilities:		

(b)

NOTES PAYABLE

INTEREST PAYABLE

INTEREST EXPENSE

(d)

Name | Problem 11-3A
Section
Date | Del Hardware

(a)

Del Hardware
Payroll Register
For the Week Ended March 15, 2008

Employee	Hours	Earnings		
		Regular	Over-time	Gross Pay
Joe Devena	40			
Mary Keener	42			
Andy Dye	44			
Kim Shen	46			
Totals				

Deductions				
FICA Taxes	Fed. Inc. Tax	State Inc. Tax	United Fund	Total
			$ 5	
			5	
	60		5	
	61		5	

Net Pay	Store Wages Exp.	Office Wages Exp.

Name

Section

Date

Problem 11-3A Concluded

Del Hardware

Date	Account Titles	Debit	Credit
(b)			
Mar 15			
15			
(c)			
Mar 16			
(d)			
Mar 31			

Name | Problem 11-4A
Section
Date | Armitage Company

Date	Account Titles	Debit	Credit
(a)			
Jan 10			
12			
15			
17			
20			
31			
31			
(b) 1.			
Jan 31			
*2.			
31			

Name Problem 11-5A

Section

Date Blasing Electrical Repair Company

Date	Account Titles	Debit	Credit
(a)			
(b)			

(c)

Employee	Wages, Tips, Other Compensation	Federal Income Tax Withheld	State Income Tax Withheld	FICA Wages	FICA Tax Withheld
J.EcKman	59000	28500			
S. Bishop	26000	10200			

Name | Problem 11-1B
Section
Date | Payless Software Company

Date	Account Titles	Debit	Credit
(a)			
Jan 1			
5			
12			
14			
20			
25			
(b) (1)			
Jan 31			
(2)			
31			

(c)

Payless Software Company
Balance Sheet (Partial)
January 31, 2008

Current liabilities:		

Name | Problem 11-2B

Section

Date | Zimmer Company

(a)

Date	Account Titles	Debit	Credit
Jan 2			
Feb 1			
Mar 31			
Apr 1			
July 1			
Sept 30			
Oct 1			
Dec 1			
Dec 31			

(c)

Zimmer Company

Balance Sheet (Partial)

December 31

Current liabilities:		

(b)

NOTES PAYABLE

INTEREST PAYABLE

INTEREST EXPENSE

(d)

Name	Problem 11-3B
Section	
Date	Hiller Drug Store

(a)

Hiller Drug Store
Payroll Register
For the Week Ended February 15, 2008

Employee	Hours	Earnings		
		Regular	Over-time	Gross Pay
L. Steck	34			
S. Jabar	42			
M. Cape	44			
L. Wild	46			
Totals				

Deductions				
FICA Taxes	Fed. Inc. Tax	State Inc. Tax	United Fund	Total
			$	
			5.70	
	61		7.50	
	46		5.00	

Net Pay	Store Wages Exp.	Office Wages Exp.

Name

Section

Date

Problem 11-3B Concluded

Hiller Drug Store

Date	Account Titles	Debit	Credit
(b)			
Feb 15			
15			
(c)			
Feb 16			
(d)			
Feb 28			

Name

Section

Date

Problem 11-4B

Pettiegrew Company

Date	Account Titles	Debit	Credit
(a)			
Jan 10			
12			
15			
17			
20			
31			
31			
(b) 1.			
Jan 31			
*2.			
31			

Name Problem 11-5B

Section

Date R. Uhlman Company

Date	Account Titles	Debit	Credit
(a)			
(b)			

(c)

Employee	Wages, Tips, Other Compensation	Federal Income Tax Withheld	State Income Tax Withheld	FICA Wages	FICA Tax Withheld
R. Lopez	60000	27500			
K. Vopat	27000	11000			

(a)

(b)

(c)

Name

Section

Date

Metcalfe Services Inc.

(a)

Metcalfe Services Inc.

Month	Number of Employees	Days Worked	Daily Rate	Cost
January - March				
April - May				
June - October				
November - December				
Total Cost				

Payroll Costs for Kensingtown's Permanent Employees

(b)

Name

Section

Date

(a)

(b)

(c)

(d)

(e)

(f)

Total taxes:

Name

Section

Date

BE12-1	Debit	Credit

BE12-2

	Debit	Credit

BE12-3

Calculation of net income division:

	Debit	Credit

BE12-4	Division of Net Income			
	Espino	Sears	Utech	Total

Name

Section

Date

BE12-5	Division of Net Income		
	Joe	Sam	Total

BE12-6 Account Titles	Debit	Credit

*BE12-7 Account Titles	Debit	Credit

*BE12-8 Account Titles	Debit	Credit

*BE12-9 Account Titles	Debit	Credit

*BE12-10 Account Titles	Debit	Credit

Name

Section

Date

E12-1

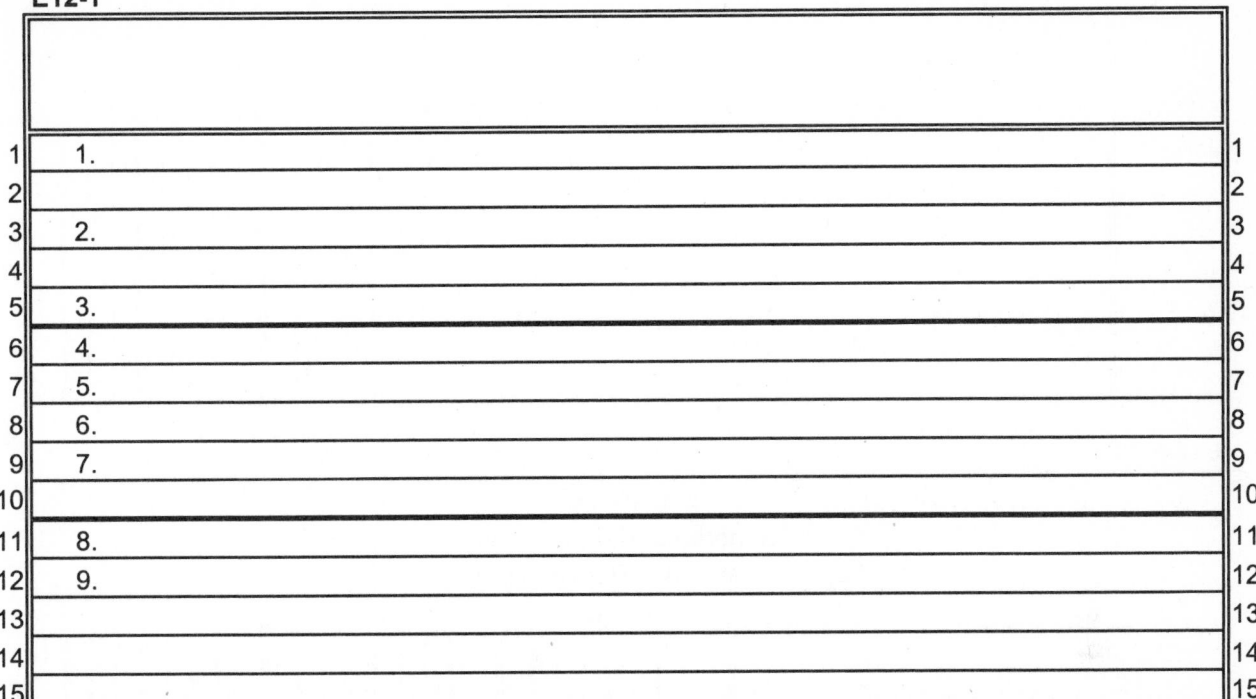

1.

2.

3.

4.

5.

6.

7.

8.

9.

E12-2

Account Titles	Debit	Credit
(a)		

(b)

Name

Section

Date

E12-3

Date	Account Titles	Debit	Credit
Jan 1			

E12-6 (a)

Starrite Co.
Partners' Capital Statement
For the Year Ended December 31, 2008

	G. Stark	J. Nyland	Total

(b)

Starrite Co.
Partial Balance Sheet
December 31, 2008

Owner's Equity		

Name | Exercise 12-4

Section

Date | F. Calvert and G. Powers

(a)

	F. Calvert	G. Powers	Total
(1) Net income is $50,000:			
(2) Net income is $36,000:			

(b)

	Debit	Credit
(1) Net income is $50,000:		
(2) Net income is $36,000:		

Name | Exercise 12-5

Section

Date | O. Guillen and K. Williams

Account Titles	Debit	Credit
(a)		
(b)		
(c)		
(d)		

Name

Section

Date

Exercise 12-7

The Stooges Partnership

The Stooges Partnership

Balance Sheet

December 31, 2008

Assets

Liabilities and Owner's Equity

Name | Exercise 12-8
Section
Date | The Best Company

The Best Company
Schedule of Cash Payments

	Item	Cash	Non-cash Assets	Liabilities	Rodriquez Capital	Escobedo Capital	
1							1
2							2
3							3
4							4
5							5
6							6
7							7
8							8
9							9
10							10
11							11
12							12
13							13
14							14
15							15
16							16
17							17
18							18
19							19
20							20

Name

Section

Date

E12-9

	Account Titles	Debit	Credit
(a)			
(b)			
(c)			
(d)			

E12-10

	Account Titles	Debit	Credit
(a) (1)			
(2)			
(b) (1)			
(2)			

Name *Exercises 12-11 and 12-13

Section

Date

***E12-11**

	Account Titles	Debit	Credit
(a)			
(b)			
(c)			

***E12-13**

	Account Titles	Debit	Credit
1.			
2.			
3.			

Name
Section
Date

*Exercise 12-12

G. Olde and R. Young

	Account Titles	Debit	Credit
(a)			

Calculation of Twener's capital account and bonus to old partners:

	Account Titles	Debit	Credit
(b)			

Calculation of Twener's capital account and bonus to new partner:

Name *Exercise 12-14

Section

Date H. Barrajas, T. Dingler, and R. Fisk

	Account Titles	Debit	Credit
1.			

Calculation of bonus to retiring partner and allocation of bonus to remaining partners:

2.	Account Titles	Debit	Credit

Calculation of bonus to remaining partners and allocation of bonus:

Name | *Exercise 12-15

Section

Date | Carson, Letterman, and O'Brien

	Account Titles	Debit	Credit
(a)			
(b)			

Name

Section

Date

Problem 12-1A

Pasa Company

(a)

Date	Account Titles	Debit	Credit
Jan 1			
1			

(b)

Date	Account Titles	Debit	Credit
Jan 1			
1			

(c)

Pasa Company
Balance Sheet
January 1, 2008

Assets

Liabilities and Owners' Equity

Name | Problem 12-2A
Section
Date | CNU Company

(a)

	Account Titles	Debit	Credit
(1)			
(2)			

Calculation to support net income distribution for (a)(2) above:

	Account Titles	Debit	Credit
(3)			

Calculations to support net income distribution for (a)(3) above:

(b)

CNU Company

Division of Net Income

	Reese Caplin	Phyllis Newell	Betty Uhrich	Total

(c)

CNU Company

Partners' Capital Statement

For the Year Ended December 31, 2008

	Reese Caplin	Phyllis Newell	Betty Uhrich	Total

Name

Section

Date

Problem 12-3A

New Yorker Company

(a)

	Account Titles	Debit	Credit
(1)			

	Account Titles	Debit	Credit
(2)			
(3)			
(4)			
(5)			

Name

Section

Date

New Yorker Company

(b)

Cash	
Bal 27,500	

M. Mantle, Capital	
	Bal. 33,000

W. Mays, Capital	
	Bal 21,000

D. Snider, Capital	
	Bal. 3,000

(c)

Account Titles	Debit	Credit
(1)		
(2)		

Name

Section

Date

*Problem 12-4A

SKG Company

(a)

	Account Titles	Debit	Credit
(1)			
(2)			
(3)			

Calculations of bonus paid by new partner and distribution to old partners:

	Account Titles	Debit	Credit
(4)			

Calculation of bonus to new partners:

Name

Section

Date

*Problem 12-4A Concluded

SKG Company

(b)

(1)

(2)

Name

Section

Date

*Problem 12-5A

FAD Company

(a)

	Account Titles	Debit	Credit
(1)			
(2)			
(3)			

Calculation of bonus to Durham in (a)(3) above:

(4)			

Calculation of bonus to old partners in (a)(4) above:

(b) (1)		
(2)		

Name | Problem 12-1B
Section
Date | Free-Will Company

(a)

	Date	Account Titles	Debit	Credit	
1	Jan 1				1
2					2
3					3
4					4
5					5
6					6
7					7
8					8
9					9
10					10
11	1				11
12					12
13					13
14					14
15					15
16					16
17					17
18					18
19					19
20					20

(b)

	Date	Account Titles	Debit	Credit	
1	Jan 1				1
2					2
3					3
4					4
5					5
6	1				6
7					7
8					8
9					9
10					10

(c)

Free-Will Company

Balance Sheet

January 1, 2008

Assets

Liabilities and Owners' Equity

Name

Section

Date

Problem 12-2B

RAF Company

(a)

	Account Titles	Debit	Credit
(1)			
(2)			

Calculation to support net income distribution for (a)(2) above:

	Account Titles	Debit	Credit
(3)			

Calculation to support net income distribution for (a)(3) above:

Name

Section

Date

Problem 12-2B Concluded

RAF Company

(b)

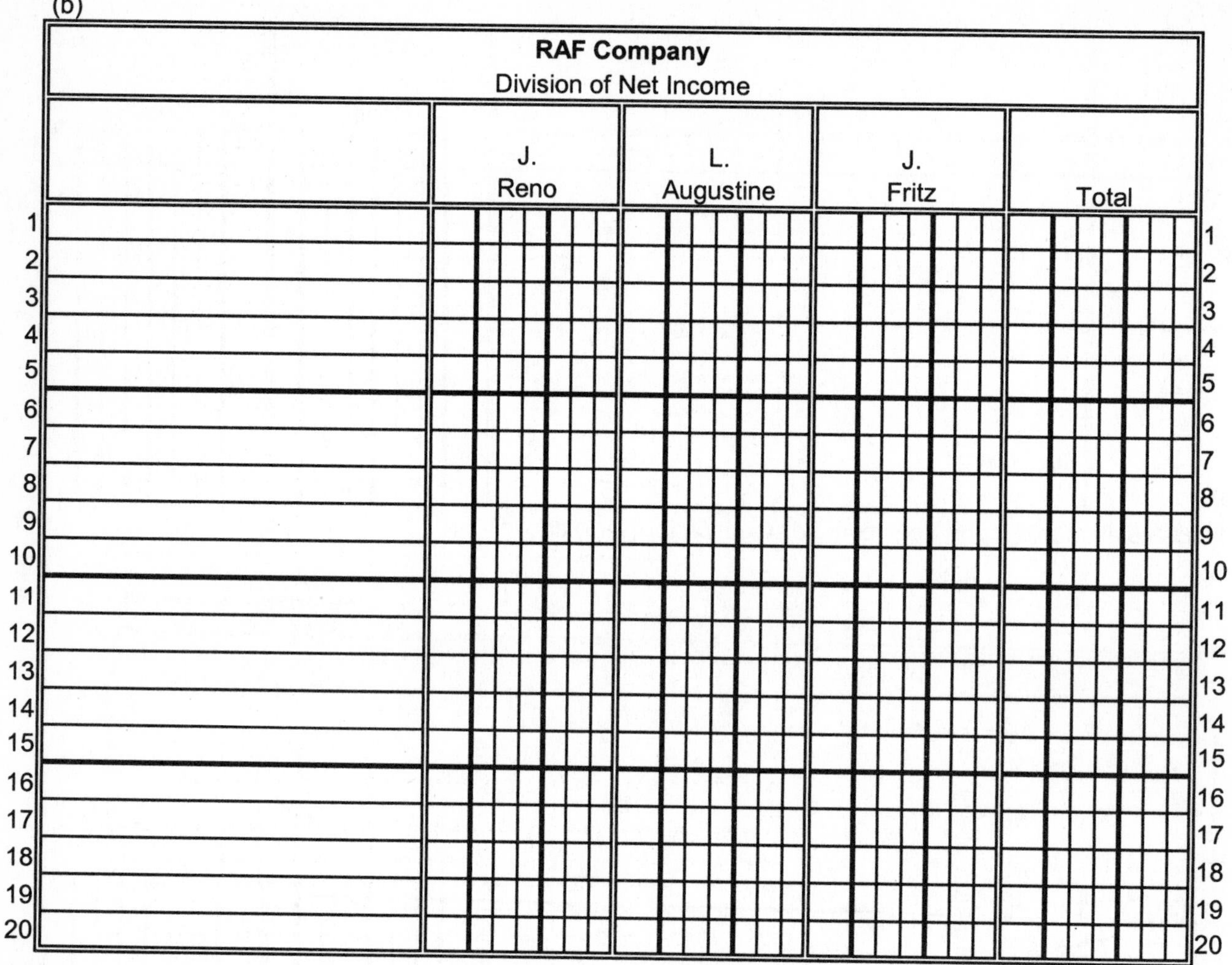

RAF Company

Division of Net Income

	J. Reno	L. Augustine	J. Fritz	Total

(c)

RAF Company

Partners' Capital Statement

For the Year Ended December 31, 2008

	J. Reno	L. Augustine	J. Fritz	Total

Name

Section

Date

Problem 12-3B

Shawnee Company

Shawnee Company

Schedule of Cash Payments

	Item	Cash	Non-cash Assets	Liabilities	Neeley Capital	Hannah Capital	Doonan Capital	
1								1
2								2
3								3
4								4
5								5
6								6
7								7
8								8
9								9
10								10
11								11
12								12
13								13
14								14
15								15
16								16
17								17
18								18
19								19
20								20

Name

Section

Date

Problem 12-3B Continued

Shawnee Company

(b)

	Account Titles	Debit	Credit
(1)			
(2)			
(3)			
(4)			

(c)

Cash

Debit	Credit
4/30 Bal 28,000	

Hannah, Capital

Debit	Credit
	4/30 Bal 11,200

Neeley, Capital

Debit	Credit
	4/30 Bal 23,000

Doonan, Capital

Debit	Credit
	4/30 Bal 4,800

Name
Section
Date

*Problem 12-4B

ANR Company

(a)

	Account Titles	Debit	Credit
(1)			
(2)			
(3)			

Calculation of bonus paid to new partner:

(4)			

Calculation of bonus paid by new partner and distribution to old partners:

(b)

(1)

(2)

Name | *Problem 12-5B
Section
Date | Poker Company

(a)

	Account Titles	Debit	Credit
(1)			
(2)			
(3)			

Calculation of bonus to Jack in (a)(3) above:

	Account Titles	Debit	Credit
(4)			

Calculation of bonus to old partners in (a)(4) above:

(b) (1)		
(2)		

Name
Section
Date

Problem 1-1A

Barone's Repair Shop

(a)

Barone's Repair Shop												
	Assets							=	Liabilities	+	Owner's Equity	
Trans-actions	Cash	+	Accounts Receivable	+	Supplies	+	Equipment	=	Accounts Payable	+	N. Barone, Capital	
1.												
2.												
3.												
4.												
5.												
6.												
7.												
8.												
9.												
10												
11.												

Name Problem 1-2A

Section

Date Maria Gonzalez, Veterinarian

(a)

Maria Gonzalez, Veterinarian

	Assets							=	Liabilities			+	Owner's Equity	
Trans-actions	Cash	+	Accounts Receivable	+	Supplies	+	Office Equipment	=	Notes Payable	+	Accounts Payable	+	M. Gonzalez, Capital	
Bal.	$ 9000		$ 1700		$ 600		$ 6000				$ 3600		$ 13700	
1.														
2.														
3.														
4.														
5.														
6.														
7.														
8.														

Name Problem 1-4A

Section

Date Miller Deliveries

(a)

	Miller Deliveries																
		Assets							=	Liabilities			+	Owner's Equity			
	Date	Cash	+	Accounts Receivable	+	Supplies	+	Delivery Van	=	Notes Payable	+	Accounts Payable	+	M. Miller, Capital			
1	June 1																1
2	2																2
3	3																3
4	5																4
5	9																5
6	12																6
7	15																7
8	17																8
9	20																9
10	23																10
11	26																11
12	29																12
13	30																13
14																	14
15																	15
16																	16
17																	17
18																	18
19																	19
20																	20

Name

Section

Date

Problem 1-1B

Matrix Travel Agency

(a)

Matrix Travel Agency													
	Assets							=	Liabilities	+	Owner's Equity		
Trans-actions	Cash	+	Accounts Receivable	+	Supplies	+	Office Equipment	=	Accounts Payable	+	Jenny Russo, Capital		
1.													
2.													
3.													
4.													
5.													
6.													
7.													
8.													
9.													
10.													

Name	Problem 1-2B
Section	
Date	Cindy Belton, Attorney at Law

(a)

Cindy Belton, Attorney at Law

	Trans-actions	Assets							=	Liabilities			+	Owner's Equity		
		Cash	+	Accounts Receivable	+	Supplies	+	Office Equipment	=	Notes Payable	±	Accounts Payable	+	Cinndy Belton, Capital		
1	Bal.	4 4000		$ 1500		$ 500		$ 5000				$ 4200		$ 6800		1
2	1.															2
3																3
4	2.															4
5																5
6	3.															6
7																7
8	4.															8
9																9
10	5.															10
11																11
12																12
13																13
14	6.															14
15																15
16	7.															16
17																17
18	8.															18
19																19
20																20

Name | Problem 1-4B
Section
Date | Geller Consulting

(a)

Geller Consulting														
	Assets							=	Liabilities			+	Owner's Equity	
Date	Cash	+	Accounts Receivable	+	Supplies	+	Office Equipment	=	Notes Payable	+	Accounts Payable	+	L. Geller, Capital	
May 1														
2														
3														
5														
9														
12														
15														
17														
20														
23														
26														
29														
30														

Name | Chapter 4 Brief Exercises

Section

Date | Ley Company

BE4-2

Ley Company
Worksheet

	Account Titles	Trial Balance		Adjustments		Adjusted Trial Balance		Income Statement		Balance Sheet		
		Debit	Credit	Debit	Credit	Debit	Credit	Debit	Credit	Debit	Credit	
1	Prepaid Insurance	3000										1
2	Service Revenue		58000									2
3	Salaries Expense	25000										3
4	Accounts Receivable											4
5	Salaries Payable											5
6	Insurance Expense											6
7												7
8												8
9												9
10												10

Name

Section

Date

Exercise 4-1

Briscoe Company

(a)

Briscoe Company
Worksheet
For The Month Ended June 30, 2008

	Account Titles	Trial Balance		Adjustments		Adjusted Trial Balance		Income Statement		Balance Sheet		
		Dr.	Cr.	Dr.	Cr.	Dr.	Cr.	Dr.	Cr.	Dr.	Cr.	
1	Cash	2320										1
2	Accounts Receivable	2440										2
3	Supplies	1880										3
4	Accounts Payable		1120									4
5	Unearned Revenue		240									5
6	Lennie Briscoe, Capital		3600									6
7	Service Revenue		2400									7
8	Salaries Expense	560										8
9	Miscellaneous Expense	160										9
10	Totals	7360	7360									10
11	Supplies Expense											11
12	Salaries Payable											12
13	Totals											13
14	Net Loss											14
15	Totals											15
16												16
17												17
18												18
19												19
20												20

Name | Problem 4-1A

Section

Date | Thomas Magnum, P.I.

(a)

Thomas Magnum, P.I.

Worksheet

For the Quarter Ended March 31, 2008

	Account Titles	Trial Balance		Adjustments		Adjusted Trial Balance		Income Statement		Balance Sheet		
		Dr.	Cr.	Dr.	Cr.	Dr.	Cr.	Dr.	Cr.	Dr.	Cr.	
1	Cash	11400										1
2	Account Receivable	5620										2
3	Supplies	1050										3
4	Prepaid Insurance	2400										4
5	Equipment	30000										5
6	Notes Payable		10000									6
7	Accounts Payable		12350									7
8	T. Magnum, Capital		20000									8
9	T. Magnum, Drawing	600										9
10	Service Revenue		13620									10
11	Salaries Expense	2200										11
12	Travel Expense	1300										12
13	Rent Expense	1200										13
14	Miscellaneous Expense	200										14
15	Totals	55970	55970									15
16												16
17	Supplies Expense											17
18	Depreciation Expense											18
19	Accum. Depreciation											19
20	Interest Expense											20
21	Interest Payable											21
22	Insurance Expense											22
23	Totals											23
24	Net Income											24
25	Totals											25
26	Totals											26

Name | Problem 4-4A
Section
Date | Disney Amusement Park

(a)

Disney Amusement Park
Worksheet
For The Year Ended September 30, 2008

	Account Titles	Trial Balance		Adjustments		Adjusted Trial Balance		Income Statement		Balance Sheet		
		Dr.	Cr.	Dr.	Cr.	Dr.	Cr.	Dr.	Cr.	Dr.	Cr.	
1	Cash	41400				41400						1
2	Supplies	18600				1200						2
3	Prepaid Insurance	31900				8900						3
4	Land	80000				80000						4
5	Equipment	120000				120000						5
6	Accumulated Depreciation		36200				42200					6
7	Accounts Payable		14600				14600					7
8	Unearned Admissions Rev.		3700				2000					8
9	Mortgage Payable		50000				50000					9
10	L. Disney, Capital		109700				109700					10
12	L. Disney, Drawing	14000				14000						12
13	Admissions Revenue		277500				279200					13
14	Salaries Expense	105000				105000						14
15	Repair Expense	30500				30500						15
16	Advertising Expense	9400				9400						16
17	Utilities Expense	16900				16900						17
18	Property Taxes Expense	18000				21000						18
19	Interest Expense	6000				10000						19
20	Totals	491700	491700									20
21												21
22	Insurance Expense					23000						22
23	Supplies Expense					17400						23
24	Interest Payable						4000					24
25	Depreciation Expense					6000						25
26	Property Taxes Payable						3000					26
27	Totals					504700	504700					27
28	Net Income											28
29	Totals											29

Name

Section

Date

Problem 4-5A Continued

Eddy's Carpet Cleaners

(b) & (c)

Eddy's Carpet Cleaners
Worksheet
For the Month Ended March 31, 2008

	Account Titles	Trial Balance		Adjustments		Adjusted Trial Balance		Income Statement		Balance Sheet		
		Dr.	Cr.	Dr.	Cr.	Dr.	Cr.	Dr.	Cr.	Dr.	Cr.	
1	Cash											1
2	Accounts Receivable											2
3	Cleaning Supplies											3
4	Prepaid Insurance											4
5	Equipment											5
6	Accounts Payable											6
7	L. Eddy, Capital											7
8	L. Eddy, Drawing											8
9	Service Revenue											9
10	Gas and Oil Expense											10
11	Salaries Expense											11
12	Totals											12
13	Depreciation Expense											13
14	Accum. Depreciation - Equip.											14
15	Insurance Expense											15
16	Cleaning Supplies Expense											16
17	Salaries Payable											17
18	Totals											18
19	Net Income											19
20	Totals											20
21												21

Name
Section
Date

Problem 4-6A

Fox Cable

(a)

Fox Cable								
(1) Incorrect Entry			(2) Correct Entry			(3) Correcting Entry		
Account Titles	Dr.	Cr.	Account Titles	Dr.	Cr.	Account Titles	Dr.	Cr.
1.								
2.								
3.								
4.								
5.								

Name | Problem 4-1B

Section

Date | Everlast Roofing

(a)

Everlast Roofing
Worksheet
For The Month Ended March 31, 2008

	Account Titles	Trial Balance		Adjustments		Adjusted Trial Balance		Income Statement		Balance Sheet		
		Dr.	Cr.	Dr.	Cr.	Dr.	Cr.	Dr.	Cr.	Dr.	Cr.	
1	Cash	2500										1
2	Accounts Receivable	1800										2
3	Roofing Supplies	1100										3
4	Equipment	6000										4
5	Accum. Depreciation		700									5
6	Accounts Payable		1400									6
7	Unearned Revenue		300									7
8	J. Watt, Capital		7000									8
9	J. Watt, Drawing	600										9
10	Service Revenue		3500									10
11	Salaries Expense	700										11
12	Misc. Expense	200										12
13	Totals	12900	12900									13
14	Supplies Expense											14
15	Depr. Expense											15
16	Salaries Payable											16
17	Totals											17
18	Net Income											18
19	Totals											19
20												20

Name | Problem 4-4B
Section
Date | Pettengill Management Services

(a)

Pettengill Management Services
Worksheet
For the Year Ended December 31, 2008

	Account Titles	Trial Balance Dr.	Trial Balance Cr.	Adjustments Dr.	Adjustments Cr.	Adjusted Trial Balance Dr.	Adjusted Trial Balance Cr.	Income Statement Dr.	Income Statement Cr.	Balance Sheet Dr.	Balance Sheet Cr.	
1	Cash	11500				11500						1
2	Accounts Receivable	23600				23600						2
3	Prepaid Insurance	3100				1400						3
4	Land	56000				56000						4
5	Building	106000				106000						5
6	Equipment	49000				49000						6
7	Accounts Payable		10400				10400					7
8	Unearned Rent Revenue		5000				2800					8
9	Mortgage Note Payable		100000				100000					9
10	G. Pettengill, Capital		120000				120000					10
11	G. Pettengill, Drawing	18000				18000						11
12	Service Revenue		75600				75600					12
13	Rent Revenue		24000				26200					13
14	Salaries Expense	35000				35000						14
15	Advertising Expense	17000				17000						15
16	Utilities Expense	15800				15800						16
17	Totals	335000	335000									17
18	Insurance Expense					1700						18
19	Depr. Expense - Building					2500						19
20	Accum. Depreciation - Bldg.						2500					20
21	Depr. Expense - Equipment					3900						21
22	Accum. Depreciation - Equip.						3900					22
23	Interest Expense					9000						23
24	Interest Payable						9000					24
25	Totals					350400	350400					25
26	Net Income											26
27	Totals											27
28												28

Name | Problem 4-5B Continued

Section

Date | Choi's Window Washing

(b) and (c)

Choi's Window Washing
Worksheet
For The Month Ended July 31, 2008

	Account Titles	Trial Balance		Adjustments		Adjusted Trial Balance		Income Statement		Balance Sheet		
		Dr.	Cr.	Dr.	Cr.	Dr.	Cr.	Dr.	Cr.	Dr.	Cr.	
1	Cash											1
2	Accounts Receivable											2
3	Cleaning Supplies											3
4	Prepaid Insurance											4
5	Equipment											5
6	Accounts Payable											6
7	Lee Choi, Capital											7
8	Lee Choi, Drawing											8
9	Service Revenue											9
10	Gas and Oil Expense											10
11	Salaries Expense											11
12	Totals											12
13												13
14	Depreciation Expense											14
15	Accum. Depr. - Equip.											15
16	Insurance Expense											16
17	Cleaning Supplies Exp.											17
18	Salaries Payable											18
19	Totals											19
20	Net Income											20
21	Totals											21
22												22

Name | Comprehensive Problem: Chapters 2 to 4

Section

Date | Julie's Maids Cleaning Service

(b) & (c)

Julie's Maids Cleaning Service
Worksheet
For the Month Ended July 31, 2008

	Account Titles	Trial Balance		Adjustments		Adjusted Trial Balance		Income Statement		Balance Sheet		
		Dr.	Cr.	Dr.	Cr.	Dr.	Cr.	Dr.	Cr.	Dr.	Cr.	
1	Cash											1
2	Accounts Receivable											2
3	Cleaning Supplies											3
4	Prepaid Insurance											4
5	Equipment											5
6	Accounts Payable											6
7	Julie Molony, Capital											7
8	Julie Molony, Drawing											8
9	Service Revenue											9
10	Gas and Oil Expense											10
11	Salaries Expense											11
12	Totals											12
14	Depreciation Expense											14
15	Accum. Depreciation - Equip.											15
16	Insurance Expense											16
17	Cleaning Supplies Expense											17
18	Salaries Payable											18
19	Totals											19
20	Net Income											21
21	Totals											22
22												23
23												24
24												25

Name *Exercise 5-19

Section

Date Green Company

Green Company
Worksheet
For the Month Ended June 30, 2008

	Account Titles	Trial Balance Dr.	Trial Balance Cr.	Adjustments Dr.	Adjustments Cr.	Adjusted Trial Balance Dr.	Adjusted Trial Balance Cr.	Income Statement Dr.	Income Statement Cr.	Balance Sheet Dr.	Balance Sheet Cr.	
1	Cash	2320										1
2	Accounts Receivable	2440										2
3	Merchandise Inventory	11640										3
4	Accounts Payable		1120									4
5	Ed Green, Capital		3600									5
6	Sales		42400									6
7	Cost of Goods Sold	20560										7
8	Operating Expenses	10160										8
9	Totals	47120	47120									9
10	Net Income											10
11	Totals											11
12												12
13												13
14												14
15												15

Name

Section

Date

*Problem 5-8A

Terry Manning Fashion Center

(a)

Terry Manning Fashion Center
Worksheet
For the Year Ended November 30, 2008

	Account Titles	Trial Balance		Adjustments		Adjusted Trial Balance		Income Statement		Balance Sheet		
		Dr.	Cr.	Dr.	Cr.	Dr.	Cr.	Dr.	Cr.	Dr.	Cr.	
1	Cash	28700										1
2	Accounts Receivable	30700										2
3	Merchandise Inventory	44700										3
4	Store Supplies	6200										4
5	Store Equipment	85000										5
6	Accum. Depr. - Store Equip.		22000									6
7	Delivery Equipment	48000										7
8	Accum. Depr. - Del. Equip.		6000									8
9	Notes Payable		51000									9
10	Accounts Payable		48500									10
11	T. Manning, Capital		110000									11
12	T. Manning, Drawing	12000										12
13	Sales		755200									13
14	Sales Returns and Allow.	8800										14
15	Cost of Goods Sold	497400										15
16	Salaries Expense	140000										16
17	Advertising Expense	24400										17
18	Utilities Expense	14000										18
19	Repair Expense	12100										19
20	Delivery Expense	16700										20
21	Rent Expense	24000										21
22	Totals	992700	992700									22
23	Store Supplies Expense											23
24	Depr. Exp. - Store Equip.											24
25	Depr. Exp. - Del. Equip.											25
26	Interest Expense											26
27	Interest Payable											27
28	Totals											28
29	Net Loss											29
30	Totals											30

Name | Comprehensive Problem: Chapters 3 to 7 Continued

Section

Date | Packard Company

(c)

Packard Company
Work Sheet
For the Month Ended January 31, 2008

	Account Titles	Trial Balance		Adjustments		Adjusted Trial Balance		Income Statement		Balance Sheet		
		Dr.	Cr.	Dr.	Cr.	Dr.	Cr	Dr.	Cr	Dr.	Cr.	
1	Cash											1
2	Accounts Receivable											2
3	Notes Receivable											3
4	Merchandise Inventory											4
5	Office Supplies											5
6	Prepaid Insurance											6
7	Equipment											7
8	Accum. Depr. - Equip.											8
9	Notes Payable											9
10	Accounts Payable											10
11	Interest Payable											11
12	I. Packard, Capital											12
13	I. Packard, Drawing											13
14	Sales											14
15	Sales Rtns. and Allow.											15
16	Purchases											16
17	Purch. Rtns and Allow.											17
18	Freight-in											18
19	Sales Salaries Exp.											19
20	Office Salaries Exp.											20
21	Rent Expense											21
22	Totals											22
23	Office Supplies Exp.											23
24	Insurance Exp.											24
25	Depreciation Exp.											25
26	Interest Exp.											26
27	Totals											27
28	Net Income											28
29	Totals											29

Name

Section

Date

(c)

Bluma Company
Work Sheet
For the Month Ended January 31,2008

	Account Titles	Trial Balance Dr.	Trial Balance Cr.	Adjustments Dr.	Adjustments Cr.	Adjusted Trial Balance Dr.	Adjusted Trial Balance Cr	Income Statement Dr.	Income Statement Cr	Balance Sheet Dr.	Balance Sheet Cr.	
1	Cash											1
2	Accounts Receivable											2
3	Notes Receivable											3
4	Merchandise Inventory											4
5	Office Supplies											5
6	Prepaid Insurance											6
7	Equipment											7
8	Accum. Depr. - Equip.											8
9	Notes Payable											9
10	Accounts Payable											10
11	Interest Payable											11
12	M. Bluma, Capital											12
13	M. Bluma, Drawing											13
14	Sales											14
15	Sales Rtns. and Allow.											15
16	Sales Discounts											16
17	Cost of Goods Sold											17
18	Sales Salaries Exp.											18
19	Office Salaries Exp.											19
20	Rent Exp.											20
21	Totals											21
22	Office Supplies Exp.											22
23	Insurance Exp.											23
24	Depreciation Exp.											24
25	Interest Exp.											25
26	Totals											26
27	Net Income											27
28	Totals											28
29												29